LINES IN THE WATER

12/06

for Pat,

with us most regards

Ben

BEN ORLOVE

LINES IN
THE WATER

Nature and Culture at Lake Titicaca

UNIVERSITY OF CALIFORNIA PRESS

Berkeley Los Angeles London

Frontispiece: Drawing of fishermen retrieving gill nets at Lake Titicaca, by Dominique Levieil.

University of California Press
Berkeley and Los Angeles, California

University of California Press, Ltd.
London, England

Library of Congress Cataloging-in-Publication Data
Orlove, Benjamin S.
    Lines in the water : nature and culture at Lake Titicaca / Ben Orlove.
        p.   cm.
    Includes index.
    ISBN 0-520-22958-4 (cloth : alk. paper).— ISBN 0-520-22959-2 (paper : alk. paper)
        1. Titicaca Lake Region (Peru and Bolivia)—Description and travel.   2. Titicaca
Lake Region (Peru and Bolivia)—Social life and customs.   I. Title.
F3451.P9 O75   2002
984'.12—dc21   2001035872

Manufactured in the United States of America
11   10   09   08   07   06   05   04   03
10   9   8   7   6   5   4   3

The paper used in this publication is both acid-free and totally chlorine-free (TCF).
It meets the minimum requirements of ANSI/NISO Z39.48–1992 (R 1997) *(Permanence of Paper)*. ∞

Dedicated to

ALBERTO FLORES GALINDO

CÉSAR FONSECA MARTEL

SYLVIA FORMAN

JOHN HYSLOP

LIBBETT CRANDON MALAMUD

THIERRY SAIGNES

MICHAEL SALLNOW

JOHN TRACEY —

colleagues and friends

who walked the paths of the Andes

and who died too young,

leaving books not written,

tales not told,

songs not sung.

Contents

	List of Illustrations	ix
	Preface: Lakes	xi
1.	Not Forgetting	1
2.	Mountains	17
3.	Names	45
4.	Work	69
5.	Fish	117
6.	Reeds	173
7.	Paths	209
	Notes	241
	Acknowledgments	277
	Index	279

Illustrations

PHOTOGRAPHS AND DRAWINGS

Morning light, Capachica Peninsula	xiii
Cirilo Cutipa on a ridge between Socca and Ilave	xviii
Two fishermen retrieving gill nets	xix
Carrying cloth from Capachica	xxvi
Cirilo Cutipa in the author's apartment in Puno	3
Family awaiting a ferry on a floating island in the Bahía de Puno	9
Fallow fields on a ridge near Santiago de Huata	12
Lake Titicaca in a flood year	23
View across the Straits of Tiquina to the Cordillera Real in Bolivia	36
Fisherman rowing near Huancané	46
Woman and children collecting dried ispi	49
Dominique Levieil at a meeting in the IMARPE laboratory in Puno	51

Woman carrying fish from shore to market   54

Using a wooden pole to push a balsa in a shallow section of the lake   66

Carachi vendors in a rural market   72

Eufracio and Hugo at the IMARPE laboratory in Puno   73

Hugo distributing slips to the fishermen participating in the selection
  lottery on Isla Soto   79

Fisherman from Vilurcuni who participated in the catch study   85

René and Hilda in the IMARPE office in Puno   86

Two fishermen returned from a night of fishing   93

Men building a house of adobe bricks   106

Vendors selling carachi in a marketplace   120

Drawing of balsa making by a villager   123

Drawing of the operation of a *wayunaqana* (trawl net)   125

Qollancha (basket trap)   128

Drawing of the construction of wooden boats   142

Preparing a field for planting in the dry season   146

Equipment in an abandoned fish cannery, Vilquechico   152

Weekly marketplace in Huata   155

Sewing old fishing nets together to make a floating cage   165

Boy harvesting totora with a scythe, Bahía de Puno   175

Drawing of annual waterfowl hunt   179

Balsa making   181

Harvesting lakeweed in the Bahía de Puno   183

Eufracio examining aquatic invertebrates along the Río Ramis   197

Flooded fields along the Río Ramis   233

MAPS

The altiplano in Peru and Bolivia   xvii

Lake Titicaca basin   19

The Ccapia route   30

Indigenous languages of the altiplano   52

Major reedbeds of Lake Titicaca   185

Lakes

Water: the most commonplace of liquids and the most essential, it quenches our thirst and brings green to our world. It is the most mutable as well. It freezes into ice, it vaporizes into steam, and, as a liquid, it assumes an endless variety of forms: a soft drizzle, a placid pond, a waterfall that can be heard for miles, a raging sea whose waves tower a hundred feet high. We can cup it in our hands and drown in its depths.

Water: the favored element of storytellers, who are drawn to its unmatched capacity to stir the imagination. The oceans bring to mind infinity. By showing the puny and fragile nature of human existence, they underscore the magnitude of the human will as it seeks to accomplish its ends. The sea is the realm that challenges and transforms the heroes of antiquity, like Odysseus, who finds the journey home as difficult as the war. It defines as well modern heroes and antiheroes, like Captain Ahab, destroyed by his obsessive quest for the great white whale. Rivers, too, are the stuff of stories. Characters can float downriver, like Huck Finn on the raft, fleeing a confining order, or they can travel upriver, like Marlow in *Heart of Darkness,* moving toward a confrontation with utter savagery. Rivers suggest movement, quests, life itself.

As I pondered the task of writing a book about Lake Titicaca, I often thought that lakes lack such dramatic power. Of the myriad attributes of water, they display only its plainness. Smaller than oceans, stiller than rivers, they simply sit, confined by their shores. Surely someone must have written an engaging book about a lake, I said to a friend one day, but the only one that we could think of was Garrison Keillor's *Lake Wobegon Days.* No wonder: a lake is a good place to spend an afternoon swimming or fishing, as is the habit of the sturdy Minnesotans whose lives provide Keillor with the material for his humor.

Troubled from time to time by such examples of the apparently prosaic quality of lakes, I feared that I would not be able to draw readers into the story that so engaged me about the fishermen of a distant lake high in the Andes. In response to this concern, I developed a plan. I would search out books about lakes and read them. They might lead me to discover some engaging aspect of lakes that had eluded me. Friends and bookstore clerks helped me assemble a list of books that provided me with my bedtime reading for several months.

I began with Theodore Dreiser's *An American Tragedy,* a book that I dimly recalled hearing of as a classic early-twentieth-century American novel. A solid, though perhaps overlong, piece of realist fiction, it centers on the life of Clyde Griffiths, who moves to a factory town in upstate New York, takes a job as a supervisor, and meets two young women: Sondra, a pretty, if vapid, member of one of the town's wealthiest families, and Roberta, a charming, vivacious worker in the factory. He attends parties with the former and has a clandestine affair with the latter, during which she becomes pregnant and is unable to obtain an abortion. She wants to marry Clyde before the baby is born, but he retains the hope that his romance with Sondra might flourish. Clyde persuades Roberta to leave the town and spend some time with her parents, while he continues to attend parties with Sondra.

Morning light, Capachica Peninsula. Photograph by Tim Kittel.

Increasingly afraid that Clyde will abandon her, Roberta presses him to see her. He agrees to join her at a lake where they can go boating. Before he meets her, he comes across a newspaper article about an accidental drowning of an unidentified man and woman in a lake. The thought of killing Roberta fascinates and horrifies him. They meet at a train station, travel to the lake, and register at an inn. When he takes her out on the lake in a rowboat, she accidentally falls into the water. He watches her flounder, he hears her desperate pleas, but he does not rescue her. She drowns. He flees; his attempts to conceal the fact of his involvement in her death are unsuccessful. The trail of clues that he has left leads the police to him. He is found, and at the end he is executed for her murder.

As the creator of a work of fiction, Dreiser could have selected other circumstances in which Clyde could have failed to save Roberta—a fall, dismemberment by factory machinery, even an automobile accident. But these alternatives would not have presented as forcefully her sense of false security in the crucial chapters. With an open view all around them on the lake, it seemed that no threat could lurk hidden, as it might in a city or a forest. Roberta is relaxed and trusting, for once untroubled by her worries that Clyde might not wish to marry her. She sings and talks happily as Clyde rows. Her cheerful mood and the mild innocence of the outing in a rowboat heighten the reader's perception of Clyde's depravity. Her death also underscores the danger that she had not seen. Her drowning is prolonged as, struggling and crying, she sinks, rises, and sinks again.

Water and journeys: *An American Tragedy* links them in a very specific way. Odysseus and Captain Ahab voyage on the ocean; Huck, Jim, and Marlow on rivers. By contrast, Clyde and Roberta travel to, not on, a lake. The lake is a destination that the characters visit and leave, rather than the setting of the novel. The outing on the lake is a single episode in the story of their romance. Oceans and rivers draw adventurers, but lakes attract vacationers, who enjoy the views across to the opposite shore and who go swimming or boating with ease and security in protected waters, undisturbed by strong currents, reassured by the land that is always in comfortable proximity should a storm develop. In *An American Tragedy* and other books, this smallness and security prove to be illusory. For Dreiser, lakes serve to demonstrate the contrast between appearance and reality. Clyde sees the dangers in a lake that looks safe to Roberta. This contrast fuels the suspense that grips many readers of the book and viewers of the films based on it: Will Roberta drown? Will Clyde escape?

The lake as a destination in a journey; the suspense that develops as the protagonist and reader grow aware of false appearances; the plot that turns as the narrator reveals that one character has been able to see beneath surfaces: these elements fit together in a variety of books. In one of the great 1940s hard-boiled detective novels, Raymond Chandler's *The Lady in the Lake*, the detective Philip Marlowe, searching for the missing wife of a wealthy man, travels to a lakeside resort in the mountains of southern California. Under a dock near some vacation cabins, he finds a partially decomposed body. Her hair, clothing, and jewelry suggest that she is another woman who recently ran off from her husband, in this case the caretaker of the cabins. Her identity changes twice in the course of the novel before Marlowe, in the final chapters, uncovers the tangled story of greed, lust, jealousy, and deception that led to several murders.

In her novel *Surfacing,* Margaret Atwood develops this contrast between appearance and reality in a different manner. An artist travels with her lover and another couple to a lake and the cabin in northern Quebec where she spent her summers as a child, but to which she has not returned for many years. The suspense lies in her search. She seeks to learn about her father, who has disappeared at the lake. As the book unfolds, it becomes evident that she is seeking as well to find her inner self and a way of being in her body (she questions both conventional and bohemian forms of diet and sexuality). Boating and swimming on the lake, she observes birds and other people and understands them very differently from her companions, who are doltish filmmakers. Diving into the lake's depths, she sees petroglyphs left by Indians and finds her father's drowned body. These hidden secrets lead her to recognitions about her past and her place in nature. Increasingly alienated from the social world of commerce, violence, and male pride, she becomes invisible to her companions. Because their filmmaking project directs their attention to artificial images and to appearances, they are often unable to see her in the water or in the bushes on the shore. In the final chapters, she decides to conceive a child and to return from the lake to society, where she will start to rebuild her life on new terms—one of the many acts of surfacing in the book. Though Atwood's characters, plot, and style are very different from those of Dreiser or Chandler, her book resembles theirs in the development and resolution of suspense through a character who travels to a lake and who sees beyond appearances.

Written with the author's characteristic restraint, Anita Brookner's *Hotel du Lac* contains less action than the other books, and it is entirely lacking in corpses. Nonetheless, it develops the themes about lakes that are present in *An American Tragedy, The Lady in the Lake,* and *Surfacing.* Edith Hope, a writer of romantic novels, travels from her home in London to a comfortable lakeshore hotel in Switzerland in early autumn. The understated suspense centers around two mysteries: why did Edith's friends pressure her to take this trip, and what is the nature of her relationship with David, to whom she keeps writing letters that she does not send? Cautious in facing emotion, Edith allows herself a series of reveries that gradually reveal the answers. She is seeking refuge from the disorder that ensued after she abruptly broke off her engagement to Geoffrey, the wealthy but dull and conventional man whose offer of marriage she had accepted not out of love or even affection, but out of dissatisfaction with her life and with her stagnating affair with David. Strolling along the lakeshore, visiting a nearby village, and eating in the hotel dining room, she reflects on her past and meets the other guests. Among them is Mr. Neville, whose wife left him a few years earlier. He courts her; he seems to appreciate her distinctive mix of reserve and wit; he proves to be even wealthier than Geoffrey, though neither dull nor conventional. He takes her on an excursion in a boat on the lake. During the trip, he proposes to her, and she agrees to marry him. Back on shore, as she gains a deeper view of the other guests and the lakeshore hotel itself, she discovers the selfish and cruel nature that lies beneath Neville's seeming sophistication and generosity. She has grown more self-aware during her brief stay at the lake. Abandoning Neville, she returns to England, resolved to live her life more fully. Like the artist in Atwood's *Surfacing*, Edith Hope is far less violent than Clyde and Marlowe, the male protagonists of the male novelists Dreiser and Chandler. Nonetheless, she encounters the elements of suspense, appearance, and discovery in the lake-as-destination theme along lines very much like those of the other three characters.

These novels held my attention with their strong characters and plots, their distinctive prose styles, and their significant elements of social critique. However, they did not allay my concerns that it would be difficult to write engagingly about a lake, since they failed to capture the qualities of their respective lakes that I wished to express in writing about Lake Titicaca. I thought back to the lake, my mind turning to Socca, the village that I had visited most often, and to Cirilo Cutipa, the local farmer with whom I stayed when I went there. I recalled the walk that we took so many times. We would descend from the slight rise on which his house was built and continue down a narrow path between fields to the lake. We sometimes followed the curve of the shore to a beach where fishermen kept their boats. On other occasions, we stayed for a while at the edge of the water, conversing or looking out in silence over the lake. Reeds grew in the shallows close to us, and beyond them were the open waters of the lake, stretching many miles to the tall mountains on the distant shore. Cirilo and I usually saw a few fishing boats, their small size

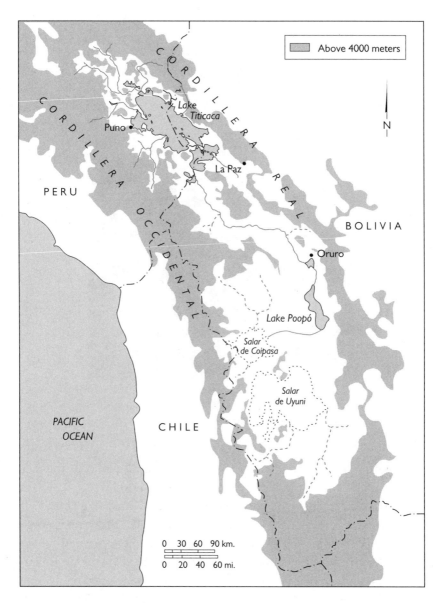

The altiplano in Peru and Bolivia.

Cirilo Cutipa on a ridge between Socca and Ilave.
Photograph by Ben Orlove.

accentuating the immensity of the lake and of the altiplano, as the great
Andean plateau, surrounded by high cordilleras, is known.

The novels, I realized, do not convey the scale of a lake like Titicaca. Its
surface area of 8,562 square kilometers makes it nearly four times larger
than Lake Mistassini, the largest lake in Quebec, where Atwood set *Surfacing;* more than fourteen times larger than Lake Geneva, the largest lake
in the Alps and the one at which *Hotel du Lac* takes place; and many times
larger than the lakes in the other novels. One looks across Lake Titicaca
not to woods or cabins or docks or small towns, as in these novels, but to
distant mountains.

Nor do these books portray the kind of mood one finds in the Andean
landscape where Lake Titicaca is situated. The novels each center on the

Two fishermen retrieving gill nets. Photograph by Ben Orlove.

theme of travelers lulled into a false ease that is suddenly disturbed by some surprise or threat. If those lakes are places of vacation and danger, Lake Titicaca is a place of sustenance and of memory. This sustenance was evident in the rhythms of the work that I saw in the village. The seasons dictated the tasks in the fields, and with the herds as well, since the cattle fed on grass on the hills above the village in the rainy season and on reeds from the lake in the dry season. The ability of the land and the lake to nourish human life was demonstrated to me at every meal. Cirilo and the other villagers ate with great relish the soups, stews, and other dishes in which the dozens of varieties of potatoes, grains, and beans appeared, often with fish or meat, in many combinations. This country fare was one of the aspects of village life that they most missed when they traveled to visit a market or to work for a while, and that they most enjoyed when they returned.

Equally evident was the centrality and immediacy of memory to the villagers. In conversation, Cirilo often spoke of his grandparents and of earlier generations, telling of the changes in their houses and their crops, of the conflicts with neighboring villages and with abusive officials. He would sometimes refer as well to more remote times, a mythic past of strange beings who lived before the Spaniards and even before the Incas in a world without a sun. Indeed, many spots in the landscape were linked to memory. It seemed that for every hill, practically for every cliff or boulder, the villagers could recount a story of an event in the past.

Routine activities such as work and meals, conversations about family and neighbors: it is in the depiction of lives of local people that the novels failed me most completely as models for writing about Lake Titicaca. The drunken caretaker in *The Lady in the Lake,* the self-effacing waiters and shopkeepers in *Hotel du Lac,* the surly, narrow-minded French-Canadians in *Surfacing* are all caricatures. Their routine and limited existence offers in each case a contrast for the suspense and discoveries of the main character. By contrast, I wanted to write about the complexity of the villagers who live on the shores of Lake Titicaca. Their efforts to maintain traditions that outsiders sought to undermine, their fiercely strong attachments to their lands and to their lake, their elaborate sense of dignity and justice, their capacity for storytelling and for humor—all these were qualities that I wanted to convey, requiring a depth utterly absent from the novels.

I found a better model for writing about lakes in a very different book, *Walden.* Neither an adventurer nor a vacationer, Thoreau remains close to home. He settles near a lake in his native Massachusetts. He undertakes many activities—building a cabin, cultivating a garden, strolling through woods, conversing with the residents of the area, simply sitting still. He does not resolve suspense but rather encounters many surprises. Walden Pond intrigues and delights him with the shifting textures of its surface, the variety of shades of blue in its depths, the course of a loon that dives and emerges again and again, and the sudden appearances and disappearances of fish. Though he comes to know it intimately, it always holds something new for him. It is as if lakes have voices and can always speak to us in unexpected ways:

> One old man, who has been a close observer of Nature, and seems as thoroughly wise in regard to all her operations as if she had been put upon the stocks [the frame on which boats are hauled out of the water so that they can be repaired] when he was a boy, and he had helped to lay

her keel,—who has come to his growth, and can hardly acquire more of natural lore if he should live to the age of Methuselah,—told me, and I was surprised to hear him express wonder at any of Nature's operations, for I thought that there were no secrets between them, that one spring day he took his gun and boat, and thought that he would have a little sport with the ducks. There was ice still on the meadows, but it was all gone out of the river, and he dropped down without obstruction from Sudbury, where he lived, to Fair-Haven Pond, which he found, unexpectedly, covered for the most part with a firm field of ice. It was a warm day, and he was surprised to see so great a body of ice remaining. Not seeing any ducks, he hid his boat on the north or back side of an island in the pond, and then concealed himself in the bushes on the south side, to await them. The ice was melted for three or four rods from the shore, and there was a smooth and warm sheet of water, with a muddy bottom, such as the ducks love, within, and he thought it likely that some would be along pretty soon. After he had lain still there about an hour he heard a low and seemingly very distant sound, but singularly grand and impressive, unlike any thing he had ever heard, gradually swelling and increasing as if it would have a universal and memorable ending, a sullen rush and roar, which seemed to him all at once like the sound of a vast body of fowl coming in to settle there, and, seizing his gun, he started up in haste and excited; but he found, to his surprise, that the whole body of ice had started while he lay there, and drifted in to the shore, and the sound he had heard was made by its edge grating on the shore,—at first gently nibbled and crumbled off, but at length heaving up and scattering its wrecks along the island to a considerable height before it came to a stand still.

Striking, too, is the difference in organization between *Walden* and the other books. Rather than consisting of a single narrative that moves forward (with occasional flashbacks or foreshadowing), it contains a series of chapters that are separate essays. Some are organized loosely around the cycle of a year rather than the forward movement of a plot; others address economic or historical themes. Thoreau's observations of nature touch off reflections that are connected to each other through their overlapping philosophical, political, literary, and scientific elements. In the other books, the lake is a destination; for Thoreau, it is a presence, one that reveals the manifold aspects of a single truth. The truth that he gradually discovers is that transcendence may be achieved through simple living, personal honesty, and direct contact with nature.

I found a few other books that resemble *Walden*. *Refuge* is a memoir by Terry Tempest Williams, a writer and naturalist whose family has lived in Utah since the early years of Mormon settlement. The book is set on the shores of Great Salt Lake during a period when the lake level is rising, threatening a bird refuge with inundation. At the same time, Williams's mother is dying of cancer. With the exception of the prologue and the epilogue, each of the book's numerous short chapters bears a double name: a kind of local bird and the level of the lake; for example, "White Pelicans. Lake level 4,209.90'." No bird's name is repeated, but the lake level in the last chapter is precisely the same as its level in the first. Some of these chapters center on Williams's seeing the bird for which it is titled; in others, the bird is not mentioned in the body of the chapter, but some attribute of it—its plumage or size or movement—underscores the chapter's mood. The variety of birds echoes the variety of feelings that sweep over Williams as she witnesses her mother's last weeks, and as she reflects on many matters: the nature of illness, the lives of her parents, brothers, and grandparents, the different facets of religion, the efforts of government agencies to manage the natural fluctuations of Great Salt Lake. By the end, the lake has returned to its normal level, and Williams has come to accept her mother's death and to accept as well the different ways in which her relatives responded to it. This acceptance is the truth whose many aspects Williams discovers at the lake where her family has lived for generations.

Thoreau and Williams describe different lakes in different centuries, and they draw on different religious traditions. Nonetheless, they both discover an enduring multifaceted truth within a lake. The very finitude of lakes highlights the nature of this truth. A different view may be seen from each point on shore, at each moment in the day and at each season of the year, and yet the lake is always the same, a single bounded body of water. The different lakes call forth the same qualities of patience, attention, and immediacy; they offer the same possibility of surprise and transcendence. If the central image of nature in *An American Tragedy* and the other novels may be termed "lake as destination," in *Walden* and *Refuge* it may be called "lake as presence."

Mark Slouka's *Lost Lake*, a collection of short stories, certainly belongs

in this latter category as well. The eight longer stories differ in their subjects: a boy discovers why his neighbor, an elderly bird-watcher, captures
turtles; an unhappy young wife has an affair with a stranger; a child
accidentally drops a watch down the hole in an outhouse; a father and
son meet several fishermen at the lake. The four shorter pieces, called
"sketches," depict a variety of objects and events. Yet the stories are
connected by the small lake in upstate New York around which a number of Czech immigrants and their descendants have settled. In these stories, the lake, in its many aspects, stirs up old memories that reawaken
longing and grief; it also creates hopes for freedom that can never be fully
satisfied. The presence that the local people discover in the lake is the
persistence of memory and the pain of exile. The lake creates a sense of
loss—one of the multiple meanings of the collection's title—that can
lead to bitterness and cruelty but also, on occasion, to the compassion
and generosity that make up the small, precious moments of redemption
in these stories.

In this series of books on lakes as presences one might even include
the Gospels. Matthew, Mark, Luke, and John each tell the life of Jesus.
Though they vary in many details, they all contain chapters that linger on
the shores of the Sea of Galilee—a lake rather than an ocean. The New
Testament has the difficult task of conveying the unfolding relationship
between the apparently contradictory human and divine natures of Jesus. This relationship has often been seen within Jesus' body—his temptation in the desert, his suffering on the cross, his ascension into heaven.
It can also be seen in Jesus' relationship to earthly and divine places. His
early ministry is linked with this lake as firmly as his birth is associated
with the village of Bethlehem, his crucifixion and resurrection with the
city of Jerusalem, and the subsequent growth of his church with the journeys of the apostles across the seas to carry his message around the world.
The presence of the lake links some of the most important miracles: the
calming of the storm, the casting out of demons, the multiplication of the
fishes and loaves, the walking on water. At this time of the early ministry,
the larger tasks—the redemption of humanity from sin, the establishment of the universal church—still lie ahead, as do the greater miracles
of the resurrection and the ascension. It is first necessary for the divine

nature of Jesus to be amply demonstrated. The most majestic features of nature—the ocean, tall mountains, the star-filled night sky—might seem better suited to this task. But it is a lake that provides the combination of finitude and variety, of familiarity and surprise, that itself parallels the awakening understanding, on the part of the humble villagers of the Galilee and the readers of the Gospels, of the divine nature contained within the man.

Perhaps even Lake Wobegon holds such a presence. Its breezes and aromas pervade Keillor's fictional reminiscences. Its shores draw young and old to many of the richest moments of their lives. Indeed, its waters gave rise to the community: during the warm spring of 1851, two newcomers were tempted to swim and uncharacteristically removed their clothes. Prudence, the New England missionary, took off her "cumbersome petticoats," Basile, the French-Canadian trapper, his bearskin garments. To their union, consummated in the waters of the lake, were born the first white children in the area. The lake's fish attracted Norwegian immigrants and continue to delight their descendants, who, along with inhabitants of other origins, go fishing in all seasons and all moods. Ice-fishing from chilly shacks, they demonstrate their stalwart persistence. Rowing out before dawn to catch sunfish for a family breakfast on a summer vacation, they show enthusiasm and optimism. The lake allows them to express their capacity to face difficulties and to enjoy small pleasures —the qualities of strength and simplicity that lie at the core of American identity itself.

This second set of books, the lake-as-presence books, assured me that it is possible to write evocatively about lakes. Each of these books portrays with considerable sympathy the people who live by lakes. For all that Thoreau is quick to judge and condemn in the wearing effects of commerce and greed on ordinary people, he finds many individuals whose knowledge of nature and whose simple lives he respects. Williams cherishes her relatives and associates, including the ones whose views differ profoundly from her own. Even Keillor, who often makes fun of Midwestern provincialism, brings a tender affection to his humorous anecdotes. Moreover, the structure of these books—their format of linked essays—suggested that I did not need to present the history of

Lake Titicaca in strict chronological order, and that I could draw broadly from my own stays at the lake, the repeated visits that stretched from 1972 to 1995 and the two periods, of nearly a year each, in the 1970s and 1980s when I lived on the shores of the lake.

In the mass of material in my study, I could see the outlines of a book like these. The thousands of pages of field notes and documents from archives reflected many aspects of the lake, aspects that can, as Thoreau indicated, be both surprising and familiar. They pointed to a single theme: the lake as a sign of the endurance of the villagers themselves. In these remote highlands, the native villagers have struggled to retain their territories and their distinctive way of life in the face of direct conquest and other pressures. They have succeeded in maintaining a fair degree of control over the fields and pastures that compose their lands, but the lake, I came to understand, embodies their tenacity with particular force. The land contains the towns with the lawyers' offices, police stations, and jails from which the government presses on them. The native languages of Quechua and Aymara, spoken openly in the villages, often acquire a taint of backwardness in town. The land contains as well the roads on which vehicles travel, bringing strangers into the villages. But the lake is wholly the villagers'. The forms of national law, even the national language of Spanish, seem not to operate out on the lake. Outsiders lose themselves in the open waters and in the wide, reed-filled marshes where the villagers move freely. The townspeople may look at the lake from afar, but the villagers observe it closely, noting every shift of the weather, tracing the annual rhythm of the lake's rise and fall with the alternation of rainy and dry seasons. They hold the lake in memory as they hold it in view. It is the recollections shared with kin and neighbors, the widely told stories of past events, that shape the history of the lake—a history that is, above all, one of continuity. Despite the many shifts—the new species of fish, the new kinds of boats and gear and markets—families have retained the established rhythms of the work of fishing, and villages have assured that local custom governs the fishermen.

My profession, anthropology, is filled with differing opinions these days. Some might argue that the only reason for an anthropologist who studies indigenous villagers to examine images of lakes in Western litera-

A carrying cloth from Capachica, with a band depicting
a trout and coots. Photograph by Ben Orlove.

ture would be to extirpate such images in order to approach the local
views more cleanly—or to recognize these images among the ones that
have been imposed on the local peoples. Such caution is salutary; in recent decades, anthropologists have become increasingly aware of the pervasive tendency to look at other cultures and to see not these cultures, but
rather the images of non-Western cultures fabricated by Western ones.
I do wish to recognize that the Andean villagers understand their lake in
ways that are distinct from the authors of these books. The individual and
family vacations in *Hotel du Lac* and *Lost Lake* are as different from the villagers' collective celebration of festivals as the detective work in *The Lady
in the Lake* is from the procedures of village assemblies that deliberate local violations of law. Nor do these books contain myths, like the accounts
of stone boats that in ancient times traveled around the lake from sacred
islands, or stories of the supernatural beings, like the *qatari*, or sea serpent, in which the villagers believe. Above all, the theme of pristine wil-
derness in most of the lake books stands in counterpoint to the theme of
conquest that is strong in the villagers' minds.

Nonetheless, in reflecting on how lakes are depicted in these books
and in the words and lives of the villagers, I am as struck by the similarities as by the differences. The idea that a lake can suggest an abiding presence does not seem to me a Western creation that I chose to adopt and im-

pose. I think of it as a theme shared in several places—perhaps in many places—and developed differently in each. If anthropology rests on uncovering and depicting cultural differences, it also rests on the common humanity of anthropologists and the people whom they study. The relation to landscape, I believe, is one of realms in which this affinity among different people is strongest. In the present era of fascination with the human body, it can be recognized that because anthropologists are born to parents, they can readily study kinship systems; because they fall ill, they can gain insight into healing practices and beliefs. It seems to me that landscape has a similar effect. Much as the capacities of the human body for sexual reproduction and for illness provide commonalities to human cultures, so too does the capacity of the human body to experience the natural world: to walk, above all, in warm weather and cold, under sunny skies and in rain; to feel the utter familiarity of established routes and the great novelty of unknown ones; to tire after long distances and to walk again with restored strength after a rest. I do not wish to assume that these experiences are identical, because they draw on meanings that are immanent in the natural world. Neither do I wish to say that the natural world is an empty vessel into which each culture pours its own set of meanings. I simply wish to suggest that these books aid rather than hinder my efforts to comprehend how the villagers of Lake Titicaca understand their landscapes and their lives; that listening to Thoreau and Williams and Slouka, and even to Keillor, helps me listen to the Andean villagers as well.

1   Not Forgetting

I was in a great hurry during my last weeks in Puno, the Peruvian city on the shores of Lake Titicaca, even though there were few loose ends to my research project on the fishermen of the lake. The study of the markets was complete. So was my collaborative work with IMARPE, a Peruvian government agency that specializes in aquatic resources. We had revised a census of the fishermen and conducted a detailed survey of their fishing trips. Moreover, thanks to my interviews and visits to archives, I had compiled the documents that I needed to trace the history of the fishing villages in the twentieth century. I had even done enough of the unstructured hanging out in villages and towns that anthropologists call "participant observation," the close-up viewing of daily life that is a hallmark of my profession.

Some of the hurry came from a quite common sort of academic nervousness. As I sat in Puno and reviewed my notes a final time, I sensed that there could be one more government official who had an interesting story to tell about conflicts between the fishing villages and the navy, one more villager whose disputes with her father-in-law could reveal new aspects of local inheritance customs. And another reason for the rushed pace was my efforts to keep at bay my sadness over my departure. I would miss the individuals whom I had come to know quite well; I would miss my two-room apartment, with its view of the sunrises over the lake and with the bustling activities of the three families around the courtyard; and perhaps most of all, I would miss speaking Quechua and the opportunities that this language offered me to converse easily with local people.

It was mostly the local people, however, who imposed the hurried pace on me. Accustomed to having relatives and neighbors leave for distant cities and new frontier areas, they would not allow anyone whom they knew to depart without some form of farewell, a *despedida* in Spanish, a *kacharpari* in the indigenous Quechua language. For the people I knew best, such as Hugo, Eufracio, and René, the biologists from IMARPE, and Tito, my hiking companion, these farewells entailed long parties. With Cirilo, there were three separate *despedidas*—a meal that stretched from the late morning through most of the afternoon in the courtyard of his house in his village on the shores of the lake, where we were joined by many of his relatives and the local fishermen; an evening meal with a few of his relatives in his son's house on the outskirts of Puno, followed by music and dancing; and a lunch with some other Americans in an open-air restaurant in an old adobe building a few blocks from the center of town.

Moreover, once word got out that I would be leaving, other people, ones whom I did not know as well, would drop by my apartment or stop me in the street. It was these unpredictable conversations that gave the harried tone to my last weeks. The local people, I discovered, had many questions to ask a departing gringo. "You must be going through Lima on your way home; could you bring a package to my cousin there?" "Could you please sell me your camera? I can offer you a good price." "My nephew would like to study in an American university; could you arrange for him to get a scholarship?" I could reply easily to these ques-

Cirilo having breakfast in the author's apartment in Puno. Photograph by Ben Orlove.

tions, but I found myself awkward, temporarily speechless, when a simpler entreaty was made: *"No me olvides," "Ama qonqawaychu"*: Don't forget me. Hilda, the woman who had assisted me in working on survey data, did not attend the farewell party that IMARPE had organized, because her husband did not want her to be away from their home that evening. When I saw her on one of my last visits to the IMARPE office, she, too, asked nothing more than not to be forgotten, though she had worked for me for nearly a year.

I heard this request frequently enough to gather that it was a standard, formulaic expression. And yet I could tell, from the strength of the tone in which it was said—many people beseeched me, nearly in tears, not to forget them—that it was not a simple mechanical response to the situation of someone's departing. Each of these people was deeply concerned that I remember him or her. At the time, it seemed pitiful to me that they did not make a greater demand. Surely there was something more that they could wish to ask for: Was I too august a figure in their eyes for them to request something more? Had colonialism and all the numerous forms of racial and class inequality in Peru rendered them so humble? Faced with this troubling request, I would stammer out a reply that I hoped was adequate. I would begin with a statement of my deep gratitude for all that I had received, and then I would promise not to forget them, ever.

Somehow I did get through the last interviews, the packing, and the parties during my final weeks in Puno. After another series of leave-takings in Lima, I returned to the United States. And I did spend a good deal of time remembering. The images in my mind were reinforced by all the records I had kept as an anthropologist—boxes of field notes, hundreds of slides, folders of copies of letters to relatives and friends. I wrote a series of academic articles about my work around Lake Titicaca, some on my own, some jointly with Dominique Levieil, a French resource economist whom I had gotten to know in Puno. He and I corresponded a good deal, shared our field notes, and debated our interpretations of the fishermen and their lives.

Several years later, when I was showing some slides of Lake Titicaca in a class, these farewell requests unexpectedly surfaced in my mind. Voices came back to me, asking not to be forgotten. I continued talking to the students, and later that day I thought back to my reactions to the urgent pleas. Had I been oversensitive? I wondered. It seemed understandable for people to wish not to be forgotten. Perhaps it was my response, rather than their requests, that needed explanation. Was I simply feeling guilty at the impossibility of repaying the generosity that I had received? No, I decided: there was a puzzling intensity to the requests. I could recall a few details of the way that they had been worded, especially the verb *ver*, to see. You have seen us, they had told me, you have seen how we live. The verb *compenetrarse* came to mind, to interpenetrate, or, as my bilingual dictionary translates it, "to (come to) share each other's feelings; to undergo mutual influence." Had they used this word, or had I only wished that they had? I was surer of the verb *compartir*, to share: they had spoken of how I had shared their meals when they fed me on trips to the villages; I had shared their houses when I slept over, and I had shared something more, it seemed to me, but what was it that they had said? As happens to all anthropologists whose field research is conducted in distant countries, I felt a strong twinge of regret. I wished that I had had the presence of mind to figure out some suitably delicate way of inquiring about the meaning of not forgetting. But I had learned to forgive myself for such ethnographic lapses, rather than to berate myself for them, and so the regret passed.

I found some clues about the meaning of these requests from a source that I had not considered as part of my anthropological work. I did not bring any tapes or a shortwave radio with me when I first did fieldwork in Peru, and so I listened only to the two local radio stations for the year and a half of my first visit, in the early 1970s, when I stayed a bit to the north of Lake Titicaca. The LPs of local music that I brought back as personal souvenirs formed the nucleus of a record collection that grew on subsequent visits. In the late 1970s, I worked as a disc jockey on the UC Davis campus radio station. I played these records often on my weekly program, *Brisas del Sur* (Southern Breezes), which ran for several years.

Returning to these records after several years of not listening to them frequently, I was surprised at how often the theme of forgetting came up—not in relation to departing foreigners, of course, but most often about lovers. In one song, a man asks,

> *qonqallawanmi nirankichu*
> *imas noqa qonqaykiman*
> *huch'uyniymanta munakusqayta*
> *huch'uyniymanta walikusqayta*

> Did you say, "He just forgets me?"
> How could I forget you,
> You whom I have loved since I have been young,
> You whom I have cherished since I have been young?

The charge to which the singer responds is not infidelity or abandonment, but, more simply, forgetting. This verse contains another clue in its use of a common device in Andean poetry and song. The two final lines are identical, except for the substitution of a synonym for one word. Such pairs of lines appear frequently in Andean folk music. The substitution of *cherish* for *love* was not very surprising, but it did direct me to look for a paired synonym for *forget*.

After a couple of hours of listening, I found one:

Maldito amor, maldito cariño,
Maldita tú, toda tu hermosura.
Que te ha pasado, que te ha sucedido,
Para que tú me hayas olvidado
Para que tú me hayas traicionado.
Seguramente te han aconsejado
Para que tú me hayas olvidado
Para que tú me hayas traicionado.

Damned love, damned affection,
Damn you and all your beauty.
What has come over you, what has happened to you,
So that you would forget me
So that you would betray me.
Surely they've told you what to do
So that you would forget me
So that you would betray me.

Traición, betrayal: a strong word to use for forgetting someone. Betrayal suggests an intentional deception, or an act of treachery involving a third party. The person who is betrayed runs a risk of some magnitude or suffers actual harm or injury. To my Western mind, a lover's betrayal implies sexual infidelity. Forgetting is at worst an unintended slight, likely to arise under circumstances far more casual than even the briefest of love affairs—for example, when someone at a party fails to recognize a friend of a friend whom he or she had met before. It is hard to imagine that someone could forget a lover altogether. But the link between forgetting and betrayal appears in another Peruvian song, interesting for its mix of Spanish and Quechua; I have used boldface to indicate phrases in the latter language and their English translation. Such switching is characteristic of music both in Quechua and Aymara, the two principal indigenous languages of the Andean highlands.

En que colegio has aprendido **kay runaq wawan munayta?**
Que profesor te ha enseñado despues de querer olvidar?
Porque pues negra traicionaste mi cariño,
Porque pues zamba traicionaste mi cariño,

Si hemos jurado amor eterno para nunca olvidarnos?
No me lamento de esta mi suerte porque ahora soy muy feliz.
Ya tengo un amor que me quiere que sabe corresponderme.

In what school did you learn **such a way to love an Indian's child?**
What teacher taught you that after love comes forgetting?
Hey, dark one, why did you betray my affection,
Hey, black one, why did you betray my affection,
If we had sworn eternal love, never to forget each other?
I don't lament this fate of mine, because now I am very happy.
I already have a love who cares for me, who is right for me.

The switch from Spanish to Quechua in the second half of the first line gives a biting wit to this song. The sarcasm is evident: Do you want me to believe that you're better than me? I know that you went to school, but I know that you know Quechua, just like me, an Indian's child—and I certainly know that going to school is no excuse for treating me the way that you have. The anger appears in the use of racial terms as well. *Negro* and *negra* (dark man, dark woman), like *zambo* and *zamba* (black man, black woman), are common terms of endearment in Peru. The skin color to which these words refer, especially the latter pair, sometimes contains a suggestion of African ancestry, of descent from the slaves brought to South America; more often, however, they simply suggest dark skin. In this context, these words hint that the singer is rejecting his lover's claim of superiority: even if I am an Indian's child, you are dark as well; you have accepted my calling you "dark one" in the past. Uneducated, an Indian, the singer nonetheless has not been defeated by the betrayal; he already has another lover.

Once I checked thoroughly, I found that the records in my collection were full of songs about forgetful lovers. They are often called *orgulloso*, proud, thinking that they are superior to the singer. One song, "Orgullosa Combapateñita"—"Proud Girl from Combapata"—mentions the name of the village or rural district from which this proud lover comes, showing in this way that the lover, someone of simple peasant stock, has been putting on airs. This song is particularly popular because of the ease with which it can be adapted: many place-names are four syllables long, so singers can denounce the pride of lovers from Capachica or Huatajata or many other locations. Forgetful lovers are accused of other faults as well. They are called *ingrato,* ungrateful, denying the value of what the singer has given them, or, worse, *pretencioso,* pretentious, haughty, stuck-up, claiming that they have no association with the singer.

As a modern American, I tend to think of forgetting as an unwilled lapse of mental function, as something that happens to one rather than something one does. These songs, though, indicate that one can choose to forget, that one can forget on purpose. They contain another surprise for Americans as well: forgetting is a social act rather than an individual one. What pride, ingratitude, and pretension have in common is the denial of social equality, rather than the rejection of emotional or erotic intimacy.

I could understand the popularity of the songs that contained this theme of forgetting and betrayal. They echoed the vulnerability felt by many listeners of the radio stations on which these songs were played. These people had been told, directly or indirectly, how inferior they were as peasants, as Indians, as uneducated boors, as residents of Peru's backward hinterlands. How easily these inferior people could be forgotten, even by the people they most trusted—even by lovers. I thought of a neighbor of mine, a man in his early twenties who worked as a shoe-maker to support his younger siblings. With little formal schooling, he spoke Spanish with a noticeable Quechua accent. He had many friends, who admired his efforts to take care of his siblings (his parents drank heavily and rarely worked) and who cheered him on at local soccer games, during which he often played goalie on the neighborhood team. He told me about a woman whom he had met and courted. They had fallen in love, but one day she suddenly spurned his attention. He told me that she did not even want to speak with him, that she acted as if she had never known him. Thinking back to his story, I could see the offenses of a forgetful one: her pride, her pretensions of superiority, her ingratitude for the small gifts that he had given her.

This social aspect of forgetting appears in relations between parents and children as well. An example can be found in one of the novels of José María Arguedas, a major Peruvian novelist, poet, folklorist, and anthropologist. Arguedas, the illegitimate son of a large landowner in highland

A family awaiting a ferry on one of the floating islands in the Bahía de Puno.
Photograph by Dominique Levieil.

Peru, was raised for much of his childhood by Quechua-speaking servants, almost as if he were their foster son. He later studied at the national university in Lima. After several attempts to find an audience for his works written in Quechua, he made a definitive shift to writing in Spanish. His novels depict the life of highland Indian peasants and the gap that separates them from the rest of Peru. They also seek to capture the cadence and force of spoken Quechua. In *Los ríos profundos,* the most autobiographical of his novels, he describes an incident in the life of his fictional self, Ernesto. When Ernesto's father, a lawyer, is forced to wander from town to town to avoid the attacks of his political opponents, Ernesto takes refuge in a remote Indian community where he has distant relatives. They welcome him warmly and treat him with great kindness. After the political persecution ends, his father comes to retrieve him. The farewell *despedida* includes fireworks, a mass, and several days of drinking and dancing. At its end, Ernesto and his father ride their horses from the plaza down a street and then follow the road up a hill, while the women sing a farewell song of the type called *jarahui*:

Ay warmallay warma
yuyayhunkim, yuyayhunkim!
Jhatun yurak' ork'o
kutiykachimunki;
abrapi puquio, pampapi puquio
yank'atak' yakuyananman.
Alkunchallay, kutiykamchu
raprachaykipi apaykamunki.
Riti ork'o, jhatun riti ork'o
yank'atak' ñannimpi ritiwak';
yank'atak' wayra
ñannimpi k'ochpaykunkiman.
Amas pára amas pára
aypankichu;
amas k'ak'a, amas k'ak'a
ñannimpi tuñinkichu.
Ay warmallay warma
kutiykamunk
kutiykamunkipuni!

No te olvides, mi pequeño,
no te olvides!
Cerro blanco,
hazlo volver;
agua de la montaña, manantial de la pampa,
que nunca muera de sed.
Halcón, cárgalo en tus alas
y hazlo volver.
Inmensa nieve, padre de la nieve,
no lo hieras en el camino.
Mal viento,
no lo toques.
Lluvia de la tormenta,
no lo alcances.
No, precipicio, atroz precipicio,
no lo sorprendas!
Hijo mío,
has de volver,
has de volver!

Do not forget, my little one,
Do not forget!
White hill,
make him return;
mountain freshet, pampa spring,
never let him die of thirst.
Falcon, bear him on your wings
and make him return.
Deep snow, father of snows,
do not harm him on the road.
Evil wind,
do not touch him.
Rainstorm,
do not overtake him.
No, chasm, terrible abyss,
do not surprise him!
My son,
you must return,
you must return!

The women's song opens with the command to the boy not to forget and closes with the injunction to return. The intermediate lines are addressed not to the child, but to the natural entities that encompass the entire territory of the community, from the snow peaks to the springs in the valley, from the sky to the earth. The women ask these entities to protect the boy from harm and to bring him home. Their song links forgetting with abandonment rather than with betrayal. I thought back to the interviews that I had conducted with fishermen, especially the older ones. When I asked them to list their children, many would mention sons and daughters who had moved to distant cities or to frontier settlements in the Amazon. Some of these children would return to attend an annual community fiesta or to help their parents during the busy potato-planting season; they would send money if a parent needed medical attention. I was surprised at how many of them returned for good after absences of many years, settling back into the rhythms of life imposed by the needs of caring for fields and flocks, by the weekly markets and the annual cycle of fiestas. A number of families, though, had a child who had not come back for years, who had not even written or sent word, who had moved beyond the social networks of the other villagers who also lived

Fallow fields on a ridge near Santiago de Huata, with the Cordillera Real behind. Photograph by Mike Reed.

in the distant areas. In some cases the parents said that they did not even know whether their child was still living. Perhaps, I thought, they did not know whether they hoped that the silence was due to an untimely death or to a deliberate act of forgetting.

To be forgotten, whether by a lover or by a child, is to be forsaken. Even the government could forget its own citizens and cast them aside: I had often heard villagers and city dwellers describe themselves as living in a *pueblo olvidado,* a forgotten town. This phrase kept cropping up; I would hear it in conversations with peasants, in speeches at village assemblies or in town squares. Officials who visited highland villages and towns would be exhorted not to forget these pueblos, these towns and villages, to remember how much they needed a school or a road or a health clinic. Reflecting on these connections, I began to understand better why officials who traveled to villages were often fed overabundantly. I recalled the enormous individual servings: a plate heaped with potatoes and topped with several large trout, a bowl of rice with big chunks of roasted mutton. In some sense the villagers were seeking to create a debt that would need to be repaid, using food, the currency at their disposal. But their concerns were not limited simply to receiving government largesse. They sought recognition that their simple fare was as good as the fancier dishes, covered with sauces, that are served in town. Most simply and most deeply, they wanted to be seen as valuable in their own right—in sum, to be remembered.

When I entered *pueblo olvidado* into the search engine of the on-line catalog at my university library, it came up with four books that had this phrase in their titles. I was struck that all of them had been written by Peruvians. Three of them are devoted to specific small towns and villages in particular parts of the highlands, and the fourth suggests that all of Peru is in essence one of these "forgotten towns." Writing at times in despair, at times with outrage, these authors stress that the degradation of these pueblos stems from the neglect by the forgetful government. Their bond to their distant homes is a kind of kinship; though they live in distant cities, they are still the "sons and daughters" of their hometowns. Their link to "the beloved homeland" creates a sense of responsibility and commitment, so they return to their hometowns for visits, and they send gifts to support the people who have remained.

Though this phrase, *pueblo olvidado,* can be understood by all Spanish speakers, none of the books were written by authors from Honduras or Venezuela or Spain or Texas. People in all these areas might wish for more attention from their governments, but they do not express such a wish with this particular idiom. In this simple and evocative phrase, the Peruvian highlanders speak of their sense that they have been overlooked, that they are not merely at the bottom of an unequal and unjust social order, but have fallen out of this order altogether.

To have devoted lovers, loyal children, generous political leaders: these forms of the wish to be remembered are widespread, as close to human universals as anthropologists, committed to the notion of cultural differences, are willing to recognize. And yet these wishes have a specifically Andean form. In this part of the world, there is always the risk of being abandoned, of having one's value not merely denied but completely ignored. The villages in which the Indian peasants live form an entire world, stretching from the high peaks to the deep valleys, a world in which one can conduct one's entire life, from birth through childhood, courtship, marriage, and parenthood to death. But they also form a part of a larger world, a modern world with cities, television, and airplanes. This vulnerability to being forgotten comes from the relations between these two worlds, from the schools in which students learn "that after loving comes forgetting," and from the beckoning cities that take children so far away that the snow-covered hills and the soaring falcons cannot bring them back.

Who could more clearly be a representative of this larger world than a gringo like me? And yet I had established ties with many individuals and with the world of the villages itself. As the people who bade me farewell had emphasized, I had seen their lives and I had shared them. I spoke Quechua, I ate simple food, I rode on the back of trucks rather than in the cab, I slept in peasant houses—sometimes even on the floor—when I stayed in villages. Like a lover, or a child, or an official, I had two choices offered to me: to esteem this world, or to abandon and betray it, simply by forgetting it. Perhaps some of the villagers had noted signs that I was not given to forgetting: the photographs of relatives and friends that I kept in my room, the stories I often told of my childhood. I think, though, that most were simply testing me as a representative of the wider world. Such strangers did not always reject them, and they could hope that I would have something to offer in addition to a camera for sale at a good price, or a chance for a nephew to receive a scholarship. I could work, in some small way, against the condemnation of their world as inferior, as forgettable. Every outsider, whether Peruvian or foreign, could be a potential ally in their struggle against oblivion.

As I reflect back, I realize that the fishermen have heeded the call not to forget. Poised between the world of the villagers and the wider world, they have faced the temptation to forget with particular force, because of the great transformations that took place in the twentieth century. Until the 1960s, the fishermen relied on ancient technologies. Fishing from rafts made of local reeds, they used harpoons, traps, and other handmade gear to obtain a small catch that they either ate at home or bartered for foodstuffs. With relatively simple technology and limited markets, they were among the poorest of the villagers—a remarkable contrast to present times, in which they have become among the wealthiest, thanks to the introduction of new kinds of boats and gear, which have increased the efficiency of their fishing, and also to the expansion of roads and markets, which allow them to sell their catch for high prices. These changes could have pulled the fishermen away from the other villagers, whose agriculture and livestock raising remain limited by the use of older tools and techniques and by static market demand. Like the lover who went away to school, or the child who left the village for the city, or the official who was passing through, the fishermen were likely to feel pride in their new position and wealth, to act with pretensions of superiority, and to forget their fellow villagers. The lakeshore villages could have been rent by divisions between the small group of new commercial fishermen and the larger populations of poorer farmers, who were more oriented toward subsistence.

That did not take place. The fishermen are very much part of village life. They converse primarily in Quechua and Aymara. They still grow their own crops, though they could afford to purchase food. They describe themselves as villagers, rather than as a separate occupational group or caste. Remembering their parents, they continue to live near their kin in the villages, rather than forming a separate neighborhood right on the shores, as fishermen in many other parts of the world do. Neither proud nor pretentious, they intermarry with other villagers. Moreover, they join in the efforts to keep their villages from becoming *pueblos olvidados* by participating actively in the efforts to obtain schools, health clinics, and other services from the government.

Many factors have sustained the ties of the fishermen to their villages. Economic and political interests connect them to the villagers who rely more heavily on their fields and flocks. By remaining part of the village, the fishermen have easier access to the protected spots on the shore where they keep their boats. Issues of cultural and ethnic identity maintain these ties as well. Fishermen, farmers, and herders all think of themselves as working people who support themselves by repetitive physical labor, conducted out of doors in all kinds of weather—unlike the townspeople, who avoid heavy manual labor and inclement weather. The power of memory itself, though, is as strong as these other forces. Like the other villagers, the fishermen remember—with surprising precision—the dense set of exchanges that are necessary to everyday life. They would not be so *ingratos* as to forget any of the individuals who helped them— who came for several days to assist them in building their adobe houses, for example, or who gave them sacks of potatoes so that they would have enough food to serve their guests at a wedding or a festival. The fishermen share as well in the lengthy past that each village possesses. This past stretches from the events of recent decades, directly observed or reported by the older generations that witnessed them, to earlier historical times, described in often-told stories—and further back, to the most remote eras that are recounted in myth. The village lands themselves demonstrate this history, since the particular location and form of rocks and hills and mountains testify to the veracity of the stories in which they figure. As new technologies and markets have allowed the fishermen to prosper, they have retained their connection with this pervasive past.

The request not to forget, then, is not always made in vain. It is not a faint plea of an overwhelmed people, but rather an injunction that demonstrates the villagers' resilience as much as their vulnerability. Strikingly, it is not an appeal to withdraw into a closed world of local custom. It is the tenacity with which the villagers hold on to the past that has enabled them to make a place for themselves in the contemporary world. The twentieth century was a time of profound changes, even in the remote Andes. It was only slowly, and in piecemeal fashion, that I came to comprehend the strength with which the villagers faced the pressures that the century placed on them—and to see that their ties to the lake itself have sustained this strength.

2   Mountains

 Soon after I moved into my apartment in Puno in 1979, I put maps of the altiplano on the wall of the larger of the two rooms. They gave it the appearance of an office or a study, thus reassuring me, when I doubted that my research was advancing very well, that I really was a serious anthropologist. Even in less anxious moments I drew some comfort from them, since they linked me to prior generations of field researchers who also had used maps as decorations. I ended up installing a large, disparate collection, justifying each addition by the fact that no single map showed in detail the entire altiplano, as the plateau that contains the Lake Titicaca basin is known. (Most maps of the altiplano are made by national governments, and each—motivated by a mix of nationalist pride and military caution— depicts the other's territory as blank space.) My favorite was a Peruvian map that showed the department of Puno. Though its dull browns and

grays lacked aesthetic appeal, it showed in great detail the configuration of the lakeshore and the lands near it. Coming in a close second were the tasteful aquatic maps that showed land in white and gray and reserved color for the lake itself, depicting waters at greater depths in successively darker shades of blue. I included as well a national map of Bolivia that indicated the country's departments not with the red, yellow, and green of the nation's flag, but with the garish substitutes of magenta, mustard, and lime.

One day, when I was taking a break from typing up notes, I got up from the piece of furniture that served as my desk and dining table and strolled over to the map-covered wall. I became interested in the largest peninsula in the lake, about seven hundred square kilometers in area. It is shaped something like an hourglass, with an unusually bulbous lower half. The bottom of the hourglass is attached to the shores of the lake; the neck is an isthmus, less than three kilometers wide; and the top projects far into the lake. The bottom half of the peninsula, I noticed, consists essentially of one tall mountain, Ccapia, whose summit, at 4,809 meters, is almost exactly a thousand meters above the level of the lake, 3,808 meters. After checking over all the maps, I realized that no place could provide a better view: other mountains are lower, or farther from shore, or behind other peaks that would block the lake. I resolved to climb to its summit. From its top I would be able to see the two main sections of the lake, the Lago Grande and the smaller Lago Pequeño, separated by the narrow Straits of Tiquina.

I would have preferred a mountain that was easier to get to. Ccapia is almost midway between Puno and the Bolivian capital of La Paz, about 120 kilometers from each. This distance was not great by the standards of industrial countries, but it meant a long trip on the dirt roads of the altiplano. I noticed that Ccapia lay near some roads, the ones that connected the larger villages on the peninsula. Wondering whether I might be able to climb this mountain, I went to the tall basket in which I kept other maps rolled up. I soon found a more detailed map of the lower portion of the peninsula. With any pretense of completing my field notes cast aside, I cleared off my table and examined the map. Drawn on a scale of 1:100,000, it indicated footpaths as thin, unbroken black lines. These lines

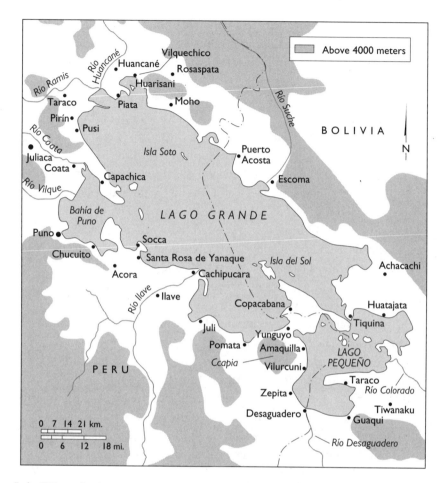

Lake Titicaca basin.

crossed the mountain and went right to the top. From my experience in other parts of Peru, I had learned that these maps were usually accurate. If they contained any mistakes, it was to omit paths, rather than to put in nonexistent ones.

I was glad to consult this map, not only to obtain the information that it contained, but also to recollect the effort that I had made to obtain it. I had seen the entire series to which it belonged in the main university library at Berkeley, and I knew that I wanted copies of the altiplano por-

tion to use in Peru. They contained valuable information on lakeshore villages, and, perhaps even more important, I knew their familiarity would
comfort me in this alien land. They bore a strong resemblance to the topo-
graphic maps on similar scales that had guided me while I was back-
packing in California. Such maps of the United States could easily be purchased in camping supply stores, but it took some doing to obtain similar
ones in Peru. There was only one place in the entire country where they
were sold: the Peruvian Military Geographical Institute, in a former mansion in an out-of-the-way neighborhood of Lima not well served by bus
lines. The room where maps were sold was just to the right of the main entry hall, in what must have been one of the formal *salas,* or living rooms,
of the mansion. Individuals who wanted to buy maps—mostly government officials who had vehicles and drivers to take them to this institute—were required to present some sort of identification. Their names,
addresses, and identity-document numbers were entered in a registry of
map-buyers. Because every copy of every map had a number stamped on
it, the government could presumably track down all the maps in case a
war broke out. (The blank obverse side of the maps bore a list of the *Obli-
gaciones del Comprador,* the duties of the purchaser, which included turning the map in to national authorities at the first signs of an outbreak of
civil disturbance.) In the case of certain regions frequented by tourists,
such as the Inca trail to Machu Picchu or the more popular peaks of the
Cordillera Blanca, the institute staff might soften the regulations and accept a hotel in Lima as an address, rather than insisting on a more permanent residence or office.

Had the changes of bus and the long walk to the institute not delayed
my arrival until late in the afternoon, when many of the staff had already
left, I probably never would have been able to obtain the five sheets of
this series, which included the portions of the border near Lake Titicaca.
I presented my passport and copies of my official *convenio,* or agreement
with the Peruvian government agency IMARPE. These documents did
not fully satisfy the clerk; he was unable to decide whether he should
sell me the maps I had requested. Would his superiors be angry with him
if they found that he had made so weighty a decision in their absence?
Was I a well-connected figure who could make trouble for him if he refused me?

After a few minutes of trying to postpone this difficult decision, he brightened. *"¿No necesita recibo, verdad?"* (You don't need a receipt, do you?), he asked. I assured him that I did not. He checked to see that the armed guard at the door was not looking in on us, then went back into the storeroom. He looked nervous as he laid out the sensitive border sheets on the counter. In too much of a rush to check my documents for the correct spelling of my sponsors, he scribbled a misspelled "IMARFE" in the space for "identification of purchaser" printed on the maps, and a second acronym, one that I have been unable to decode, "DINTE," for the "signature of permission-granting authority." He took my money, rolled the set of maps into a cylinder, thrust it into my hands, and hurried me out the door. I was delighted to have the maps in my possession and set off on the long walk to the avenue where I would catch a bus back to my hotel.

The encounter became clearer to me after I'd thought it over. Few of these maps had been sold. The clerk must have known that the registry of purchasers was checked only infrequently, so that even if the gap in these border sheets were noticed, he would be only one of several individuals on whom blame might be placed. Moreover, the acronyms he had put on my map consisted of capital letters written in block script rather than cursive. It would therefore be difficult to trace him if anyone apprehended me with the maps and doubted the legitimacy of the channels through which I had obtained them. No definitive evidence against him could be presented. In the meantime, he must have pocketed the cash that I had given him. Had he given any of it to the apparently inattentive guard, I wondered? I somehow thought that he had not, but I could not be sure.

And here in Puno, seeking to climb a mountain, my efforts at obtaining these maps paid off. This sheet, which I had previously used only to locate fishing villages and reedbeds, showed the routes to the summit of Ccapia. I asked Hugo and René, the younger biologists at IMARPE whom I saw regularly, if they'd like to join me. I had accompanied them and Eufracio, the director, on two or three trips to the peninsula, first to the remote village of Vilurcuni to select fishermen for our catch survey, and later to complete other surveys. And the IMARPE staff was always ready for an excuse to visit the border town of Yunguyo, on the peninsula's isthmus. With a smaller government presence than Desaguadero, it was a good place to pick up contraband, especially small electronic items that had been smuggled all the way across Bolivia from Brazil, and the much prized *café de los yungas,* the dark, strong-flavored coffee from the lowland Bolivian valleys between the Andes and the Amazon. But mountain climbing seemed a bit strenuous to them. Urban dwellers at heart, they liked to take their vacations in cities. Their idea of a pleasant outing in the altiplano was a visit to a hot spring or an excursion to a town with some local food specialty such as roast lamb. I kept talking up the possible climb, and it became a bit of a joke. The other biologists would tease Hugo, the shortest and fattest among them, suggesting that a run up the mountain would be a good way for him to burn off his excess kilos. He would retort that he was *gordito pero agilito,* plump but quick on his feet— a truth they had to recognize, since he was one of the best players on the IMARPE soccer team. He achieved a double balance with this response, since he knew that I never accepted the invitations of the IMARPE biologists and technicians to join in one of their games. Aside from Amanda, the one woman biologist, they were all at least competent at the sport, having played it since their boyhoods, and some of them were quite good. By contrast, I was a very poor player and did not want them to see how awkward I was on the field. This unwillingness of mine to play soccer balanced with their reluctance to climb a mountain; we were even. They were as glad as I was to have the pair of unmet invitations as a reliable and safe source of banter.

If not with my IMARPE friends, then with whom could I climb Ccapia? Though Cirilo was a sturdy walker, he was in his sixties and had limited vision. The climb might be too strenuous for him. Tito was a possibility. I had gone on outings to pre-Inca ruins and colonial churches with him. He shared my curiosity about the altiplano and my fondness for hikes, in part, I think, because he was a bit of an outsider in town himself. He was the son of the owner of one of the largest hardware stores in Puno, the grandson of Italian immigrants—and hence, by local standards, someone who was clearly a newcomer. His old Volkswagen could take us to the foot of Ccapia as reliably as the IMARPE Toyota Land Cruiser could. We discussed the trip, but it never materialized. Ccapia

Lake Titicaca in a flood year, with water covering the fields on either side of the railroad line between Puno and Juliaca. Photograph by Tom Love.

was much higher than the hills we had scrambled up to see ancient burial towers, and even Atojja, the one sizable mountain that we had climbed, was not as high. It was a good bit farther from Puno as well, and it would have entailed an earlier departure than Tito was accustomed to.

I needed some other plan. I knew that the base of the mountain was easy to get to, and that I would pass by it on one of my trips between Puno and La Paz. Occasionally, I traveled between these two cities by the routes that did not pass the mountain. I sometimes spent two or three days on the narrow winding roads on the northeast shore of the lake, with long delays in the squares of small towns while I waited for a truck to take me on the next leg of my trip. On two occasions, I went directly across the lake by steamer. This form of travel was the most enjoyable: it was comfortable, it had the best views—the sunrise over the snow-covered peaks of the Cordillera Real took on an added beauty when reflected in the waters of the lake—and the steamer itself was a wonderful old ship, the glamour it must have had in the 1930s still evident in its old brass fittings and worn velvet curtains. But these alternatives were slow, so I usually took the main road on the southwest side of the lake, and this is the road that passed by Ccapia. It was the widest of the roads around the lake, although, like all the others, it was not paved. With two full lanes, cars and trucks did not need to slow down very much to pass each other. Running through flatter terrain, it was less likely to get washed out and was more quickly repaired when it did. On this road, buses could cover the 240 kilometers between Puno and La Paz in ten hours, sometimes in eight.

This road went south from Puno through a series of small towns: Chucuito, Acora, Ilave, Juli, Pomata. These had been former *cabaceras,* or chiefly villages, of the Lupaqa nation, both when it was an independent kingdom and after it was conquered by the Incas and became a province of their empire. The towns had been parishes under Spanish rule, and they became districts soon after independence. When the road reached Pomata, at the base of Ccapia, it divided in two. The principal branch continued to the southwest along the base of the hourglass peninsula. It passed below Ccapia and reached first Zepita (the sixth of the Lupaqa settlements) and then Desaguadero, a town named for the river on whose banks it had been built. This river marks the border between Peru and Bolivia, and Desaguadero is the easiest place to cross between these two countries: the Peruvian border station is only a few blocks from the river, and the Bolivian station is right next to the modern cement bridge. The Bolivian portion of the trip to La Paz passed quickly on the flat road that climbed slowly up the altiplano away from the lake until it reached the lip of the canyon in which the city stands.

The other fork of the road from Pomata offered a slower, more scenic route to La Paz. Following the edge of the lower half of the hourglass, it hugged the shore, circling around Ccapia to Yunguyo, the seventh and last of the Lupaqa towns, and to the border, two kilometers farther on. Passengers were not permitted to ride between the several hundred meters that separated the border stations, but instead had to walk, a process that often created a certain amount of confusion and delay. Seven kilometers past the border lay the first Bolivian town, Copacabana, the site of major shrines since pre-Inca times and now the seat of a cathedral and the home of the Virgin of Copacabana, Bolivia's patron saint. The name of this town has traveled far, carried first in the early sixteenth century by the Portuguese explorers to the beach near the city of Rio de Janeiro and second in the mid-twentieth century by North American businessmen to their nightclub on East 60th Street in Manhattan. From Copacabana the road wound up the ridge that formed the central part of the upper half of the hourglass. The flat top of this ridge, less than half as high as Ccapia, afforded spectacular views, but I recalled it principally for the sense of foreboding that it evoked. At several bends in the road, hungry dogs would run up to the bus, yapping loudly. The local people, rather than ignoring them as they usually would, opened windows and tossed pieces of bread down to them. These dogs were *almas perdidas,* they explained to me, lost souls: souls that had escaped from purgatory and taken animal form, souls capable of retribution against those who denied them their wishes. From this haunted ridge the road curved down to Tiquina, where the lake narrows to a strait less than a kilometer wide. The buses queued up here for their turn to take one of the ferries, flat wooden boats barely larger than the buses themselves. The road on the other shore had another ridge to climb and descend before it finally reached the flat portion of the altiplano that led to La Paz.

I could not easily select between the alternatives of approaching the mountain from the Copacabana road or the Desaguadero road. The former would let me begin the climb from a town where I could ask for directions, since the route from Yunguyo to the peak was short. The latter would require me to ask the bus driver to drop me off somewhere in the potato fields and pastures roughly midway between Pomata and Zepita. Despite that difficulty, however, the second route had some advantages: it had more traffic, and it would take me through an area of great historical interest. I was curious to see this area between Desaguadero and Pomata, a key route across the altiplano for centuries, and as such, a battleground. It was the site where the Incas quelled the largest rebellion that they had ever faced. The altiplano, with its autonomous Aymara-speaking kingdoms, was one of the most difficult regions for them to conquer. The Pacajes, the former kingdom to the south of the Lupaqa, rose up around the 1470s. It was not subjugated until the Incas staged a decisive victory around 1488. In 1538, still not fully under Spanish rule despite the military successes of the conquistadores against the Incas elsewhere in the Andes, this place saw a set of battles between the Spaniards and Lupaqa, who had retained a distinctive identity even after their incorporation into the Inca empire. In this fighting, the Spaniards received some support from the Colla, the Aymara kingdom to the north of the Lupaqa, which they controlled more tightly. In 1823 this area witnessed one of the key events in the Wars of Independence on this part of the continent. As schoolchildren in both countries know well, the republicans under General Santa Cruz defeated the royalists in the Battle of Zepita. If I were to hike through this area, I thought, I might find some evidence of the fortifications in the region. At the very least, I would be able to imagine more concretely the troops that had fought here in earlier centuries.

Neither the convenience of the Yunguyo route on the Copacabana road nor the interest of the battlefields on the Desaguadero road were attractions strong enough to make me select one over the other. The routes were similar in their difficulty. They both had an elevation gain of a thousand meters, and the round-trip distances were also very close: twenty-five kilometers for the former, twenty-three for the latter. Moreover, they both shared a key logistical difficulty: I would not be able to take the detailed map with me, since these maps were sensitive documents, and I had to consider the possibility that I might be searched if I were to hike so close to the border. I took this risk seriously, since I had had a difficult encounter with a policeman at the border earlier that year. After he saw me taking photographs of the Río Desaguadero, he wanted to confiscate my camera. It required all my rhetorical abilities to convince him to let me keep it. I was not a spy, I told him, but an anthropologist. This river fascinated me for its ecological and historical significance—look how small it is, considering that it is the only outflow of the lake; that's because much more water leaves the lake by evaporation than by flowing down the river. Did he know that the Incas had maintained a pontoon bridge there, constructed of reed rafts, and that such bridges were maintained throughout the colonial period and well into the nineteenth century? Either impressed by my reference to his nation's pre-Columbian heritage or eager to escape my babbling, he let me keep the camera, but I did not want to meet him, or any colleague of his, while I was illegally transporting a document. I thought of the alternatives: if I rolled it up and brought it with me in the cardboard tube that I ordinarily used for carrying maps, it would be conspicuous enough to attract attention. If I folded it and concealed it in my bag, it would certainly wear along the creases. Moreover, if it were found there, I would have a more difficult time pleading innocence. Better to leave it in Puno, where it would remain safely for me to consult in the future.

The thought of a mapless ascent troubled me. I recalled one such hike that I had taken on my own. It took me longer than I had anticipated to climb the ridge that separated two small towns, Luribay and Sapahaqui, in valleys halfway down to the lowlands east of La Paz. Leaving Luribay just after sunrise, I had to retrace my steps several times to find the correct route out of the valley. I arrived in Sapahaqui not late in the afternoon, as I had hoped, or even at nightfall, but in the middle of the following morning, exhausted from a night spent in an uncomfortable bivouac near the crest of the ridge, and very thirsty as well. Unwilling to drink from the springs that I knew might be contaminated by sheep and llamas, I had nothing to supplement the two quarts of water that I had brought, other than the moisture I could extract by chewing the cobs of the fresh-boiled corn that, along with a roll, some cheese, and some figs, had been the food I was given by the family with whom I'd stayed in Luribay.

As with so many undertakings in the altiplano, then, the climb up Ccapia would depend on personal contacts, on finding someone who could lead me to the summit. I added the bottom half of the peninsula to my mental list—already quite lengthy—of places in which I wanted to meet local residents. The IMARPE biologists introduced me to an employee of the Ministry of Fisheries from Yunguyo, Diogenes Choquehuanca. He described with enthusiasm the many times he had made the climb as a boy, and the wonderful view from the top. I could visit his parents, he told me; he was sure that one of his brothers could accompany me to the peak. I willingly agreed to the favor that Diogenes requested in return, to bring an *encargo*—a package of some sort—to his parents.

Several weeks later, when I was preparing to travel from Puno to La Paz, I looked up Diogenes at the Ministry of Fisheries office. I returned the next day to receive the item he wanted me to deliver. I was pleased to find that it was only an envelope. On the following morning I picked up a bus in Puno. It traveled through the lakeshore towns that had become familiar to me. I was always struck by the well-preserved square in the first town, Chucuito, and its most striking feature, the churches. With their massive bulk and the long arcaded walls that surrounded their courtyards, they retained something of the authority that they must have had at the time of their construction in the decades after the Spanish conquest. The plaza contained a *rollo* as well. This fluted column, erected in the mid-1500s, served as a pillory under the Spaniards: Indians who violated the law could be punished by being tied to the *rollo* and whipped. Though such *rollos* had been placed in many towns, few survive to the present.

After Chucuito the road continued through the flat lakeshore zone, the land a patchwork of cultivated and fallow fields, with clusters of low adobe houses scattered among them. Other towns came every half hour or so. Like Chucuito, they had features that had become familiar to me: the bridge in Ilave over the river of the same name, the largest of the streams that flowed down into the lake from the Cordillera Occidental; the four fine churches in Juli; the small cluster of food vendors near Pomata, where the bus would always stop at lunchtime and where I would buy a bowl of soup with several large potatoes and a hunk of meat. The roofs of Yunguyo were visible at some distance as the bus worked its way across the flatlands near the lake. Once I arrived in the town, I quickly found the house of Diogenes' parents. I was not sure which of several possible factors accounted for the warmth with which they received me. Had the envelope contained some check or document that they had been awaiting? Had he written very positively about me? Did they hope that I would somehow promote his career? Or were they simply hospitable people, glad for the presence of a visitor to add some variety to their lives? In our conversations later that afternoon, I learned that they included other foreigners in the circle of their acquaintances; they showed me the collection of Christmas cards, some of them several years old, pinned to one wall of their living room, including ones that they had received from a Peace Corps volunteer who had lived in a nearby village.

I have a clearer sense of the motives of Diogenes's older brother in agreeing to lead me up the mountain the next day. Dante—like his brother and their other six siblings, named for a literary figure rather than a saint, as is more common in the altiplano—had studied at a university but had not finished his degree. He had lived for a while in Arequipa, the largest city in southern Peru, where he had worked as the assistant manager in a store, only to find that this job did not turn out the way that he had hoped. He had plans to return to Arequipa in a few months on a business deal that involved a few partners. In the meantime, he was back in Yunguyo, living with his wife and children in two rooms in the back of his parents' house, helping out occasionally in his parents' store, and altogether a bit bored. He welcomed an educated outsider with whom he could talk, and he had nothing to do the next day that could not be postponed. His father seemed pleased, as much to give his older son the chance to spend some time out of the town from which he wanted to move permanently as to return to me the favor of having brought the envelope from his younger son.

We arose early the next morning and had a large breakfast—habits that I associate with Aymara-speaking households, whether rural peasants, as most of them are, or prosperous urban merchants like the Choquehuancas. Dante's older child, a boy of about eight with the undistinguished name of Juan, was eager to join his father and this exotic stranger and came along as well. Out the door, down the street: two blocks later and we left the town behind. The cement street turned into a dirt road with some ruts left by the few trucks that occasionally traveled on it. Because the land sloped upward so gradually from the lake, I would have had no sense of climbing at all for the first half hour, if it had not been for the massive presence of Ccapia, looming larger as we approached it. We continued onward among the fields, brown at this time of year. Some of them contained parallel lines of ridges and furrows, dotted with clumps of barley stubble. Others were covered with large clods of earth, which were left after potatoes had been dug from the ground. There were occasional bare patches of whitish ground, too prone to flooding to per-

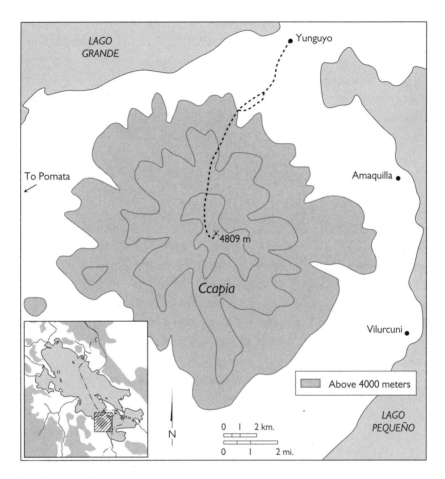

The Ccapia route.

mit cultivation. Every few hundred meters we would pass a family compound—a few adobe houses clustered near one another, linked by a low adobe wall with a doorway leading into the courtyard.

After an hour or so, we reached the first hills, dotted with eucalyptus groves, that flanked the mountain. The road continued between two ridges that descended from the mountain to bound a small field-filled valley, an extension of the flatlands around the lake. We did not go very far into this valley, but rather swung up onto the ridge on our right. After a short, steep climb on a path that went between stone terraces, we decided to take a break and sat down on some boulders. Though Dante was not, I thought, a regular consumer of coca leaf, the mild stimulant used throughout the Andes, this rest stop struck him, as it did me, as a good spot at which to chew some leaves. Juan watched with surprise to see a gringo retrieve from his pack a plastic bag containing dry green leaves a few centimeters long, but he seemed familiar with the process of chewing itself—the adults passing the bag back and forth, thoughtfully selecting leaves and placing them in our mouths, then biting off a little corner of the cake of *llipt'a*. This gray lump, made from the ashes of stalks of certain plants, contains the alkaline substance that invariably accompanies coca-chewing. Though Dante did not blow on the leaves or offer blessings to the mountains, as more traditional people might, he did pick them carefully from the bag and hold them between thumb and forefinger in a little fanlike arrangement before adding them to the quid in his cheek. We all sat quietly for a few moments, before Dante proposed that we resume our climb.

We continued up the ridge, leaving behind the last of the potato fields about the time that we reached its crest. In this part of the altiplano, agriculture is confined to the shores of the lake and the areas immediately adjacent to them, where the climate is milder than in the surrounding highlands. This crest ascended more gently than the sides of the ridge, leading us to broader, more open country that rose steadily but not steeply toward the peak. The climb was not difficult, I realized, despite the elevation of the summit. Ccapia is hundreds of meters higher than the tallest peaks in the lower forty-eight states; as I later discovered, it reaches a few meters higher than Mont Blanc, the highest mountain in the Alps. Nonetheless, it was proving to be what my climbing friends in California call a walk-up.

This uncultivated land looked quite different from the flat areas below us. The slopes of the mountain were covered with *ichu*, the perennial grasses that grow in clumps half a meter or so across, each composed of hundreds of blades of grass, cylindrical rather than flat, rising up a quarter to half a meter. The clumps of *ichu* stretched for kilometers on either side of the narrow path we followed, with occasional low, tiny-leafed shrubs scattered among them. This landscape, the *puna,* as the grasslands are known, had little in common with the Amazonian forests that lay only eighty kilometers to the northeast of us, and four kilometers lower. It was much more like the distant steppes of Siberia, or like northern Canada, another region of vast open landscapes, of tough perennial plants adapted to a cold, harsh climate. The steppes and the *puna* are the homelands of herds of large ruminants, animals whose bodies are large enough to prevent rapid heat loss, and whose multiple stomachs can digest the rough vegetation. Reindeer and caribou in the steppes support pastoralists of the more domesticated varieties, hunters of the wilder ones. Animals and people live in close association in the *puna* as well. Here on Ccapia, we saw flocks of sheep off in the distance. Llamas and alpacas, I knew, were more numerous in the higher portions of the cordilleras, and vicuñas, though much reduced by hunting, were still found in remote zones.

This empty country invited the pace that we adopted: steady and fairly fast, but not hurried. Up on the slopes of the mountain, the trail was narrower than the paths between the fields down near the lake. We fell into the most comfortable order: Dante in front, his son Juan close behind, and I in the rear. Even if the trail had been wider, I do not think that we would have spoken much in this open grassland. The empty expanses of the *puna* corresponded to the silence in which we walked.

After a couple of hours, we reached a spot where the rock outcroppings, which so far had been quite low, grew large. We rounded a bend and came to a tiny pond, a few hectares in area. This seemed a good place for lunch, with a distinctive feature of landscape, some large boulders to sit next to, and a clear view of the town of Juli and a broad stretch of lakeshore below us. Though he had been hiking uncomplainingly, Juan seemed particularly glad to stop. We shared the bread, chocolate, and oranges that I had brought and the cheese that Dante carried, and we chatted for a while. They had some questions about the United States, and they wanted to hear once again about my project with the biologists at IMARPE and my link to Diogenes. Then Dante spoke of the pond and its legends. The pond is surprisingly deep, he told me. Some people say that it contains treasure; the old people believe that ducks made of gold appear on its surface for a few moments each year. I reflected on these stories, wondering how seriously he took them. I was not sure whether he was more eager for me or for his son to hear them. Perhaps he wanted his son to hear him tell these stories to a foreigner like me, so that he would take some pride in the old tales. But my mind did not linger on these possibilities. I was content to look down at Juli and pick out the churches, and then to gaze off across the lake. We sat for some time and then realized that we still had a good bit of distance to cover.

We set off and resumed our firm pace. As we rounded a corner, a breeze picked up. I noticed that the sun had begun to swing down. It was already early in the afternoon, later than we had expected, when we reached the summit, a little rise atop the mountain's broad crest. For the last portion of the climb, we had been hiking with our backs to the lake, not stopping to look behind us. When we turned around, the whole altiplano appeared before our eyes: the enormous sheet of the lake below us, beyond it a spread of dry grasslands rising to long chains of snow-covered peaks. For all my anticipation of this view, I still was unprepared for its immense scale. The lake itself was far bigger than I had expected. The opposite shore, sixty kilometers to the northeast, seemed very remote, and the most distant portions of the lake, near the delta formed by the Río Huancané, lay beyond the horizon, even though we stood a full thousand meters above the lake's surface. From our vantage point atop the highest point on the peninsula, the lake seemed to stretch around us. Filling 240 degrees of the view, it could not be taken in all at once. If we looked immediately below us at the southwestern shore near Juli, we had to turn our heads to see the Río Desaguadero.

Only one small portion of the eighty-one hundred square kilometers of the lake's surface was obstructed from view. The upper half of the hourglass peninsula contains a broad ridge that blocks the view of the Straits of Tiquina. This narrow, canyonlike channel, less than a kilometer wide and four kilometers long, separates the Lago Grande from the Lago Pequeño. Had I not known that these two were connected by the straits, I might have taken them for two bodies of water, separate and distinct. The Lago Pequeño was not only smaller, but filled with many more islands; the uninterrupted expanse of the Lago Grande seemed almost oceanic in scale. I recalled the Bolivians whom I once had heard discussing whether Lake Titicaca was so large that it should not be termed a *lago,* a lake, but rather a *mar continental,* an inland sea. From this vantage, I had no doubt that it merited such a name.

I began to pick out some of the specific features in the lake. The town of Copacabana, quite close to us, was easy to find, and immediately offshore from it was the largest island in the lake, with its distinctive steep cliffs. This island appears as Isla Titicaca on old maps but is now known as the Isla del Sol, the Island of the Sun, for the temples that the Incas built on it to commemorate its importance. Viracocha, the creator, had made the world and peopled it with a race of giants, but had left it in darkness. Dissatisfied with the giants, Viracocha caused a great flood, whose waters still remain in Titicaca. After the flood, he decided to remake the universe in a different way. He created the sun and the moon on the Isla del Sol, giving light to the world, and then went to Tiwanaku, where he formed animals and humans.

Other islands were in view as well. That more distant one must be Soto, the island near the deepest portion of the lake, where many fishermen caught trout and carried them illegally across the border from Peru into Bolivia. How brave they seemed, crossing the broad open waters in five-meter boats. And those hills were the pasturelands of Chuquiñapi, a village that I had traveled to several times. Its position on the corner of a large peninsula could not be confused with any other place, even though its shores were blocked from view by a ridge. But which was that distant town on the Bolivian shore beyond the Isla del Sol, the few roofs distinct among the fields? Was it Escoma or Puerto Acosta, or could it even be Moho, on the Peruvian side of the border, across the lake? And was that distant small fleck of land the island of Socca, Cirilo's home, the village that I had visited so many times?

I tired of these efforts at identification and let my eyes rest on the vast lake itself. I could see many shades of blue on its surface, and as I looked more closely, I could note the play of rougher and smoother patches of water as the winds shifted. I stared for a long time at the distant horizon, where the sky met the lake. And then my gaze was drawn back nearer me, and upward, not merely to the cluster of mountains that I had expected, to Illimani and the other high peaks near La Paz, but to a long, gleaming sweep of white, the full extent of the Cordillera Real. Here I could see the sections that, to people standing on the shores of the lake, were hidden behind lower ranges, and here, too, I realized to my astonishment, I could see other mountains glinting far to the northeast in the distant Cordillera de Carabaya. These two cordilleras form the local portion of the eastern cordillera, the Cordillera Oriental, the great eastern flank of the Andes that stretches from Venezuela and Colombia down into Patagonia, the wall that separates the highlands from the Amazonian forests immediately beyond. Puffy clouds had begun to build over a few of the summits, suggesting the humidity of the forests that lay behind the mountains. We had climbed a kilometer up from the level of the lake, but the highest peaks reached two full kilometers above us. *Majestic* is surely an overused adjective, and yet these ranges did possess the quality of solemn grandeur that that word evokes. It was as if I had come not before a king or queen, but before an entire assembled court whose imposing stateliness derived equally from the presence of a few exalted figures and from the dignified array of many other, lesser, yet still noble personages—the other peaks, which, though lower than the tallest ones, still stood higher than I did.

Dante and Juan relished the attention that I gave to the Cordillera Real. Dante's travels had left him with an awareness of how little Yunguyo mattered to people from large cities and foreign countries, so he was pleased to find a gringo who was so evidently impressed by these local attractions. Still, both he and his son were surprised not that I could identify Illimani, but that I knew so few of the other mountains' names. Juan took these mountains' importance for granted and seemed not to believe my statements of ignorance when I asked his father which peak was Illampu, which one was Huayna Potosí. It was like standing with New Yorkers in view of the Manhattan skyline and asking them to point out the World Trade Center and the Empire State Building. These mountains were familiar to them not merely as reference points on the horizon, but as more immediate presences as well. The mountains send the winds that blow across the altiplano. Each wind bears the name not of the cardinal direction from which it comes, but of the mountain that is its source.

View across the Straits of Tiquina to the Cordillera Real in Bolivia. Photograph by
Mike Reed.

Dante and Juan identified a few of the other major peaks that I asked
about and then turned to the part of the view that most held their attention.
Had there been a city in sight, I think that they would have pointed it out
to me, but there was no town with more than ten thousand inhabitants in
the eighty thousand square kilometers before us. La Paz lay deep in a
canyon, and both Puno and Juliaca, the two sizable cities on the Peruvian
altiplano, were far to the north, beyond the curve of the horizon. They
showed me instead the nearby towns of Pomata, Zepita, and Desaguadero; that space far below us, surrounded by buildings, was the plaza of
Yunguyo, and those tiny specks were the town's market, its two churches,
its secondary school. Amid the darker shade of the cultivated lands right
near the lake were the villages, all of whose names Dante and Juan knew.

As the day progressed into mid-afternoon, I sensed their impatience
(they must have recognized that they would have to be the ones to propose starting our descent), but I had one last thing to do. I wanted to look

at the Cordillera Occidental, the western cordillera, the other main chain of the Andes. We turned our backs to the lake and the Cordillera Real. Surely the western cordillera must be more impressive than this, I thought. And there must be something worth looking at in the huge expanse of dry *puna* that stretched away from us to the western range. Dante agreed with me that the white spot on the horizon, so small as to be barely recognizable, must be Sajjama, at sixty-five hundred meters the highest peak in that part of the altiplano. Like a novice stargazer trying to locate the Pleiades or the Andromeda galaxy, I stared and speculated. Could that peak be Parinacota, a volcano on the border between Peru and Chile? I liked that mountain because I understood its simple Aymara name, Flamingo Lake: in that dry zone were many shallow saline lakes containing the crustaceans that supported enormous flocks of the brightly colored birds. Could I expect to see the mountains immediately beyond Arequipa, Chachani, Pichu-pichu, and Misti? I had climbed more than halfway up Misti nine years earlier, only to be turned back by unexpected clouds, which thickened during my descent and which dispersed the next morning to reveal the peak covered with the season's first snow, unusual both for its early date and its great extent.

Though Dante and Juan stood quietly, I sensed that I was testing their patience with these questions. (Weeks later, back in my apartment in Puno, I resolved them myself with more map study: I probably had seen Parinacota, but not Misti.) Even if we had had far more time, though, their attention would not have been held for long by these western mountains, which are less important in local folktales and are less striking visually than their eastern counterparts. It was not that they are lower than the Cordillera Real and the Cordillera de Carabaya. In fact, some of its peaks are higher. Rather, it was that certain climatological facts, with which I was familiar, leave them less interesting to look at. Cloud-laden air masses travel westward from the Amazon, dropping heavy rains and snows on the eastern cordillera, the first mountains they encounter. Though the second barrier of the western cordillera succeeds in intercepting virtually all of the clouds that reach it—to the west of it lies the Atacama Desert, the driest place on the surface of the earth—it still receives a smaller share of the moisture than the eastern cordillera. Because of the more frequent and heavier storms to which it is subject, then, the Cordillera Oriental has a much lower snowline than the Occidental. As we stood atop Ccapia, to our northeast lay the broad white swath of the eastern cordillera; to the southwest were the peaks of the western cordillera, many of them higher than their snow-covered counterparts (some of them reach above fifty-eight hundred meters), but all of them appearing as dry heaps of rock or, at most, small zones of snow. Indeed, the western cordillera contains the highest snow-free mountains in the world—a feature that attracts some ice-averse mountain climbers, but that does not give it great visual appeal.

Finally, it was time to go. I was as ready to start down as Dante and Juan. Even if we had somehow been able to camp at the summit and return to Yunguyo the next day, I would not have sat still and gazed steadily at these mountains for the hours that our climb down the mountain required. I would have grown too cold and restless. The steady pace of our descent—like our ascent, the trip down was made in silence—provided just enough warmth and motion for me to enter a pensive state in which I became mesmerized by Illimani and the other mountains whose names I had just learned: Illampu and Huayna Potosí, their snowy crowns turning opalescent as the afternoon drew on. I felt a satisfaction that came not only from physical effort, not only from the successful completion of a long-anticipated endeavor, but also from a feeling of wholeness linked to the wholeness of the mass of the mountain we had climbed, to the wholeness of the altiplano we had seen. As we came lower down, we saw the shepherds and their flocks returning home, and then a truck driving down a road with a long plume of dust trailing behind it. Far off, barely within earshot, a donkey brayed.

If we had begun our descent earlier, or if Ccapia were not so large, we could have chosen a different way back to Yunguyo, perhaps seeing some other villages, but the lateness of our return required us to follow the same path we had taken up. Dante led us on a route that differed from our ascent in only one detail: to reach the little valley that formed an extension of the flatlands near the lake, we dropped down from the last ridge not at the spot where we had stopped to chew coca, but at a higher point, taking a little-used trail with numerous switchbacks. This trail took us through a sizable stand of eucalyptus, perhaps a few hundred trees. I had seen many such groves before, but never had I reacted to them this way: the gray-green leaves, with their hard, waxy coats, had often seemed harsh to me, but after the hours spent in open grasslands, the slight rustle of the leaves and their fresh, aromatic fragrance struck me as lush and appealing.

I noticed a change in Dante and Juan once our trail left the ridge and joined the main path down the valley. Although it was nearly dusk, their pace slackened a bit, and they began to speak more. In his tone, if not in his words, Juan seemed relieved to get off the mountain while it was still light, as if he had been troubled by the thought of remaining in that wild place after dark. Dante, I thought, had been able to sense his son's fear because he had felt it himself. He, too, had been eager to return to the lower zone of fields, of wider paths, of greater human presence. We could now walk side by side, and we began to speak of the hike as if it were over, even though Yunguyo was still five kilometers away. Despite the growing darkness, we could easily follow the path. It was wide (or at least it seemed so, after the narrow trails on the mountain), fairly straight, and lighter than the fields on either side. We sensed the houses along the path as much from the barking of a dog or the sudden scent of burning dung as from the sight of their black forms against the night sky, which was rapidly filling with stars. Tired but content, we trudged easily along, knowing that we would be back to Dante and Juan's house in less than an hour. I felt a great sense of comfort from the completion of the long day, the security of our return, the anticipation of the meal that awaited us, and above all, from the poignancy of the many small reminders of human habitation down here. The climb had been a vivid reminder of something I had known intellectually for a long time, that the strip of land right on the shores of the lake, for all its droughts, frosts, and floods, is the only hospitable section in the immense, barren steppe of grass and rock that stretches from one cordillera to the other. This narrow ribbon of farmland is home to the villagers. Within its confines they build their houses, cultivate their fields, and set out in their tiny boats onto the waters of the lake, whose vastness I now could comprehend.

When we arrived in Yunguyo, the pavement and the faint illumination of the streetlights made it seem like a city. We passed a few stores that were open, each spilling a wedge of brighter light into the street. Dante greeted someone who passed us but did not stop to talk. We were welcomed in his house with a flurry of concern for our late arrival. Dante's parents gladly received our apologies and my willing acceptance of responsibility for our delay. Though Dante's younger siblings had already eaten, his parents and wife had waited for us to have a late dinner of soup and a dish of meat and noodles. After we ate, the two women went back to the kitchen, where Juan soon joined them. Dante turned his chair slightly toward his father and talked with him. I was relieved to have a few moments to be alone with my thoughts. I drifted into a reverie, but it did not last long. Dante, apparently as tired as I was, soon proposed that we go to sleep.

We all awoke early the next day. After breakfast and the exchange of a long series of farewells and promises to write, I set off for La Paz. A truck carried me through the two border stations without delay and dropped me off in the plaza in Copacabana, where I found a bus that would be leaving soon for La Paz. It wound its way up the ridge, pausing for the passengers to toss bread to the dogs, and then worked its way down to the ferry stop at the Straits of Tiquina. I was glad when the bus completed the series of switchbacks up the next ridge. Ccapia came back into view, accompanying me for all of the long last leg of the trip.

I looked out at Ccapia and noted again its broad rounded shape, so different from the sharper peaks of the eastern cordillera that loomed a few dozen kilometers off the road. Enormous geological forces have been at work to create these mountains. The most important element of the geology of this region is the convergence of the continent of South America with the bottom of the Pacific Ocean. This portion of the Andes has been shaped by the operation of plate tectonics—the movement of the plates, or large sections of the earth's crust, and the uppermost mantle in relation to one another. The South American plate, which includes nearly all of South America and the western half of the bottom of the South Atlantic Ocean, has been pulling away from Africa, to which it had formerly been attached, and moving generally westward for the last 150 million years. Along most of its western margin, it meets the Nazca plate, the plate that carries portions of the bottom of the South Pacific Ocean east-ward. The mountainous Andes are the result of this impact, in which two enormously massive objects move toward each other at an enormously slow rate. The Nazca plate is thrust under the South American plate, slip-ping beneath it at an angle of about 30 degrees. As the South American plate rides up over this huge obstacle, the entire altiplano region is lifted up, and certain portions—particularly the eastern cordillera—have formed folds perpendicular to the direction of motion, much as the hood of a car would fold under such an impact. Along lesser folds and faults, blocks slide past each other, one side moving up, the other down. It is this movement that accounts for Lake Titicaca's great depth in places—more than 280 meters in spots—as well as for the steep cliffs on many of its islands and peninsulas. Moreover, as the Nazca plate plunges into the mantle, pools of magma form and rise, creating some small volcanoes within the altiplano (Ccapia is one such extinct volcano) and the higher volcanoes of the western cordillera. In recent years, geologists have stud-ied this uplift in detail, examining regional variation in these mountain-forming processes in the crust and the interactions between the crust and the mantle that underlie them.

The most recent chapter of this long history, two or three million years in length, is the time for which there is strong evidence of the pres-ence of lakes in the altiplano. In geological terms, lakes are ephemeral. It is not much of an exaggeration to compare them to puddles that disap-pear soon after they form, since it takes a delicate balance of factors for lakes to endure over long periods. Minor shifts in climate have large con-sequences for lakes. For example, lakes shrink rapidly in dry, warm peri-ods, faced with both a reduced input of water and an increased loss from higher rates of evaporation. Even in cool, moist periods, lakes may not be permanent. The rivers that bring water to them also carry sediments that deposit on the bottom. As these sediments accumulate, lakes become shallower and can eventually fill up altogether. The rivers that carry wa-ter out of lakes are also part of this steady process of material moving downslope; they erode their own banks and eat away at the basins of lakes. Because of these processes of sedimentation and erosion, lakes are scarce in some of the rainiest parts of the world. The age that is required

for a lake to be termed "ancient" is only a few hundred thousand years—
an age at which a river would still be in its youth, and a mountain range
in its infancy. Few areas of the world have the specific combination of
topography and climate that is required for lakes to reach even this age.
A large proportion of such lakes is located between parallel steep mountain ranges in regions of the world with fairly moist climates. Titicaca is
found in such a setting, as is the world's oldest lake, Baikal, in Siberia,
and the lakes of the Great Rift Valley of Africa: Malawi, Tanganyika, and
the smaller Albert and Turkana.

Like these other ancient lakes, Titicaca has undergone great variations.
During the Ice Ages of the Pleistocene, when the earth's climate was
cooler and moister, there were lakes in the altiplano larger than present-
day Titicaca. Their presence can be inferred from fossilized diatoms and
mollusks, as well as from the remains of former shorelines, now standing
on hillsides above the lake. Half a million years ago, one of these lakes,
known as Lake Ballivián, was about fifty meters higher than Lake Titicaca. At this time, Ccapia was an island. In periods between the glacia-
tions, the lakes shrank considerably. The Straits of Tiquina may have dried
up, separating the Lago Pequeño from the main lake. The history of the
lakes in the region over the last twenty thousand years or so can be as-
sessed more precisely through an examination of the sediments at Titicaca's lake bottom. The pollen and minerals that slowly accumulated in the
muck record changes in the depth, temperature, and salinity of the lake.
These records suggest that the level of Titicaca shifted by tens of meters
in this period, assuming its current level only a few thousand years ago.

This most recent geological evidence overlaps with the oldest archaeological record. The earliest archaeological sites in the altiplano are about
eight thousand years old. They consist of small hunter-gatherer settlements in the *puna* above the lake, probably inhabited by people who traveled up from the Pacific Coast. For many decades, archaeologists believed
that humans reached the Americas about eleven or twelve thousand years
ago, crossing from Siberia into Alaska when ocean levels were lower and
the Bering Strait was dry. The earliest sites are difficult to locate, since
human populations were small and the few remains they left have not
always survived the intervening millennia. However, in recent years,

archaeological sites that are as much as fifteen thousand years old have been discovered in southern Chile, leaving open the possibility of earlier settlement in the altiplano as well. The question of the age of settlement in the Americas thus has been reopened. Even so, it is certain that the history of humans in the altiplano is only a fraction of the history of Lake Titicaca, much as the age of the lake is only a fraction of the age of the Andes—and the Andes, in turn, are geologically quite young compared to the age of our planet, calculated to be between four and five billion years.

3 Names

In its most basic outline, the story that I want to tell about Lake Titicaca is a simple one. If I were to reduce it to a paragraph, it would run like this: Through the first half of the twentieth century, fishermen set out from shore in small balsas made of reeds. Sticking close to land, they used many kinds of traditional gear designed to work in shallow waters. Each village managed its own onshore fishing grounds through a system of customary laws. There was very little traffic in the open waters of the lake. Around the middle of the century, fishermen acquired wooden boats and nylon nets. They traveled farther from shore to the deeper waters, where they could catch trout and silverside, two commercially valuable species that recently had been introduced into the lake. As they moved into this offshore zone, they encountered a new political force, since the Peruvian state had become more active in its efforts to patrol and govern the lake.

A fisherman rowing a boat near Huancané. Photograph by Ben Orlove.

The small navy base at Puno had expanded, and others were opened, and other agencies, such as the Ministry of Fisheries, had established offices in Puno. The central government claimed to be the only body that could grant permission to travel or fish on the lake. On the basis of this claim, it established regulations to control access to the lake. The offshore waters became disputed territory: would they be controlled by the villagers or the government? The conflicts took many forms. The two sides often refused to acknowledge each other, but sometimes they fought violently. By the 1980s, the local villagers, possessed of a remarkable tenacity, gained control of the offshore waters and kept their customary hold on the onshore waters. Both of these zones remain in the hands of the fishermen to the present. The fish bring them a good income. Moreover, as a number of ecological surveys have shown, they manage the lake well: the populations of fish, birds, and plants are all stable.

This story is a local version of events that are taking place around the world. There are more people in the world than ever before, and they are demanding more goods, putting pressure on our planet's finite resources. The earth's empty spaces are filling up. Local people are often displaced by outsiders: in the Amazon, by government-sponsored settlement schemes, petroleum corporations, and wealthy ranchers; in islands in the Caribbean and the Pacific, by tourist enterprises; in the grasslands of East Africa, by game preserves and national parks; even in many farming regions of the United States, by large corporations and suburban developers. Unlike local people who seek to preserve their lands for future generations, these newcomers frequently do not look beyond their next annual report or the next election. They often use resources at an unsustainable rate. In this context, the story of the Lake Titicaca villagers is unusual and important, because the outsiders are usually the ones who win.

Before I begin telling the story of the fishermen in greater detail, though, I must complete a preliminary task: choosing the names to describe the groups of people about whom I write. This problem of names sometimes struck me with particular force when I spoke to groups about my research at Lake Titicaca. I must have delivered several dozen such talks, if I include presentations to undergraduates and graduates in classes as well as lectures at other universities, meetings of academic societies, and a few invitations from fisheries experts and development agencies. On most of these occasions, the discussions after the talks were limited to scholarly issues. There were a few times, however, when I received a more direct sort of question. Someone in the audience would object to my use of the word *fisherman* on the grounds that this gender-specific word reinforced gender inequalities in Peru and in the United States. I would always begin my reply by saying that men did virtually all the fishing on Lake Titicaca. It was rare for a woman to set out with boats and nets. A woman might wade into the lake with a dip net attached to a long pole and scoop some fish out of the shallow waters right offshore, but even such small efforts were unusual. At this point, the conversation would shift onto one of a series of possible tracks. My challenger and I would sometimes collaborate in the effort to replace *fisherman* with a gender-neutral alternative, along the lines of the substitution of *letter carrier* for *mailman* or *firefighter* for *fireman*. Other people in the audience would sometimes join this discussion. I could use *fishing village,* a term that seemed familiar, and *fishing household* as well, but I still needed a term for the "persons-who-fished." *Fisher* was the one term that would quickly come to mind, but it sounded rather artificial. Were we to adopt it nonetheless and hope for its acceptance, or continue our search for an alternative? *Fisherfolk* seemed a more satisfactory substitute for the plural *fishermen*, but it carried a sense of a category rather than of a set of individuals. We could accept "The fisherfolk of Latin America are faced with growing demand for their catch among urban populations" more readily than "Three fisherfolk stood on the shore." By the time the conversation had made it about this far, other people in the audience, more eager to discuss issues of profitability or sustainability than to continue unpromising efforts to eradicate one instance of sexism, would begin to wave their arms. I felt an obligation to receive their questions, and my challengers, usually moved by a spirit of participatory democracy, would accede to the request to give someone else a turn to speak, despite the failure of their quest for a new term.

On other occasions, I would consider the use of the word *fisherman* in a different fashion. I would sometimes trace the sources of the male exclusivity of fishing on Lake Titicaca, emphasizing that much of the fishing takes place in the early morning and in the late afternoon, the times when women and girls are busiest with the preparation of meals; in some cases, I would continue, men had easier access to money to purchase boats and nets. More often, however, I turned to the involvement of women in the fishing economy, since this latter theme seemed to interest my audiences more than the former. I sometimes explained that women processed the fish: not only did they prepare the catch for the members of their households to eat, but they also readied it for sale by sorting it according to species and size and, when it was not to be sold fresh, by drying, baking, or cooking the fish. This pattern is similar to the division of labor in agriculture, I would continue, in which the women store the harvest and divide it into portions to be eaten, sold, or saved for seed. Then I would move from the specific details of the Lake Titicaca fisheries to more general issues. I sometimes went on to describe how some anthropologists see these arrangements as an indication of deeply held indigenous Andean cultural patterns of gender complementarity, which differ sharply from the gender hierarchies found in Western societies. On

Woman and children collecting ispi, a native fish, that have been left to dry in the sun. Photograph by Tim Kittel.

a few occasions, this point led to a discussion of the relations between gender hierarchies on the one hand and colonialism and imperialism on the other: was the image of an unsullied egalitarian indigenous order a reflection of past realities or of present utopian impulses?

At a few talks, I shifted direction in response to the question of whether to retain or replace the word *fisherman* by proposing that the audience and I consider the terms that the local people themselves use to describe the villagers who catch fish in the lake; perhaps I could translate these words into English. If I were to find that the local term did refer explicitly to men but not to women, I might claim that *fisherman* was the best translation of the local term. This choice would be a conceptual shift: I would use the word not as a social scientific term that denoted a certain category of persons, but as an English equivalent of a local word without any claims to generalizability. This effort did, indeed, prove to be of assistance, but not in the way that I anticipated. By looking at usage in Spanish and in the Andean languages, Quechua and Aymara, I found that it was impossible to come up with a consistent pattern of terminology to duplicate the local ways of referring to persons-who-fish—suggesting that it was not only contemporary Americans but people in the altiplano as well who contend with different systems of categorization.

I explained that the fishermen understood the Spanish word *pescador,* "fisherman," at least in some instances. I offered as an example one particular type of occasion: my visits to fishing villages early in the main period of my research, from 1979 to 1981, when I was accompanied by several of the biologists from IMARPE. In conjunction with Dominique Levieil, a Frenchman who was working in IMARPE headquarters as a consultant to the FAO (the United Nations Food and Agriculture Organization), the IMARPE staff and I worked out a joint research project to study the levels of activity of the fishermen on the Peruvian side of the lake, and to measure their catch. (A brief digression is necessary here: *IMARPE* refers to the Instituto del Mar del Perú, the Peruvian Marine Institute, an autonomous branch of the Ministry of Fisheries. IMARPE's main offices are in Callao, the port city that lies close to Lima. Its activities have focused on Peru's large but troubled maritime fisheries, which suffer from overexploitation, poor and unsystematic regulation, and the impact of El Niño events that reduce fish stocks. During most of the time of my research, IMARPE maintained three regional laboratories for freshwater aquatic systems as well, one of which was in Puno, the capital of the Department of Puno and the largest town on the shores of Lake Titicaca. This office's principal responsibilities are scientific, though the lack of budgets and equipment impede sustained research efforts.)

With IMARPE staff, Dominique and I sometimes traveled out to lakeshore villages, where we had set up meetings with *pescadores,* fishermen. The IMARPE biologists would remind the villagers that they had come out in 1976 and conducted a census of the *pescadores.* They checked the census to see whether there were any new *pescadores* and whether any of those who had been counted in the past had ceased fishing. These questions made sense to the villagers. Both those who fished and those who did not could understand our efforts to establish a list of *pescadores.* They might mention a *pescador* who could be taken off the list because he had sold his boat and nets and moved to Lima. Some *pescadores,* they would tell us, were not present: one had gone that morning to a market in a

Dominique Levieil at a meeting in the IMARPE
laboratory in Puno. Photograph by Ben Orlove.

nearby town; another had left the previous day to take his son to high
school in Puno and might not return for a few days. No women presented
themselves as *pescadoras*. With the list of *pescadores* thus worked out, we
could conduct our interviews.

The villagers, then, had an understanding of the term *pescador* in the
sense that they could use it in conversation. I later found out that IMARPE
had not introduced the official use of this term to the region. The first
state agency that used it in dealings with local persons-who-fish, as far as
I have been able to tell, was another branch of the Ministry of Agriculture, which set up a School for Indian Fishermen (Escuela de Pescadores
Indígenas) in 1962 to instruct the villagers in the use of gill nets. *Pescador*

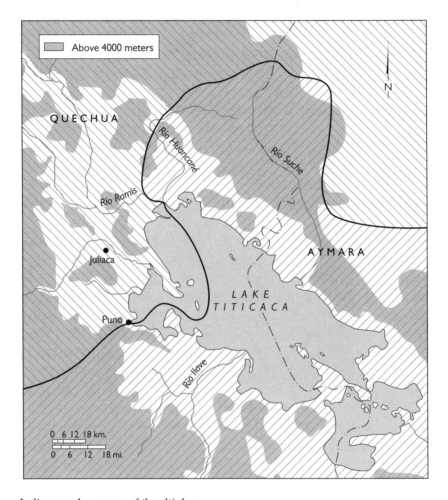

Indigenous languages of the altiplano.

was certainly the term that IMARPE staff used for them, so frequently that the simple letter *p* became the abbreviation for the word in their informal memos and drafts of documents.

Before I proclaim the equivalence of *fisherman* and *pescador*, though, I should note the lack of any equivalent term in Quechua and Aymara. At first glance, this lack, in sharp contrast to the villagers' familiarity with the Spanish word *pescador*, is puzzling. One might expect that there would be a simple term to distinguish the minority of households in lakeshore villages that have members who fish (about one in ten) from the majority of households, which do not. An examination of the linguistic structure of the Andean languages can offer a partial explanation of this absence, of some relevance to the issue of the gender-labeling of work and of great significance to the central themes of this book.

The word *fisherman* can be divided into three syllables, which are also three morphemes, the smallest meaningful units of language. Beginning with the first of these morphemes, I note that there is a word that means "fish" in both Quechua and Aymara, as might be expected from the inhabitants of a region where fish have been eaten for centuries. In both languages, though, this word, *challwa*, functions as a noun only and is not used as a verb. For example, the English sentence "They fished" cannot be translated word-for-word, but must be replaced by a sentence in which *fish* is the direct object of a verb. To illustrate, I offer examples from Quechua. (Quechua and Aymara have similar enough structures that examples from one will suffice to make the point. I use only one language for the sake of brevity and choose Quechua rather than Aymara because I am much more familiar with it.) In Quechua one could say, *challwata hap'iranku*, "They caught fish," but even here the translation is imperfect. Though *hap'iy* can mean "to catch," it refers more broadly to any kind of rapid taking or seizing. A fisherman might use it when shouting to a child on board his boat to "grab" a fish that was about to slip back into the water. Moreover, while in English there is only one verb—*to catch*—directly linked to securing fish, there are several such verbs in Quechua. People not only *hap'iy* fish: they also *horq'oy* (take) or *hoq'ariy* (take out) fish from the lake, or *apay* (bring) them to their houses or to market. These verbs refer not only to catching fish, but also to other activities, such as transporting or carrying fish.

The differences between the subtleties of English and Quechua are illustrated by the corny joke of the two men who return from a fishing trip, one having caught many fish, the other none. The unsuccessful one asks his companion not merely to give him a fish but to toss it to him "so that I won't be lying when I tell my friends that I caught it." I heard a number of jokes around Lake Titicaca that follow the same basic structure: they

A woman carrying fish from shore to market. Photograph by Ben Orlove.

open with an individual faced with a predicament, move on to a potential solution, and close with a punch line that reveals the clever ruse through which the individual resolves the difficulty. Despite the overlap in cultural patterns of humor, however, this familiar joke could not be translated into Quechua, because its ruse is based on language-specific wordplay. This joke, or an equivalent one about putting the fish into a sack so that he could *hoq'ariy*, take it out, would not strike a Quechua-speaker as funny, since the different meanings of *hoq'ariy* grade into one another, rather than being sharply distinguished like the two senses of *to catch*, and since there are many verbs associated with getting fish, rather than a single primary one.

Whereas the difficulties of rendering the *fish-* of *fisherman* into Quechua arise from the complexity and multiplicity of alternatives, the difficulties with *-er* come from the simplicity and ubiquity of its Quechua equivalent. All of the numerous ways of saying "to catch fish" can easily be turned into "fish-catcher" by the addition of the brief morpheme *-q* to the verb stem. This suffix, one of the many that Quechua-speakers append to words in their language, is what linguists term the "agentive," the form of a verb that denotes the performer of an action. Of the plethora of examples of the use of -*q* that I have at my disposal, I will select the one likely to be familiar to the largest proportion of the readers of this book. Most people who have seen the film *Star Wars* recall the barroom scene: the young Luke Skywalker and the old Obi-wan Kenobi convince the pilot Han Solo to take them to the planet Alderaan; the discussion takes place in an alien-filled bar. After the deal is struck, they leave, and Han encounters Greedo, a "slimy green-faced alien" sent by the crime lord Jabba to kill him. Some people may remember how hideous Greedo sounded, not only because of his nasty tone but also because of the electronic modification of his voice and, I believe, the unfamiliar and—in this context—sinister consonants of the foreign language he spoke (this scene is the only one in the movie with subtitles). Very few people know that this "alien language" is Quechua.

As Quechua-speakers tend to do, Greedo uses the agentive suffix -*q* with some regularity. Late in the scene, for example, Greedo says, *"Jabaq wañucheqnin hamushani. T'aqtani wañu usqhaq."* These sentences can be translated as "I'm coming as an assassin for Jabba. I'll obliterate you and you'll die quickly." A closer look at the second sentence shows that it consists of three words, each based on a single root: *t'aqtay* (to pound down), *wañu* (death), *usqhay* (to hurry). The agentive -*q* turns *usqhay* into *usqhaq*, a "hurrier," so a *wañu usqhaq* would thus be a "death hurrier" or, more colloquially, someone who sends people to early graves. This chilling construction suggests the ease with which verbs in Quechua can be nominalized—turned into an equivalent of the -*er* form in English. (My translation is, I believe, more accurate than the one that appears in the blatantly overdramatized subtitles: "Jabba's put a price on your head so large that every bounty hunter in the galaxy will be looking for you.") Greedo and Han carry their conversation on for a few moments longer. Han shoots Greedo and leaves the bar, and the movie continues with a number of exciting but Quechua-less scenes.

The suffix -*q*, the equivalent of our -*er*, occurs in more ordinary conversation as well. All Quechua-speakers attach -*q* to verbs and verb phrases more freely than English-speakers use the agentive -*er*. It would be quite ordinary to speak of someone as a *siwilla qoriyaq*, though the English equivalent, "onion weeder," sounds odd. However, there is a difference in the way the two languages use these agentives. Simplifying the complex patterns in both, it could be said that where the English -*er* suggests regular or frequent performance of an action over a certain period, the Quechua -*q* conveys that the action takes place at the same time as another action. Drawing examples from a Quechua verb phrase whose agentive form, unlike "to hurry death" or "to weed onions," has a close English equivalent, we may examine "to play soccer," *wayra hayt'ay*. In English we would add -*er* to a verb when we wanted to state generally that "My neighbor is a good soccer player" but would not for a specific instance such as "My neighbor has gone to the field to play soccer." The obverse is generally true of Quechua, where the -*q* would be used only in the second, as *wasimasiy kanchaman wayra hayt'aq riran*: word-for-word, "Neighbor-my field-toward soccer play-er went"; here, the "soccer player" phrase means that the neighbor has just gone to play soccer, but does not imply that he plays soccer regularly. For the first case, Quechua-speakers would not use the -*q*, but would be more likely to say instead, *wasimasiyqa pasaqlla wayra hayt'an*, "My neighbor often plays soccer." To describe someone who fishes a great deal, a Quechua-speaker might say, *pasaqlla challwata hap'in*, "He often catches fish." *Challwa hap'iq*, "fish catcher," would ordinarily be used only in phrases such as *manan wasimpi kanchu, qochaman challwa hap'iq riran*, "He isn't at home; he went to the lake to catch fish."

So in Quechua there's no verb *to fish*, and the agentive is used differently from -*er*; the word for *man*, the third part of *fisherman* and the stimulus of the discussion of names, is also treated differently in Quechua than in English. English and Quechua both have words for adult male (*qhari*, "man") and adult female (*warmi*, "woman"). There is currently some instability in the generic English term for "adult," since the word *man*, which formerly had been used unquestioningly, has fallen into disfavor as its inseparability from its masculine referent has become recognized, but it has not been fully replaced by alternative terms such as *human* or *person*. By contrast, Quechua does have a widely used generic term, *runa*, which means "person" or "human," sometimes with the connotation of Indian or rural person. It is used at times simply to denote people (*askha runa qhatuman rishanku*, "Many people are going to market"), at times to distinguish human and nonhuman domains (*runa ñan*, "human path," a path people walk on, as opposed to *makina ñan*, "machine path," railroad, or *taruka ñan*, "deer path," deer track). Unlike the English *man*, the Quechua *runa* does not carry implications about gender, following the tendency of Quechua not to mark gender in circumstances where some other languages, such as English and Spanish, do. (A single pronoun, *pay*, corresponds to *he* and *she*, and nouns and adjectives in Quechua, unlike their Spanish equivalents, are not marked for gender.) The key difference, though, is not whether the morpheme (*man* or *runa*) that is added to the other morphemes is truly gender neutral, but whether such a morpheme is added at all. In English, this morpheme is often added, and in Quechua it is only rarely. Where English combines *fore*- and -*man* to make the word for a person who leads or directs a group of workers, Quechua simply uses *qollana*, also connoting a forward or primary position, without adding *runa*.

This consideration of the local equivalents of *fisherman* has revealed a curious bifurcation. In certain Spanish-speaking contexts, villagers use *pescador*. In contexts in which they speak the indigenous languages, they discuss fishing without recourse to a single label for fishermen. The villagers have adopted some Spanish occupational labels into Quechua and rejected others—a selectivity that they show in many areas of life. *Chofer*, "driver" (derived from the French *chauffeur*), and *profesor*, "teacher," are widely used in Quechua, while *tejedor*, "weaver," like *pescador*, is not. *Comerciante*, "trader," coexists with the Quechua words based on *qhatuy*, "to buy or sell at a market." This selection is made on the basis of several criteria. Quechua terms are retained for work that takes place within the territory of the village and that produces food and other basic necessities. Such work often seems more rural than urban, because it requires sustained or heavy effort or because it entails close contact with the soil. Spanish words are adopted for work that takes place outside the village and for which a salary is paid. This work often leads to involvement with government authorities. Drivers and teachers, for example, cannot carry out their occupations without official licenses. Though fishermen occasionally interact with government agencies (for example, when IMARPE made visits to lakeshore villagers), the work of fishing lines up fairly well with the Quechua end of the criteria, rather than the Spanish end.

In sum, this consideration of local terms failed to provide me with a clear resolution to my dilemma about what word to use for "persons-who-fish." I decided to retain *fisherman*, the alternative that worked best for the majority of people with whom I discussed the matter. This attention to the interplay of indigenous and European languages led me to reflect on a second matter of names. What term should I use for the people who live in the countryside around Lake Titicaca? This second set of people is a much larger group that includes not only the fishermen, but also their relatives and neighbors, and indeed all the residents of the villages in the lakeshore region. It may seem unproblematic to use the labels "Spanish" and "Quechua" when discussing the two languages, and it might even be adequate to use "Spanish-speakers" and "Quechua-speakers" in considering conversation and jokes, but other terms present themselves in an examination of social life. In selecting a broader term for "Quechua-speakers," I could choose between the two main alternatives that are open to people who write about the Andes. I could call the villagers "Indians" or "peasants." These two alternative views of Andean villagers are often passionately held. It is not merely an analytical choice between two anthropological labels, but in some sense a moral one as well. The adherents of each often feel strong commitments to documenting the great injustice of Andean society, whether framed as mestizo domination in the former view or economic exploitation in the latter, and they frequently support political activities to redress this injustice.

The term *Indian* and its Spanish equivalent, *indígena*, emphasize the position of the villagers within a society that contains different cultural and ethnic groups. Years ago it had been the term most used by anthropologists and by Spanish-speaking Peruvians, since it captured very simply the distinctiveness of local custom, belief, and practice. It fell out of fashion for a while, especially in the 1960s and 1970s. To call people Indians appeared to be a way to make them exotic. It suggested that they were cut off from the rest of the world. By emphasizing the links of present-day Indians to pre-Columbian civilizations, it implied a look backward to the past, rather than forward to the future. It was not clear what the future of Indians might be—perhaps acculturation and assimilation into national society, or the formation of a kind of hybrid culture.

The term *peasant* and the Spanish cognate *campesino* seemed a powerful corrective to these difficulties. Where *Indian* implied cultural distinctions, *peasant* indicated economic relations—exploitative relations in which wealthy classes benefit from the poverty of the people who work the land. It placed the villagers squarely on the political agenda, since it indicated that some transformation was needed to end such inequality. This transformation might be agrarian reform programs, socialist revolution, or a more conventional sort of economic development. It is not an entirely unjust caricature to say that a generation of researchers felt that the term *Indian* placed the villagers in museums, while *peasant* scripted them into revolution.

In recent years, the term *Indian* has regained a good deal of popularity. The resurgence of nationalism in many parts of the world has directed attention to the ethnic identities that lay beneath the surface for long periods, identities that are visible in the lingering effects of colonial rule. Movements of indigenous peoples around the world have expanded, while peasant movements carry less weight than they did in the past. In Latin America, class-based movements have not ended inequality and exploitation, but activism by people of indigenous and African origin has grown.

Having felt at various points the appeal and the difficulty of each of these labels, I use both *Indian* and *peasant* on occasion, when the ethnic or class elements seem particularly strong. However, for this book I have decided to use the simple term *villager*. Rather than merely being a safe— if not a cautious, or even cowardly—means of sidestepping a long debate, the word *villager* has many advantages. It seems accurate enough, since the fishermen live in small rural communities, with an average population around a thousand inhabitants and an average area of about thirty square kilometers. Moreover, unlike *Indian,* which refers to culture and ethnicity, and *peasant,* which indicates class and exploitation, the term *villager* points to space. It directs attention to the local dimension of human life and interaction. The word *village* can refer to several things at once. Depending on context, it can denote the people who live in a particular place, the houses in which they live, or the lands that they inhabit. This overlap captures an important aspect of life in the altiplano that the other two terms do not. Whereas *peasant* suggests that political tensions emerge from conflicts over agriculture, *villager* permits a wider range of resource-based politics that involves control over forests, grasslands, or in this case, a lake. Whereas *Indian* implies a cultural difference with mestizos, *villager* points to the spatial opposition of countryside and city that also underlies this ethnic separation. It might be added that *villager* does not suggest that social life or even politics is restricted to the scale of an individual village. Large groups of villages can seek to control entire regions, or to move broadly toward decentralized politics.

The fishermen themselves use place-based labels more than terms related to class or ethnicity. The word *campesino* comes up from time to time, as do the labels for Indian, whether *indígena* or the linguistic and ethnic categories Aymara and Quechua. However, the fishermen are more likely to identify themselves as residents of a specific place rather than as members of a social category. When speaking to one another, people from different sides of the lake refer to their home provinces, Huancané or Chucuito or Puno. Those who live a bit nearer to one another mention their districts of origin, and close neighbors speak of their villages or even sections of their village. Accustomed to thinking of people in terms of the places from which they come, the lakeshore villagers draw as well on a rich series of teasing nicknames for people from particular districts. Those from Pomata are called *huk'ullkapa*, "tadpole catchers," for their lack of prowess at fishing; those from Vilquechico are called *kapachqeri*, "bag slitters," a reference to their alleged predilection for cutting open sacks and stealing their contents. The term for the people from Moho, *hawas phuspu*, "bean boilers," implies that they do not have enough potatoes to eat—a sign of great inferiority in the altiplano.

There are some occasions, though, in which the villagers use labels that have at least a bit of an ethnic tinge to them. I knew that *runa*, though often meaning "human," could convey a sense of Indianness when it was used in opposition to *misti* or *q'ara*. One of these terms appears in a phrase that I heard two or three times, the Quechua equivalent for *drizzle: misti manchachi*, "that which frightens the mestizo." The term implies a description of a scene: those mestizos, it says, they run inside the moment a few drops fall, while we remain outside, working in our fields until the rain really starts to come down; aren't they a silly bunch of softies?

I reflected on how I liked the phrase for *drizzle*. I was harvesting potatoes with some villagers on a cloudy afternoon when I first heard it, as a few raindrops began to sprinkle on us, and I remember how pleased I was to have it used in my presence. I was gladdened as well by the self-confidence that it implies. As I think about it now, I realize that this phrase offers another suggestion as well. The richest verbal expressions of identity do not necessarily come as individual words, the choice of terms or labels for social categories, but in more extended use as well, in phrases, sentences, and entire stories.

While teaching classes about Latin America, I have often turned to another anthropologist's work for an example of more extensive self-labeling. In her book *Food, Gender, and Poverty in the Ecuadorian Andes*, Mary Weismantel describes the social, cultural, and economic tensions that arise within Indian households as women attempt to construct meals from two inadequate food supplies: the local foods, especially potatoes and barley, that they grow in their fields, and the Western foods that their male kin, who migrate to work in urban areas, purchase with their earnings. The foods differ not only in their price and nutritional value, but in their meaning as well. They convey distinct understandings of what is proper comportment for Indians and whites, for husbands and wives, for parents and children. Major arguments take place in rural homes over whether to serve Indian foods such as *máchica*, toasted barley flour, or Western bread and rice. Weismantel describes one stage of her fieldwork:

> I had been trying for weeks to elicit some term that people of the area use to identify themselves as an ethnic group or distinct population, but aside from the Spanish *naturales*, used even when speaking Quichua, and the derogatory *longo* and *runa*, I had found none. One afternoon the old man [about whom she had written in a previous paragraph] initiated again a conversation about airplanes, a topic of which I was heartily sick. "What is it like to be in one? What could you see?" He looked at

me as if guessing my impatience and said, "What would we know about airplanes, we who eat *máchica?*" I was struck by the aptness of the phrase, this self-appellation "we who eat *máchica."*

Weismantel's insight, that food can express different dimensions of identity, emerged from a conversation that she at first had thought was unimportant, merely a tedious repetition of a topic that underscored her arrival in Ecuador rather than her integration into a specific community in that country. Responding to such questions was little more than an awkward and burdensome, though necessary, phase that permitted social ties between anthropologist and local people to be established, and real ethnographic fieldwork to take place. One of my most significant encounters—it cannot even be called a conversation—with a person from a lakeside village also took place in this sort of contact zone, a setting peripheral to what I conceived of as my fieldwork, in a place that was as far as possible from the site of the fishing and subsistence agriculture that interested me: in the entryway of a house in one of the wealthiest neighborhoods in the largest city in the region, La Paz, Bolivia's capital.

During my first months of fieldwork, I spent most of my time on the Peruvian side of Lake Titicaca, establishing the fishermen surveys with IMARPE and making visits of several days or a week to different lakeside villages. I made two trips, each a few weeks long, to Bolivia, where I hoped to establish what I then conceived of as the Bolivian half of my research. I was eager to compare Peruvian and Bolivian fishermen. Since they had generally similar economic and cultural patterns, but participated in different national political systems, I expected to find some interesting parallels and divergences in their histories. The most striking contrast, though, was not the one that I expected. After several months, it became clear to me that the Peruvian fishermen were much easier to study than their Bolivian counterparts. In particular, the regional surveys that were a key part of my work proceeded fairly well in Peru, because of my collaboration with IMARPE; but I established only fragmentary relations with Bolivian groups, because of the greater political tensions in that country at the time. There were several coups during the period of my main fieldwork. Nonetheless, I do not regret the travels to lakeside

villages in that country, or the long hours spent in Bolivian peasant organizations, universities, government offices, development agencies, and
navy bases. From that time I learned of the strong similarities between
villagers on both sides of the border.

On my first trips to La Paz, I stayed in the home of Philip Blair, an
American anthropologist who was conducting field and archival research and was working for development agencies. His house was a comfortable place, with several spare bedrooms on the second floor, a number of interesting people from his wide social networks to meet, and a
good location on a pleasant side street in Sopocachi, an upper-middle-
class neighborhood a bit up a hill from the main downtown area of the
city. My usual morning routine in the house was briefly interrupted one
day. I had taken a shower, dressed, eaten breakfast, and gathered up my
notebook and pen. I was about to go out the front door, catch a bus, and
begin my round of appointments, when I saw Dora, the maid, standing in the entryway near a table with the telephone. "Excuse me, does the
telephone work in Aymara?" she called to Phil, who was in the next
room. I paused, nodded good-bye to her, and continued out the door, in
too much of a hurry to hear Phil's reply or even to let her question register with me. It was only as I walked down the hill that I recalled her
question and began to reflect on it. It struck me as funny. How could anyone think that the telephone would not work in Aymara? I mentioned the
story to a few other Americans later that day, and they were as amused
as I had been. Checking with some of the people in the house that evening, I found that Dora had wanted to talk to a relative—an aunt, if I recall correctly—who had just arrived in La Paz from Chuquiñapi, their
village in Omasuyos province on the Bolivian shores of Lake Titicaca. Phil
had assured her that the telephone did work in Aymara, and she made
her call. Despite her strong Aymara accent, Dora spoke Spanish fairly
well, but her aunt did not, we gathered, so Dora had thought it necessary
to check whether they would be able to carry on a conversation over the
telephone. The story struck us as an example of nothing more than the
unfamiliarity with modern technology of recent migrants to cities.

I repeated the story a few times during the following week, then nearly
forgot it altogether. Only later, after I returned to the United States, did

it come back to me, and I thought about it a good deal. Did Dora know all along that the telephone could function perfectly well in Aymara, and was she simply asking, in an indirect and deferential way, for permission to make a personal call on her employer's telephone? That possibility did not square with the other images that I formed of Dora during my stay. She was anything but reticent: I recalled her autonomy in making decisions about what to cook or when to do the laundry, her forthright requests for extra time off, the ease with which her relatives could stop by the house. Moreover, had she known that the telephone did work in Aymara, but been reluctant to request permission to use it, it would have been easy for her to postpone her call until she had been alone in the house. Nor could I assume that she was dismayed by the thought of using a strange electronic appliance. Having seen her at work around the house, I knew that she was familiar with a number of machines that she had not grown up with in Chuquiñapi. Phil's house had not only some of the cheaper appliances, such as blenders, that Dora might have seen in the houses of rural migrants to cities, but more expensive ones as well: a refrigerator and even a washing machine. I could not believe that she was intimidated by modern technology, and at any rate, she had more than a passing acquaintance with the telephone. She had seen many people use it, and she had taken messages for Phil on a number of occasions.

After a good deal of reflection, I decided that her question came from her sophistication about electronic communication, rather than from her unfamiliarity with it. Dora was certainly accustomed to hearing radio programs in both Aymara and Spanish, since radio stations in La Paz were some of the first on the continent to begin broadcasting in indigenous languages. Audiocassette recorders were still new in the late 1970s, but they were beginning to be popular in La Paz, a city with a long history of black-market trade and at that time the recipient of a good deal of inexpensive Asian electronic equipment. Soon after the arrival of this equipment, villagers began to record festival music, the words clearly sung in Aymara. A market also sprang up for cassettes of Andean music.

Dora also knew, from her experience with Phil's large color TV and with smaller black-and-white sets in other houses, that television programs were broadcast exclusively in Spanish, whether they were imported Argentine or Mexican soap operas or low-budget local news, talk, and game shows. I am less certain about the films she may have seen. Most of them would have been either shot in Spanish or dubbed, but she might have seen some English-, French-, or Italian-language films with subtitles, or might have somehow gone to one of the films made by left-wing Bolivian directors with dialogue in Aymara or Quechua. It is also quite possible that she saw *Star Wars*. Whether or not she had seen Aymara-language films, or films with scenes of Aymara dialogue, though, she surely knew that all electronic media transmitted Spanish, but that only some carried Aymara.

Dora's question about the telephone, then, was a sensible and practical one. Wishing to get in touch with a relative in another neighborhood of the city, she considered the possibility that she might carry on a conversation in Aymara on the telephone, even though she might well have never heard one. Her question suggests that she wanted to know whether she would be able to speak easily to her aunt; otherwise, she would need to speak in halting Spanish or seek an interpreter at the other end. Dora phrased this question, which now seems reasonable rather than comic, in a way that interests me. Faced with the personal and immediate wish to speak with her aunt, she asked a more collective and longer-term question: "Does the telephone work in Aymara?" This choice of words, it seems to me, raises issues of collective identity. Weismantel was asked about the opposition between barley eaters and airplane passengers, and I heard Dora ask Phil a question that raises similar broad issues: Do monolingual speakers of Aymara, like her aunt, belong to the world of telephone users? Must monolingual Aymara-speakers learn Spanish in order to take part in telephone use?

The entryway of the appliance-filled house in the wealthy neighborhood in La Paz may not be as different from the villages on the shores of Lake Titicaca as I'd first imagined. Telephones in the former, wooden boats in the latter: these new technologies raised similar questions. Much as Dora recognized that she did not know which languages a telephone could transmit, the fishermen faced questions about the use of boats. The lakeshore villages established the rules for reed balsas, in which the waters closest to each village formed part of its territory. Would these rules

Using a wooden pole to push a balsa in a shallow section of the lake. Photograph by Tim Kittel.

be extended to the wooden boats and to the portions of the lake, farther offshore, in which they traveled, or would government agencies be the ones to create and enforce new regulations for these new boats and new fishing zones? Much as Dora could ask whether Aymara conversations could take place over the telephone, the fishermen wondered whether customary village law, enacted in assemblies, could be extended farther out into the lake. These are both issues over the control of space, broadly understood: communicative spaces for the telephone, legal spaces for the boat regulations.

The details of this control of space varied from one instance to another. As Dora discovered, a telephone can transmit one language and then switch to another a few moments later. Legal systems cannot be picked up and dropped so easily. Even in the circumstances in which two different entities share authority, considerable negotiation is required to establish a framework for joint administration. Moreover, the aspects of identity that surface in these two cases are not the same: the difference between Aymara and Spanish is linguistic, or perhaps ethnic; the difference between customary and national law is juridical, or perhaps political. Nonetheless, the cases of telephones and boats both show how identities, however firm they may appear, can be called into question. They suggest that the task of the anthropologist may not be to determine the labels that best fit particular groups, but rather to witness the different grounds on which these groups encounter one another. It is in the history of such encounters that identities are made and transformed—in the accumulation of moments in which barley eaters see planes fly overhead, or maids call their aunts, or fishermen buy boats and row them far into a lake.

4 Work

I arrived in Peru in 1979 with a plan for a research project and with the knowledge that I would change this plan. The plan was laid out in a grant proposal that I had written to obtain funding from the National Science Foundation. It described the procedures that I would use to answer a question of interest to anthropologists and ecologists: what factors influence the amount of fish caught in Lake Titicaca? I knew that I would not follow every step I had outlined. Fieldwork always presents anthropologists with surprises that force them to drop some components of their projects and entice them to add others. A proposal could not serve as the blueprint for a house that I intended to build, even if it specified the size of the building, the layout of the rooms, and the materials I would use. I knew that it was more like a preliminary sketch that would be modified as I came to know the site and the local building codes and found some unexpected materials.

There were only three elements of my plan that I could not imagine giving up, aspects of my dream house that I would insist upon. The first, a list of the price of fish, seemed simple enough. The second, a complete census of the fishermen, might prove trickier, and the third would be hardest of all: a detailed record of the fish that the fishermen caught. Still, I could not conceive of ending the project without knowing the number of fishermen, the volume of fish they caught, and the value of this catch.

My first days in Lima left me optimistic. I visited the headquarters of IMARPE, the Peruvian Marine Institute, where Pete Richerson, a biologist colleague of mine, had worked in previous years. The head of the Inland Waters Division told me that only three years earlier, the biologists at the Puno laboratory had conducted a complete census of fishermen, and that this census could easily be updated. He expressed great enthusiasm for my idea of a survey to determine the level of catch. We drafted and signed an agreement to collaborate on the research and celebrated with a lunch at the nearby Club Canottieri, an old sailing club right on the ocean. As we ate course after course, served on heavy china decorated with the emblem of the club, I occasionally would look out the window across the harbor to the islands offshore. The clear blue sky and the brilliant sun that reflected off the water seemed auspicious. I left the restaurant feeling pleasantly sated and thoroughly optimistic about the future of the research.

This optimism lasted until I reached Puno. I looked up Edgar Farfán, the laboratory director whom I had met on earlier visits to Puno, and whose friendly, cheerful manner I recalled. However, I learned that he had recently been fired. The new director, Eufracio Bustamante, was more officious. He had the habit of bringing his hands close to each other, almost palm to palm, and tapping all five pairs of fingers together. I soon learned that this gesture, accompanied by a nervous smile, indicated that he was about to pass on bad news. Eufracio told me the laboratory budget had been reduced. They had not been able to pay their bills, so their telephone service had been cut off. Their research boat was not working, and their vehicle, a Toyota Land Cruiser, was in such poor condition that he was unwilling to have Victoriano, the driver, take it anywhere except on the one stretch of paved highway that linked Puno with an airstrip in the nearby city of Juliaca. Eufracio liked the idea of my project, he told me, but he would need me to provide additional support for the laboratory before he could work with me.

During my first weeks in Puno, as Eufracio and I hammered out a plan to study the levels of catch, I discovered that even finding out the price of fish was a more complex matter than I had anticipated. I could not even tell all the fish apart. I already knew what trout and catfish looked like, and a few of the other species were easy to learn: the sleek silverside, with an iridescent, metallic stripe on its flanks; the tiny sardine-shaped ispi; the long, thin boga. I was distressed, however, that I could not distinguish the different types of carachi, the most common of the native fish. All of these lumpy gray fish were small, ten centimeters or so in length, and all of them had the up-curved lower jaw that gave them perpetual frowns. Their shapes were similar as well: a humped back from which a small fin stuck out, a thick belly, and a square tail. It took me nearly a month to learn the subtle differences in the shades of gray: the slightly darker shade of the black carachi, the pale belly of the white carachi, and the bigger hump and larger scales of the yellow carachi.

I had to learn not only the kinds of fish, but also the units by which they were sold and the items for which they were exchanged. The largest fish—trout, catfish, silverside, and boga—were usually sold by the kilogram and exchanged for money. The smaller fish were sold sometimes by the kilogram, sometimes by groups of three or four fish, and sometimes by the *huk'a*, or heap—a little mound of fish weighing, as I discovered by purchasing them, a few hundred grams. Though often sold for cash, the fish were also bartered for foodstuffs, principally potatoes and barley. Moreover, the prices varied from market to market, although they were always trending upward during this period of rapid inflation.

Once I learned these details, I was able to take a truck out to a market in a town square or in a village, walk over to the line of women who sat on the ground, their fish displayed before them on carrying cloths or plastic sheets, and simply ask them how much their fish cost. This question often struck them as humorous, since their usual customers were local women, not a foreign man like me. My inquiries would provoke the vendors into badinage. To the amusement of everyone within earshot, they

Carachi vendors in a rural market. Photograph by Ben Orlove.

often did not reply to my questions, but rather asked me whether I had a wife at home to cook for me. When I told them that I was single, the vendors made even more pointed remarks about the possible reasons for my continued bachelorhood. I enjoyed these encounters, which continued on and off through my fieldwork, though it was my research assistant, Cirilo Cutipa, a less conspicuous figure, who gathered the bulk of information about fish prices.

The second task, the census of the fishermen, might have been formidable. It was a minor request to direct questions about fish prices to a market vendor, already offering to the public her husband's or brother's or son's catch. It would be a far greater intrusion to travel to a village and ask about the number of men who went out to fish. Moreover, it would be a vast undertaking to visit all the villages spread around the shores of the lake. Fortunately, IMARPE had conducted its census only three years earlier. Seeking to provide me with something to compensate for the additional budget outlays to which I had just agreed, Eufracio offered to give me access to this data, which had been compiled at considerable ef-

Eufracio (left) and Hugo meeting in Eufracio's office at the IMARPE laboratory in Puno. Photograph by Ben Orlove.

fort. It took eight months for Eufracio and Hugo Treviño, a biologist who worked in the laboratory, to complete the task, since they needed to meet with an assembly of household heads in each village to obtain approval for their study. The fishermen generally cooperated, since they thought they might receive in return some kind of government largesse, such as a credit program that would allow them to purchase boats or nets, or perhaps bags of cement to build jetties. IMARPE also had the good sense to use local contacts to introduce them into the villages and to ask only a few simple questions about the craft and gear of the fishermen. Despite the political tensions elsewhere in the region at the time, they were able to complete the census. Their work established that there were a total of 3,040 fishermen distributed in 151 lakeshore villages.[1]

Eufracio, Hugo, and I were confident that this census was still quite

1. The data from this census of fishermen, and more recent censuses in the 1980s and 1990s, are available in electronic form at http://www.des.ucdavis.edu/faculty/Orlove/ book/appendices/fman_census.xls.

accurate, since the turnover of fishermen was low and fairly evenly balanced between gains and losses. A few of the oldest men had stopped fishing, and some young village men, who had learned to fish as boys, had acquired boats or balsas of their own and begun to fish. A handful of new fishermen had moved into lakeshore villages, poor men with little or no land of their own who had come to live with their wives' parents and thus were able to petition village assemblies to grant them fishing rights. Some fishermen had left the villages and migrated in search of better-paying jobs, leaving the altiplano for a coastal city, or the agricultural frontier in the Amazon Basin, or a mine. However, in most cases a relative had replaced them, usually a son or a younger brother who had assisted them, so there would not have been a change in the total. Dominique Levieil resurveyed thirty-four fishing villages in 1980 and found that the number had increased by 0.8 or 0.9 percent per year. Later surveys in 1984 and 1993 showed that this slow rate of growth continued through the 1980s and into the 1990s. It was about half the rate of population growth in the department of Puno as a whole, which was 1.6 percent per year.

The third task, measuring the amount of fish that were caught, appeared to be the most challenging, even after Eufracio and I had devised a new working agreement. The parameters of a catch survey could vary greatly. I knew that I would take only a small sample of the total population. How many fishermen should I contact? I thought that I would want to record their catches over at least twelve months, since it was important to see whether there were any seasonal variations. But would this prolonged contact with a research project somehow change the way they fished?

My contacts with the main office of IMARPE proved to be helpful in resolving these questions. Soon after I had arrived in Puno, several fisheries researchers had come to IMARPE from one of the major branches of the United Nations, the Food and Agriculture Organization, or FAO. They had been hired to advise IMARPE on the management of Peru's marine fisheries, in which millions of tons of anchovies were processed into fish meal that was sold in Europe and the United States for animal feed. Once they had familiarized themselves with the marine fisheries, these experts were also curious to travel from the coast to the highlands in order to learn about the fisheries of Lake Titicaca.

As they informed me, the FAO had considerable experience in the study of small-scale fisheries in underdeveloped countries. They had developed guidelines for "catch surveys," the term that I quickly learned applied to this sort of project. The methodology could work anywhere in the world. It mattered little whether the fishermen lived in Malaysia or Zambia or Tonga, since fisheries could be reduced to simple elements that were found everywhere. Research manuals published by the FAO laid out the details of the methods by which any fishery could be divided into "fishing economic units," the independent entities that owned and operated fishing boats. These fishing economic units could be as small as an individual or as large as a corporation. To conduct a catch survey, a researcher takes a sample of the total number of fishing economic units and trains the members of this sample to record their catch. The researcher also directly measures the catch of another sample of such units to provide a reliability check, since local fishermen may be inaccurate in their self-recording. Whether intentionally or not, they might exaggerate or minimize the amounts. Once the fishermen's own reports have been corrected, it is a matter of simple statistics to extrapolate from the reports the catch of the entire population.

One of the FAO consultants, Don Chapman, happened to have a few spare days during his stay in Peru and decided to visit Puno. His presence seemed to raise the importance of my project in Eufracio's eyes and also gave me much needed assistance in research design. He helped Hugo and me prepare a short survey form on which the fishermen could record data about the kind of craft and gear that they used, their travel time, and their catch of different species. There was one major dispute in this process. I wanted to use the local units of weight, since I was curious to know about the use of these measures for different species in different parts of the lake. Hugo and Don, trained as biologists, insisted on using kilograms. I gave in on this issue, because I had already extracted one concession from them—I wanted the fishermen to record the amount of the fish they sold, the amount they bartered, and the amount they ate, a topic that did not interest my colleagues.

We reviewed the form with the fishermen who worked for IMARPE as field assistants and then tried it out in a nearby fishing village. After a few changes in wording and format, it was ready for use. Chapman decided that fifty fishermen would be a satisfactory number and designed a three-step sampling procedure. The first two steps took place one afternoon in the IMARPE office. We first divided the lake into four zones from which we wanted samples. Two of these were the smaller, shallow basins at either end of the lake, the Bahía de Puno, or Puno Bay, in the west and the Lago Pequeño to the east. The other two were the north and south shores of the larger, deeper Lago Grande, or main body of the lake. The different characteristics of the shoreline and lake bottom in these areas meant that fish populations would vary. The uneven distribution of road networks around the lake also meant that fishermen might have different access to markets. We allocated the fifty fishermen to the four zones so that the proportion of the sample in each zone would be the same as the proportion of fishermen in that zone to the overall number of fishermen in the most recent census.

The second step was to select the villages that we would study. Chapman had seen the difficulties that arose when surveys were conducted among widely dispersed fishermen. It was hard to train them and hard to stay in touch with them. If we selected our sample entirely at random, we might end up contacting people in thirty or forty villages, with one or two fishermen from each. We decided to aim for three or four villages per zone, with an average of four fishermen per village. Some simple statistical techniques allowed us to make sure that we did not introduce a bias in favor of fishermen from larger or smaller villages.

With the IMARPE fishermen census and a random-number table in front of us, we settled in to choose villages. Suddenly the conversation took a serious tone, as if the catch survey were a very weighty matter. Hugo and Eufracio were relieved when one of the villages from the Urus islands in the Bahía de Puno was chosen; they would have been disappointed not to travel out to these famous islands, which consisted of enormous mats of reeds that floated in the lake more than five kilometers from the shore. We continued to the northern portion of the Lago Grande. I was disappointed that Piata, the village that I had first visited, would not be included. There was a pleasant surprise, though, when Isla Soto was selected. As one of the rainiest spots in the altiplano, it was reputed to be much greener than other areas, but its distant location made it hard to visit. Had it not been selected, I might never have had the chance to travel to it.

The random-number table also failed to give us the sites that we hoped for on the south shore of the Lago Grande. Cirilo's village of Socca was not chosen. And when Cachipucara was selected, Hugo seemed nervous. This village was twenty-five kilometers from the main road out at the tip of the Río Ilave delta, the largest in the lake. Its fame as a home for smugglers extended beyond the altiplano. An article in *Caretas*, a national newsmagazine, described it as a key node in the cocaine economy that linked coca growers in Bolivia with clandestine laboratories in Peru. If the villagers refused to work with the survey, we could turn to an alternative site, but such deviations from our first random sampling might diminish the value of the study.

After several hours, we completed the selection of sites. With his characteristic confidence, Hugo assured me that the fishermen around the lake would remember him from the census that he and Eufracio had conducted. There was no need to worry, he told me. He would set up meetings and visit all of the thirteen villages that we had selected in the four zones. The pretest of the survey had gone well, he reminded me.

Nonetheless, I was filled with concern as we went out to one of the first villages. We left Puno before dawn in the IMARPE Land Cruiser, repaired with some money that I had contributed from my grant. It was late in the morning when we reached Conima, the last town before the Bolivian border on the north shore of the lake, and boarded a boat to ferry us across a strait to Isla Soto. The village authorities met us at the dock on the island. They walked with us into the small settlement a few hundred yards from the beach. It was with great relief that I saw the flag raised in front of the schoolhouse, the sure sign that an assembly had been called. The islanders did remember Hugo, as he had predicted. After the customary welcomes, Hugo thanked them for responding to the messages that he had sent in advance to call for this meeting. A short, rotund man, dressed in a denim jacket and jeans, he moved almost continuously as he spoke. We wanted to study the fishing in the lake, he explained, and had decided on Isla Soto as one of the communities that we wanted to have participate, along with a number of others from areas around the lake. He pointed to Isla Soto on a large map that we had brought with us and waited until he heard a soft murmur of recognition from the assembled villagers before he continued. We would select five fishermen from this community, he said. They would work on the survey for fourteen months, telling us how much they caught each time they went into the lake. They would have to report only on what they caught; we were not hiring them to fish more than they ordinarily would. Waving his arms as he walked back and forth in front of the silent villagers, he indicated that the payment for this work would be low, fifteen hundred *soles* per month—the equivalent of six dollars in U.S. currency—but the fishermen would have other advantages. They would receive a diploma at the end of the period, which would state that they had worked on an important international project, and if IMARPE expanded, they might be hired as technicians. He paused before delivering the clincher: the participants would have a chance to win a prize. Eight fishermen, selected in a lottery at the completion of the project, would receive twenty thousand *soles* each. This sum, worth eighty dollars, was a strong incentive not to quit before the end of the project.

A discussion ensued. The men, some sitting on benches, some standing, slowly took turns to speak. A few of them addressed questions to Pedro Castillo, one of the fishermen who worked for IMARPE, who had come with us. The women, sitting on the ground at a short remove, spoke occasionally as well. Hugo's explanation and Pedro's elaborations seemed to have satisfied both groups. They agreed to take part in the survey after only a half hour of deliberations, practically breakneck speed by local standards.

The process of selecting the participants then took place. Hugo asked the *pescadores*, the fishermen, to come forward. None of the men seemed unsure about whether he was included in this category. Thirty-five of them gathered at the front of the assembly. Standing to one side of them, Hugo made a show of arranging pairs of numbered slips of paper on a table. The fishermen came up one by one and picked up a pair of slips. Once a fisherman had satisfied himself that the numbers on the two slips were the same, he would drop one in a metal drum mounted on a board

Hugo distributing slips to the fishermen participating in the selection lottery on Isla Soto. Photograph by Ben Orlove.

and sit down. With a bit of the manner of a carnival barker, Hugo told them to hold on tight to their slips. Once all the fishermen were settled down again, he called for a *loro,* a parrot. The villagers understood him at once (his request struck them as humorous), but it took me longer to grasp his meaning. Hugo wanted a child to come forward to select numbered slips, much as fortune-tellers in marketplaces have parrots put their beaks into a container filled with scraps of paper to pluck out one that foretells a customer's future. The tone in the room shifted from serious listening to some joking. Several people pushed forward a boy about ten years old, so bashful that he could not raise his head to look at the crowd. He acceded to Hugo's request to blindfold him, though, and he pulled out five slips, one at a time. The fishermen with corresponding numbers stepped forward, and all five agreed to participate. They signed forms that Hugo had prepared and received a thousand *soles* for their travel expenses for a training course to be held in Puno.

After the drawing, we climbed a hill to a flat expanse where community members, anticipating our visit, had set up tables. Over a long lunch, the village leaders thanked Hugo. They were glad that he had returned after his census visit a few years earlier. We heard many stories of life on the island. Though the climate was mild enough to permit farmers to grow maize and even to raise gladioli for sale in markets, the amount of land was limited, so many people had moved to San Juan del Oro, a frontier settlement in the eastern lowlands. The fishermen felt themselves to be fortunate. They did not need to migrate from the island in order to earn a decent cash income. We found ourselves unable to finish the huge bowls of potatoes, maize, and trout that had been placed before us, and our hosts insisted that we take the leftovers with us. The IMARPE staff, anticipating this need, had brought plastic bags to carry them back.

We chatted a bit more, then went for a stroll around the island. It was indeed one of the greenest places I had seen in the altiplano, with flowering vines and shrubs planted in abundance around many of the houses. Even more striking to me was the absence of the dogs that in other places would run out to bark at me. There were no thieves on this small, close-knit island. The village authorities led us to the highest point on the island and showed us the sunken plazas there. In ancient times people had traveled in balsas made of stone, they told us, all the way from the Isla del Sol, the Island of the Sun, the place where the creator-god Viracocha had brought light to the world. We lingered at this spot, from which we could look down to the lake in all directions.

Eventually, the lengthening shadows reminded us that it was time to head back to Puno. The village authorities accompanied us down the dock and spoke with us about their hopes for the progress of their island. Then they let us take our leave. Satisfied with the outcome of our visit to the island, we sat quietly in the boat as we crossed. The steady chug of the outboard motor provided a sound that relieved any impulse to converse in order to fill a silence. The boat progressed smoothly across the calm waters of the lake. We might not have known that we were in motion, that we were not suspended at a point between the star-filled sky and the mirroring star-filled lake, had it not been for the cool breeze on our faces from the boat's movement, and for the black masses of the mountains above the horizon that grew higher as we approached the mainland.

The visits continued, village by village, a process that took more than a month. The most tense moment came in Cachipucara. We were greeted at the edge of the village lands by two young men on motorcycles, who escorted us to the village center for the meeting. Mixed in with ordinary village houses were other houses, mansions in fact, with large trucks parked in garages. We had the discretion not to inquire whether this escort and evident prosperity were linked in any way to drug smuggling. Our meeting went much as it had on Isla Soto, and we drove, one motorcycle ahead of us and one behind, back to the boundaries of the village. Hugo, Eufracio, and I were pleased that we had been accepted by all thirteen villages that we had selected in our random sample. This level of cooperation was unusual for such research projects. We were fortunate in the project's timing, since regional and national politics were relatively calm. As important as the broader political context, though, was the positive impression of IMARPE that the villagers had formed during the census, and that they still retained.

As planned, Hugo and I conducted training workshops at the IMARPE laboratory for the fishermen who had been selected. We held four workshops, one for each zone. Since many of the fishermen had to travel long distances to reach Puno, the training lasted two days. One by one, the fishermen from each village arrived and sat down as a group in the largest room at IMARPE, the former living room of the apartment that had been converted into offices and a laboratory. The IMARPE staff, which had worked long enough with villagers to understand the importance that they placed on food, provided them with a much appreciated lunch (ham sandwiches on packaged white bread, as many as they wanted, followed by coffee). Hugo explained to the fishermen how to record their catches in small spiral notebooks, and how to transfer this information to the catch report forms. We took some minutes to develop a system for the illiterate fishermen: they would each identify a younger relative with more schooling who could enter the information for them. As we reviewed the forms, we found that we had to explain several times how to transfer the weight of the catch from the notebooks to the forms. Because the fishermen were accustomed to local measures, we had to explain again and again that the *arroba*, a unit of weight, corresponded to about 11.5 kilos (or 25 pounds), and that the *lata*, a large oil or lard can, equaled 20 kilos.

Another question arose. A few fishermen told us that they were thinking of working outside the altiplano for a month or two during the period
of the study. Hugo and I told the fishermen just to have the catch recorded by the brother or cousin or other relative who would use their
boats in their absence. We knew that migration was common in this region—in a sense, the fishermen are migrants themselves, having colo-
nized the offshore waters of the lake—and we knew as well that families
with migrants arranged among themselves to make sure that the boats
and nets would not remain idle, just as they found someone to plant crops
in fields that belong to migrants.

As we were finishing the first day's training session, the fishermen from
Huarisani began to talk softly among themselves. One of them raised his
hand and asked a question: Since they were working for an official government program, would they now be permitted to fish in the waters that
belonged to other villages? They were very close to Cohasía, the village
that controlled the rich fishing grounds near the mouth of the Río Huancané, and they were not too far from the island of Taquile and the deep
waters nearby, reported to have large stocks of trout. The fishermen from
Isla Soto had told us how they would chase away intruders who sought
to catch trout in their waters. Would we be weakening their hand by suggesting that we could grant permission for fishermen from Huarisani to
travel the long distance there to fish? The fishermen from other villages
waited attentively for our response. Hugo and I looked quickly at each
other. I nodded to him, knowing what he would say. No, he told them,
don't go to those other places. It's important for us to know just how you
fish. Just keep fishing in the same places, he said.

If there was any disappointment on the part of the fishermen from
Huarisani, or relief on the part of the ones from Isla Soto, they did not
display it openly. Moreover, they all were in a hurry to finish the meeting
and leave the IMARPE laboratory. As we had learned while we were talking in the morning before the meeting began, the fishermen were planning to stay with relatives in town. They would combine the unspent portion of their stipend with other savings and make purchases in the stores
and markets of Puno, where some goods were cheaper than in the small
towns near their villages. They were particularly eager to go to the large

hardware stores to buy items for their boats—nails or putty or paint—
and to visit the stalls near the markets, where they could find clothing.

The meeting on the second morning was shorter. After a quick review
of the data collection, Hugo described the monthly visits that IMARPE
staff would make to the villages to pick up completed forms and to drop
off new ones. We then shifted to the distribution of materials. The fishermen lined up and came to the desk in front, one by one, and each received
a notebook, the first month's set of forms, a spring balance to weigh fish,
and two pencils. Each one signed, or made a mark, in a register that
IMARPE kept for its own accounting. This distribution, conducted with
great ceremony, took nearly half an hour, giving me a chance to drift into
my thoughts. We could not expect the fishermen to make any outlay of
cash, even the smallest, for this project. Some of them might not even
have pencils or other writing implements in their houses; of the ones who
did, a number might seek to conserve the pencils as long as possible for
their children to use in school assignments. If we did not keep such
records, the fishermen might pester us with requests for additional supplies that they might use for other purposes, or even sell. Nor should I assume, I realized, that the townspeople were prosperous. The IMARPE
office staff and scientists also spoke of the difficulty of making ends meet,
and I could understand that they, too, might be tempted to pilfer the project's supplies.

Still, the formality of the event impressed me. It was not just the poverty and the temptation to steal that imposed the detailed record keeping, but an odd sort of office ritual that I had seen many times and in
which I was now participating. As I watched them file up to the desk
and stand patiently while Hugo and Rosalía, the office secretary, handed
them the items, it seemed to me that the workshop had contained many
moments that demeaned the fishermen. We had been treating them as if
they were uneducated boors, strangers in the world of government agencies, printed forms, and standard measures. In the gratitude with which
the fishermen accepted a few sandwiches, in their hesitation to ask questions, I sensed an acceptance of this assumed inferiority. And yet the fishermen were also in some sense being honored by their inclusion in the
project. As I write now, I view all the documentation—the notebooks

and forms, the registration of the survey fishermen, the diplomas that would be granted—more broadly. It represents not merely a chance for the fishermen to earn some money, but also an opportunity to garner recognition for themselves, for their villages, for their entire way of life. In the patience with which the fishermen waited to be registered, I see an element of their commitment not to be forgotten, a step in the fight against oblivion.

Once the fishermen had been trained, the data collection proceeded smoothly. Hugo traveled with the IMARPE vehicle for the first month to make spot checks of the data forms that the fishermen had completed. He found only a few minor errors. Some of the fishermen would omit the units of the catch, perhaps in their confusion between the customary units with which they were familiar and the new ones that they were required to use, and some of them reported the total catch, rather than the catch in each net, as IMARPE had requested. Others left out some details of the amount of time they spent fishing. By the second month, though, the forms seemed quite accurate.

After the first month's set of forms had come in, I began to design a system to allow the computer analysis of the data. It was easy enough to create a series of numerical codes for the fishermen, the villages, the fish species, the kinds of gear, and all the other information that the forms contained. One afternoon, when I was showing Hugo a draft of the code-book, he suggested that I could hire someone in Puno to transfer the data from the forms onto coding sheets—yet another detail of the project that I had not anticipated. Once I had found someone for this task, Hugo pointed out, it would leave only the work of transferring the data from the coding sheets into a computer, a step that we knew would take place in my university. (The IMARPE laboratory did not have a computer, and I had not brought one with me.) He recommended Hilda, and when I did not recall anyone by this name, he explained to me that she was the wife of Victoriano, the driver of the IMARPE truck. This detail brought her to mind. I recalled the pretty woman with dark curly hair. She had struck me as one of the shiest people I had ever met: she would stand with her eyes turned downward when she waited for her husband just inside the door of the IMARPE office; when she spoke, even to the IMARPE em-

A fisherman from Vilurcuni who participated in the catch study, preparing to sign his name to acknowledge receipt of his monthly stipend. Photograph by Ben Orlove.

ployees she saw regularly, her voice was barely audible. Her husband was quite different, a proud, almost cocky man. Unlike other ministry drivers, who would put on a dark blue uniform of work clothes when they carried out any activity that might get them dirty, Victoriano made a show of washing the vehicle in his good clothes, keeping them dry and clean as he carried buckets of water around. He often talked about the prizes that he had won in regional folk dance contests. As he spoke, he would perform a few of the steps that had impressed the judges. The contrast between Hilda and Victoriano was most striking when he left the office. Seeming to ignore her, he would stride briskly through the door, knowing that she would follow him.

Hugo told me that Hilda had recently lost her job as a secretary at the Ministry of Education because of a budget cut. She seemed like the kind of person I might be looking for, he said—responsible, hardworking, intelligent, and in need of a job. He did not need to state the obvious:

René and Hilda in the IMARPE office in Puno. Photograph by Ben Orlove.

I could do IMARPE a favor by hiring her, since Victoriano would be more content with his low salary if his wife could also earn some income. And Hugo could do me a favor by finding me a person with whom I could remain in touch when I was away from Puno. Moreover, Hilda could work at a spare desk in IMARPE, so that the data forms would never have to leave the office. I hired her, and as we anticipated, the coding proceeded smoothly, as did the data entry, which I supervised when I returned to California to teach for two trimesters before returning to the altiplano for the second year of fieldwork.

It was the process of checking the data that I found most laborious. I realized that there were four points where errors could have appeared: when a fisherman recorded catch in his notebook, when he transferred data from the notebook to the catch survey form, when Hilda entered the data on the coding form, and when the research assistant entered the data into the computer from the coding form. Some apparent errors were easy to fix. For example, if an unknown code appeared for the number of a fishing village, I could simply replace it with the correct number for the village for that particular fisherman. Sometimes I looked at sequences of records: if two trips were reported for the same time on a Monday, and the next trip was reported for the same time on a Wednesday, I would change the second trip to Tuesday.

With other cases, I was unsure whether the apparent anomaly was some sort of error, or whether it was simply an unusual fishing trip. For example, fishermen typically took between five and ten nets when they went into the lake. A few might take as many as twenty. There were occasional reports of thirty, forty, or even fifty and more. These large numbers being multiples of ten, I could attribute them either to a coding error or to the common tendency to round off large numbers. If I saw a case with forty or fifty nets, I checked with other records from the same fisherman to judge whether to accept the number or to remove the final zero. Similarly, many fishermen reported that they went out onto the lake at night and returned the next morning. A few might stay out for two nights. Would I count a three-night trip as an error, or as a very long trip? These exceptional cases troubled me. I wanted to correct or eliminate the records with coding errors, but I felt with equal urgency the importance of retaining the genuine cases of unusual behavior. How was I to avoid misrepresenting the fishermen by imposing my own views? I did not want to have my preliminary impressions of them lead to a misuse of their own reports of their own catches. My views could lead me to detect errors that might lie in the data, but they also could cause me to treat unusual cases as errors.

I knew that my decisions would not make a large difference. There were fewer than two dozen problematic cases among the total of more than a thousand records. Still, I was reluctant to discard any of the records, and I considered each one carefully. Late one Friday afternoon, I spent some time trying to decide whether one particular trip had been unusual. It reported that many kilos of catfish had been caught, along with a few of carachi. Since the catfish are rare, and the carachi are abundant, there seemed to be a mismatch of species and the amount of catch. Or had an error been made in recording the species? I paused and looked over my desk, on one side the printouts that signaled the possibly incorrect data, on the other the codebooks and stacks of forms, filled out in Hilda's precise handwriting. The task of handling the data appeared

endless, the fishermen seemed remote, and the entire project struck me
as absurd.

Suddenly, fishing boats filled my mind, a precise image from one of
the hills above Piata, a few small rowboats against the vast expanse of
sparkling blue water, a high ridge in the distance. There was a cut in my
mental movie, a closer shot of a man in a boat, a man who wore a sweater
and was pulling hard on the oars. I could see the nets curled in the bottom of the boat, the small carachi glinting in the sun. What is the point of
all these printouts? I wondered. Why am I spending so much time at this
desk? The notion of a science-fiction movie came to me. It was set in an
alternate universe in which the reality conformed to the printouts rather
than the other way round. Any change made in the coding forms would
immediately replicate itself in the altiplano. I could see a fisherman's surprise as one hundred carachi, suddenly expanding and elongating, transformed into one hundred silverside. Twenty kilos of trout mushroomed
into two hundred, nearly upending the boat. By changing the code for a
province from 03 to 02, I could make the boat leap out of the water and
fly through air to a distant spot in the lake. "It's been too long a week,"
I decided, and got up from the desk to head home.

I calmed down over the weekend and realized that my fantasy was not
merely the product of fatigue or overwork. I did have a certain power
when sitting at my desk: a chance to tell the story of the Lake Titicaca
fishermen any way that I wanted to. I might send drafts of papers to the
IMARPE office, I might write to Cirilo with specific questions, but the final version would be up to me. I came into the office on the following
Monday and reviewed the list of possible errors. There were fewer than
ten that I could not resolve. I explained them in a letter to Hugo and
Hilda. Hugo checked with the fishermen and answered the questions. He
also mentioned his eagerness to receive the preliminary estimates of the
catch. Julián, another one of the lab researchers, had already tabulated
some by hand. In a few weeks, I gave him the average catch per trip for
each of the fishermen, broken down by species. I gave him averages for
the four zones of the lake, for boats and for balsas, and for different types
of nets. My report also indicated the proportion of fish that was sold,
bartered, or eaten at home. This data covered only the first two months of

the catch survey but was sufficient to make a strong impression. The catch was somewhat higher than the IMARPE staff had expected. The figure of about eleven kilograms per fishing trip and just over twenty trips per month yielded a total annual catch of around eight thousand metric tons. This respectably large figure would suggest the importance of lake fisheries and therefore of IMARPE's continued operations around the lake. Another package of forms arrived in California each month. The entering and cleaning up of data became simpler, and there were fewer cases to ask Hugo to check.[2]

Hugo and Eufracio were satisfied with the estimates of the weight of the catch. The findings fit in well with their responsibilities in a provincial office of an organization dominated by biologists. The catch estimates appeared again and again in the steady flow of research reports, work plans, and budget requests that they sent to their superiors. When they sought to compete with other branches of IMARPE for a share of the limited budget, they could point to the large size of the total catch and claim that they needed to conduct further research to support this important fishery, which contributed the equivalent of about three million dollars annually to the economy of the altiplano. Of importance as well was the notion that on the whole, the fisheries were not being overexploited. The echo-sounding work that the FAO had carried out provided an estimate of the fish biomass in the lake that was well above the amount needed to sustain such a catch; other aquatic ecologists, including my colleagues at UC Davis, could use their measurements of photosynthesis in the lake and their knowledge of food webs to corroborate this point. IMARPE could also advise the local branch of the Ministry of Fisheries on regulations to protect the few species, such as the catfish and the boga, that appeared to be relatively scarce.

For Dominique and for me, however, these catch surveys could not stand alone. Other components had to be added. Dominique's graduate studies made it clear to him that an economic dimension was missing. He

2. The data from the catch surveys are available in electronic form at http://www.des .ucdavis.edu/faculty/Orlove/book/appendices/Fish_Dist.xls, http://www.des.ucdavis .edu/faculty/Orlove/book/appendices/Seasonality_fishing.xls, and http://www.des .ucdavis.edu/faculty/Orlove/book/appendices/canneries.xls.

had completed his position with IMARPE by this time and was already working on his dissertation in marine resource policy at the University of British Columbia, one of the leading programs in fisheries management in the world. His professors had trained him in a well-defined paradigm that analyzes fisheries as involving the interaction of biological and economic systems: It was not enough to measure the amount of fish that were being caught at any given time, and to compare this figure to the overall size and growth of the fish stocks. One needed to know as well the economic parameters that shaped the decisions the fishermen made. In this view, the fishermen were like any other small-business owners. They had a certain amount of capital and a certain amount of time. They would invest their money in boats and gear if they could repay their loans and generate a satisfactory profit. In parallel fashion, they would spend time fishing out on the water as long as they could meet their expenses (gasoline for the motor, wages for the crew, and so on) and still make enough additional money for it to be worthwhile.

This view developed in the 1950s and 1960s as a response to the growing evidence of a similar problem in fisheries around the world, a problem that Geoffrey Waugh, an Australian economist, has aptly named "the persistent tendency towards depletion." This term refers to a course of events that has occurred in many places. The sequence opens with a small group of fishermen whose level of catch is fairly low. At this point, the fish are abundant and profits are high. The next step is for the fishery to expand. The fishermen might use their equipment more intensively, or they might purchase more equipment, or new individuals might begin to fish—or, as is most common, all three might happen at once. Though the size of the fish stock might diminish, the levels of profit remain fairly high. The fishery continues to grow, in terms of the number of fishermen and the amount of capital invested in equipment, but the great dilemma is that the investments grow as the resource itself shrinks. Though fishermen experience lower returns on their capital and on their labor as the fishery becomes more crowded, new individuals and new money can still be drawn into the fishery for a while. As Waugh points out, the sequence ends with "low catch rates, poor economic returns [and] unnecessary accumulation of capital investments." In other words, there are no longer enough fish, and there are too many fishermen and boats. Such collapses have occurred many times: with cod and herring in the Atlantic, with sardines and anchovies in the Pacific, and with other species elsewhere. The move toward depletion is pressed onward by an inexorable force. It is particularly easy for fisheries to become overcrowded and over-exploited, because they are usually "open-access resources"—anyone can buy a boat and start fishing.

For Dominique, this account had the advantage of being readily expressed in a series of equations and graphs, the models that still fill articles and books on fisheries management. These models show that the rate of depletion is affected by biological factors, such as the rate at which the fish reproduce, and economic factors, such as lower interest rates, which would make the stock decline more quickly, because fishermen could invest more readily in new boats. Because of this combination, this account is often called "bioeconomic modeling." Biological and economic parameters are present throughout. The declining rate of profit is as important as the declining size of the fish stock.

This account also had the appeal of a coherent, well-told story. The characters were simple, familiar actors with straightforward motivations, caught in a situation beyond their control. The plot in which they were involved would move forward to an inevitable tragic conclusion. Like many other stories, this one also had a moral: the need for regulation. If additional characters could be added, the plot might move to a happy ending. These new characters would be fisheries biologists, fisheries economists, and government regulators, who would find some way of slowing down the expansion of the fishery. A government could give out a limited number of licenses, or prohibit fishing entirely at certain times, or set a total amount of catch that could not be exceeded. Though these measures might be unpopular among some people, they would prevent the depletion of the fisheries in their shift toward sustainability, which would improve conditions overall.

But that was not the only way the story could reach a happy ending. The fishermen themselves could join together, establishing and enforcing rules that would limit the total catch in some fashion. This local control would convert open-access resources, available to all, into "common property" resources, managed jointly by a local community or population. A number of researchers, notably the political scientist Elinor Ostrom, have documented the conditions under which local users can keep common-property resources from being overexploited. Some anthropologists have reported that local fishermen's organizations exist in Japan, in atolls in the Pacific, and in other areas. Since Lake Titicaca appeared to be a similar case, Dominique was eager to document such self-regulation. This task would require measurement of economic variables. If the fishermen were earning a good return, that would provide economic support to the biological claim from the echo-sounding studies that the fish stocks were sizable and not declining.

Once we were both back from the altiplano, Dominique traveled from Vancouver to California, and we spent a busy month on these questions. The bioeconomic models had seemed like a mail-order kit with attractively simple instructions: easy to assemble at home, no special tools required. We thought it would be straightforward to calculate the returns to the investment in capital and time in fishing. Instead, as with most such kits, some parts fit readily together, but others took more effort to insert.

The formation of boat crews was one of the easy bits. We knew that many fishermen took someone along in the boat, almost always a son or a younger brother. This pattern was much like the informal, family-based apprenticeship through which villagers learned to farm, raise animals, and build houses. When the fishermen discussed their reasons for taking relatives along, they occasionally spoke about assistance in handling nets or about other contributions to the work itself, but more often they emphasized that they wanted to show their sons and brothers how to fish and, moreover, that they simply liked having someone along. If the fishermen had paid these crew members, we would have had an extra expense to keep track of. Since they did not, our calculations were much easier. At most, we usually could just add the assistant's time to the work hours, since he was part of the same household.

It took us more effort to decide how to tally up the time spent with the gill nets, the type of gear that accounts for more than four-fifths of all fishing trips. A fisherman would row out on the lake and hang the nets in the water. At some later time, he would haul the nets up, with fish in them. It took us a while to notice that there were three different sequences. On some trips, fishermen stayed out on the lake next to the nets

Two fishermen who have just returned from a night of fishing, sitting under a reed sail and eating soup. Photograph by Ben Orlove.

and returned when some fish had been caught. We termed these "overnight trips," because they lasted from one evening until the next morning. On other trips, fishermen would set the nets and return at once to shore. They would retrieve their nets usually the next day, sometimes a day or two later. These we named "double trips." The third sequence differed from the first two in that the fishermen removed the fish from the nets while they were still out on the lake and would hang the nets in the water again before coming back to shore. We called these trips "check trips," since the fishermen were checking their nets for fish.

We found that the fishermen were catching about 1.6 kilograms of fish per hour, which we could convert to an economic return of 340 *soles* per hour. However, this figure was the gross return, without subtracting any of the fishermen's expenses. To calculate expenses, we used the other surveys that we had conducted. Once we knew the price of the boats and their average useful lifetime, we could estimate their effective annual cost. Similar calculations could be made for the nets. We proceeded with the expenditures for maintaining the boats (Dominique prudently had inquired about expenses for nails for attaching loose boards, putty for filling cracks, and the like). We could then recalculate the returns to fishing time on an annual basis, taking the total value of catch, subtracting the total expense, and dividing by the total number of hours. The returns proved to be 121 *soles* per hour. Since the exchange rate at the time was 250 *soles* to the dollar, the returns worked out to just under half a dollar an hour.

This figure provided a key to Dominique's dissertation. He could compare the return to similar figures for other economic activities in the region. Though very low by the standards of industrial economies, it was higher than the returns to other activities, and it made good economic sense for the fishermen to continue in this line of work. Moreover, Dominique could argue in his dissertation that there was some factor that "limited fishing effort," to use the terminology of bioeconomic modeling. If more money could be earned in the altiplano by fishing than by growing potatoes or selling fruit in a marketplace or making reed mats, why did people not spend more time fishing and less in these other activities? The conventional economic theories in use at the University of British Columbia suggested that wages should reach some sort of equilibrium, and that people would move from lower-paying jobs to higher-paying ones if they could. We knew that government regulations, very weak in this area, could not be the factor that excluded potential fishermen.

Dominique and I discussed and then rejected one possibility: that credit limited the number of fishermen. From our calculations about the cost and depreciation of boats and nets, we knew that the equipment was not too expensive. Still, perhaps there was a large group of potential fishermen who were unable to start fishing simply because they could not buy a boat or balsa and the nets that were necessary. It was difficult for villagers to get loans from banks, and private moneylenders charged exorbitant interest rates. But credit did not seem to be a problem. The capital usually came from livestock. As the villagers told us, many families owned a few head of cattle, and most sold a calf or two a year. In a *yarqa wata*, a hunger year, a year of poor harvests, this money might be used to purchase food, but in an *allin wata*, a good year, a year of normal or abundant harvests, it could be spent on a boat.

For Dominique, the barriers to entry were clear. He was well aware that lakeshore villages excluded outsiders from fishing in their waters. He had spoken to many fishermen about this and had heard from them how each lakeshore village had a section of water, adjacent to the lands that it owned, that it used for fishing. We had heard the fishermen refer to these territories during the training sessions for the catch surveys. The name that Dominique used for this system was "territorial use rights in fishing." It was simple and clear, and it had an easily remembered acronym: TURF.

His argument struck me as reasonable. Villagers from other parts of the altiplano might well have wanted to move into the lake fisheries, much as they had moved to frontier zones in the Amazon and into cities, but the systems of territorial use rights had been a major factor in limiting their entry. It gratified me to know that the case of the Titicaca fisheries would be of interest not only to academic social scientists like me, but also to more applied researchers like the resource managers who came to Dominique's program from many parts of the world. I was well aware of the tensions between people who view environmental problems as technical matters to be resolved by experts and those who see them as social issues that require broader participation. As Dominique argued in his dissertation, the success of the TURFs could lend support to those who believe that local people should become involved in the management of the areas in which they live. He indicated that this general notion is applicable not only to fisheries but also to forests, to watersheds, to the protection of habitat for endangered species.

In the years since 1987, when Dominique completed his dissertation, I have been glad to see that other people have drawn this conclusion. Review articles on fisheries management have cited his work to support the participation of local fishermen in management. Indeed, the case of the Lake Titicaca fishing grounds meets certain basic principles that correspond in many ways to Ostrom's model of successful common-property management. The grounds have clearly defined boundaries and are governed by locally appropriate rules for management, and effective means are in place to draw participants into decision-making procedures. The rules are easy to monitor and have a set of graduated sanctions for their enforcement. When conflicts do emerge, they can be resolved. Only in the final principle that Ostrom lists—at least minimal recognition by the state of the right of the participants to organize themselves—might one find an exception, yet even here the state does recognize many lakeshore villages as communities, though it grants them rights to administer only the terrestrial portion of their territories, not the aquatic portion.

Still, I felt that something was missing from the account of TURFs. From my earlier work elsewhere in the Andes, I knew how strongly villagers defended their territories—fields and pastures above all, but other kinds of bounded resources as well: the water that they are entitled to draw from irrigation channels, the spots in town squares where village officials have customary rights to sit during religious festivals. The villagers' control of their fishing grounds is not an Andean case of fishing territoriality, I thought; it's a fishing case of Andean territoriality. I recognized that it was important to present this control in terms that could be compared to other fisheries. However, it seemed equally important not to take this rich, complex case and carve off all the historical and cultural factors that made it unique, until all that was left was a kernel that could be compared to other cases that had undergone similar excisions.

My ambivalence centered on the acronym TURF. Its cleverness amused me, and I recognized that it served as a successful mnemonic. But I also disliked its breezy wit. The joke worked well in English, but there were few people in the altiplano who would appreciate it, other than foreigners and a small number of cosmopolitan Peruvians. It occurred to me that I was ambivalent about acronyms altogether. I recognized that I could not dismiss them out of hand. The history of the twentieth century cannot be told without speaking of the USSR and NATO, of the FBI, the CIA, and the KGB. The pithiness of acronyms allows these entities to be mentioned rapidly. It represents the swift pace of the century itself: the bold brevity of the headline, the rapid voice of the newscaster. To eliminate acronyms would be to eliminate much that I valued in this century. FDR and JFK would lose some of their presence and stature if they had to be called only by their last or full names. Any genuine account of the civil rights movement of the 1960s speaks of the NAACP, CORE, SCLC, and SNCC. Still, I realized, my impulse is to reduce rather than to expand the scope of acronyms. I would be glad if no advertisement ever asked me to check out the new fall programs on ABC, NBC, and CBS. In my more utopian moments, I believe that American landscapes might be less cluttered with sprawl, American air less fouled with automobile emissions, if people did not yearn to own a BMW or an SUV; that public discussion and imagination could create simultaneously a more effective health care system and a more appealing name for it than HMO. Above all, work life would be more pleasant and, I suspect, more productive if a simple direct vocabulary would replace the tedious acronyms that every corporation and government agency spawns and uses to fill its e-mails and memos.

I realized, however, that the villagers might not share my ambivalence toward acronyms. Perhaps they liked them more wholeheartedly, or simply were less familiar with them. I thought over the years that had passed since I'd first visited the altiplano in the early 1970s. Much as the Spanish words for occupations have been borrowed selectively into Quechua, only some acronyms have entered local conversation, and even they never remained for long. I had heard a few fishermen speak of IMARPE, though that was in conversations focused directly on my research. Some political parties, government agencies, and peasant organizations, known by acronyms, had been widely discussed for certain periods, especially during the agrarian reform of the 1970s and again during the conflicts of the late 1980s and the early 1990s that involved the Shining Path guerrillas, left-wing parties, local civic organizations, and the military counterinsurgency. These acronyms faded from memory after a decade or two, however. The turnover of administrations and ministries often hastened this disappearance, the names not lasting in conversation much longer than the posters and graffiti that also contained them. This evanescence, I realized, was the quality that made acronyms seem inappropriate for the village control of fishing, which rests on the enduring attachments that link villagers and landscapes.

I looked back to the way that Dominique had based his account of TURFs on the economic activity of the villagers. His arguments rested on the villagers' earning more when they fished than when they carried out other forms of work. This income gap demonstrated that the fishery was indeed profitable, and that some mechanism—the TURFs, in this case—kept the fishery from expanding too much. But the concern with profitability seemed to be as partial and alien an account of work as the TURFs were of spatial control. If fishermen were so concerned about profits, why did they all continue to grow crops and herd animals? Not one of the fifty fishermen in the catch survey had given up his fields, even though they could earn more by fishing full time. Moreover, the fishermen were just a fraction of the villagers who lived next to the lake. What kept the rest of the villagers, who also had access to fishing grounds, from cutting back on their agriculture and putting more time into fishing? Above all, I wondered, if the success of the village fishing grounds lay in the profits that fishing provided to the villagers, then why did the villagers not speak of fishing in terms of income? To be sure, the fishermen were practical people; they repaired worn nets, and they selected the most productive fishing spots. However, they did not raise issues of monetary value when they discussed fishing.

The profitability issue lingered in my mind. I reviewed the variables that Dominique and I had measured in order to calculate the returns for fishing. Our goal had simply been to calculate a ratio for each fisherman, a fraction whose numerator was the net economic returns and whose denominator was the total amount of time spent fishing. Though there might have been some details that were cumbersome to pin down, the basic task had been a simple one. First we established the net economic returns by taking the gross economic returns (defined as the weight of the fish times the price of the fish) and subtracting the expenses, both short-term outlays and longer-term depreciation of equipment. Then we divided each fisherman's net economic returns for the year by the total number of hours that he had worked. On the side of the returns, I was confident that we had good data. The weight of the fish seemed reasonably accurate, since the fishermen had learned to make the conversions from the *arrobas* and *latas* that they recorded in their notebooks to the kilograms that they entered in the reporting forms. We certainly had detailed information on the price of fish.

But what about the labor input? I reread my field notes one more time.

It struck me that the fishermen used their own system of reckoning, one that differed from modern scientific measurement in more subtle ways than did their measurement of weight. Hugo and I could not help noting that the fishermen would report their catch in *arrobas* and *latas*, but it was harder to detect the distinctiveness of time measurement. The fishermen, the IMARPE biologists, and I all understood that there was such a thing as a total catch, though we might report it in different units of weight. Any questions about what was to be counted as "catch" seemed trivial. A few fishermen would occasionally find a frog in their nets, but these totaled only a few kilograms; it was not worth debating about "nonfish catch." Nor did we think it worthwhile to track the few ispi or carachi that might slip out of the nets. There seemed to be no problem at all with the measurement of total work, since it was obvious to everyone that it would be reported in hours. The agreement over the unit of measurement, however, concealed a difference about the total quantity that was being measured.

This point had surfaced early on. In the training sessions at the IMARPE laboratory in Puno, Hugo had asked the fishermen to describe a typical fishing trip and to fill out a form for this trip. The fishermen often listed their work as beginning when they pushed their boats or balsas from the shore, rather than when they left their homes. For the calculations of the returns, however, time that a fisherman spent going from his house to the shore was important, since it was time that could not be spent in other economic activities. (Perhaps, I thought, the fishermen are like commuters, rather than like migrants.) Hugo understood our concern. At the training sessions and again during his early visits to the villages to collect the survey forms, he explained to the fishermen the importance of keeping track of the time they spent walking.

The definition of "work" came up in other ways as well. Had it not been for Hilda's care in coding the data, I might have missed this point altogether. To my good fortune, Hilda took the coding very seriously and reported even apparently minor discrepancies to me. One issue that came up concerned the variable for crew size. We asked the fishermen to report the number of people who went out with them on each trip and some basic information on these crew members. The fishermen had indicated whether someone else went out with them or not, Hilda said, but they had not put in the other information. From a fisheries-economics perspective, the size of the crew was a matter of fundamental importance. Dominique and I had spent enough time out in the villages to know that fishermen often took along a younger brother or a son. The boats and balsas, around five meters long, were too small to hold comfortably more than two people and the gear. I told Hilda to simply insert a "1" for the number of crew members, and a "99," the code for "missing data" for the other information. We found that it was slightly more common for a fisherman to be accompanied than to be alone.

Hilda had other concerns as well. She was uncertain how to code the data that the fishermen reported for the amount of time they spent repairing and mending their nets. Though they often indicated on a catch form that they had fixed their nets since the previous trip, they rarely put down the number of hours this task had required. Once again I told her to insert simply a "missing data" code. She still seemed dissatisfied, so I assured her that Dominique, Hugo, and I would interview a number of fishermen and establish the number of hours that a typical net-repairing session would take.

These minor gaps in the data did not prevent us from estimating the net returns to fishing. If they had any consequence at all, they led us to increase the number of hours, thus reducing the catch per hour and providing a conservative estimate of the difference between fishing and other activities. Many of the additional crew members were young boys, who would have contributed relatively little to the fishing—perhaps helping a bit to pull nets in. In some cases, they might actually have reduced the overall catch, because their weight would have slowed the boat down as the fishermen rowed it through the water. The fishermen had a standard way of phrasing the presence of these crew members. A relative would *acompañar*, "accompany," them rather than *ayudar*, "help," them. This difference was particularly important in the case of a younger brother who lived in another household. Had the younger brother "helped" his older brother, a social debt would have been incurred, and the older brother would be expected to offer some kind of help in return. Merely "accompanying" his older brother, though, did not engender such an obligation. In the face-to-face world of village economic relations, "accompanying" was remarked upon and remembered much less than "helping." In similar terms, the repairing of nets did not really count as work. Quechua-speakers distinguish between *llank'ay*, "to work," and *ruway*, "to do"; the difference seems to exist in Aymara as well, though it is not marked as explicitly.

What makes one person's presence "help" and another's "company"? Why would one be "working" when engaged in one activity and "doing" in another? From the fisheries economics perspective, work is an objective fact: the allocation of human effort in ways that measurably yield a product, in this case, fish. The local categorization of work, though, takes on a social reality: a visitor who arrived at a house would be received more leisurely if the people were "doing" rather than "working," much as "helping" and "keeping company" yield different obligations.

As I thought over the meaning of terms like *work* and *help*, I recalled the *diarios campesinos*, the peasant diaries that a development project had collected in the late 1970s and early 1980s from Bolivian villages on the shores of Lake Titicaca, and in lower valleys. I had looked through them only once and then set them aside, disappointed by their content. Now, at last, they might be of interest. They might provide the key to the ways that villagers spoke about economic activity, to the cultural concepts that influenced their work lives.

To my knowledge, no other set of such diaries had been written by Andean villagers. When I heard about them I contacted the project and learned that its staff members had typed up the handwritten notebooks in which a number of villagers had kept daily entries about their lives. For nothing more than the cost of photocopying and mailing, I could have copies of the seven diaries from the lakeshore villages. I felt that I had been granted a stroke of good fortune. The diaries would have been of great interest to me even if they had been written by villagers who lived in some distant part of the Andes, rather than just over the border in Bolivia in lakeshore villages much like the ones I was studying in Peru. I ordered a set and eagerly awaited its arrival.

My initial excitement at receiving a large cardboard box, filled with hundreds of pages of typescript, soon turned to boredom. I glanced through the pages and saw that they contained the diaries kept by seven individuals—all men, as their names revealed, and all married with children, as I could tell by reading the first entries. These diary-keepers, I discovered, described their lives in very routine terms. Ramón Mamani said nothing more for May 9, 1980, than, "Today we went to harvest potatoes we got 11 *arrobas*." For another day a few months later he stated, "My wife herds the sheep I sew a skirt."

Even the fullest entries seemed monotonous. Tomás Hoyo gave the most detailed description of his household's activities:

> On Tuesday, the whole family woke up very early, we had tea and soon after that we ate a meal. Afterwards, we went out of the house to work and we loaded the tools on the donkey. We also drove the cows, the sheep and the pigs to the place where they would feed. There, we prepared the soil for the entire field for this year's potato crop. At midday, as we always do, we had a meal and drank some water to refresh ourselves. After lunch, we began to work again and in the afternoon we rested, we loaded all the tools on the donkey and this way we returned home. At home we prepared supper, we listened to radio programs and soon after we went to sleep.

And so it continued for more than a thousand typed pages. Relentlessly repetitive, the diaries were nearly as unreadable as a telephone directory. Their entries presented a routine of steady labor, the only changes seeming to be between the forms of labor as the diary-keepers and their family members moved from work in the fields to caring for animals or craft production, such as spinning and sewing. A fraction of the entries touched on other events—births, weddings, deaths, festivals, a visit of government officials to villages, political demonstrations, trips to the city—but these topics were reported in the same flat tone as the work. I did not spend even a full morning with the diaries.

When I thought back on it later, I realized I was so disappointed in the diaries because I was accustomed to thinking of diaries as accounts of private experience, as windows into the inner world of selfhood. In retrospect I realized that I had no reason to expect that the villagers, capable of articulate expression and even eloquence in conversation, in song, in collective performances such as dance, and in political action, would use diary-keeping as a means of self-exploration. Nonetheless, like most modern readers, I realized, I thought of a diary as the means and the record of an individual's journey toward self-awareness. Anne Frank's diary is memorable not merely for the facts that it contains about the daily routines of individuals who lived in hiding from the Nazis, but for the distinctiveness of the author's voice, the precision of her perceptions, and the vivid path of her development as an individual. These Andean diary-keepers, by contrast, did not present themselves as having any inner lives at all. From what they wrote, one would assume that they did not feel or think. They simply worked, ate, and slept. Even the very act of keeping a diary did not seem to stir them into reflection. The diary-keepers identified themselves only by their names and villages, without even so simple a claim to personal distinctiveness as a profession. The few who provided a reason for keeping the diary did nothing more than describe the first meeting at which they were given instructions on what to write and a schedule of payments. Pedro Maquera mentioned that "we would write a book that would be a memoir for our children, and we would all be the authors of this book." And Ramón Mamani recalled that he was instructed "to write each day about how a family lives and works." The only other references to the diaries within the diaries themselves consisted of listing "writing in the notebook" or "my notebook task" in precisely the same terms as any other kind of work.

It did not surprise me that the project that had collected the diaries did not use them as the basis for any report or document. (The justification for commissioning the diaries was to collect information on appropriate technology, a topic much in favor in development circles at that time.) At most, it seemed to me the entries could be summarized to provide a simple annual calendar of work activities and a description of the division of tasks by gender and age, but such information was already available in other anthropological studies. And so I set the diaries aside, taking them out only a few times to show some pages to students. One student was appalled by the unrelieved tedium they presented. Another, noting the diverse range of crops, animals, and crafts, found a note of bucolic charm in this simple life. Caught up in a sudden burst of enthusiasm, she suggested that the diary-keepers exemplified the virtues of Taoist sages: autonomy, contentment, and wisdom. As we perused a set of entries, we recognized that the diaries did point toward autonomy in the form of economic self-sufficiency, but that they suggested contentment only in the lack of complaints and ambition. The wisdom, if not lacking, was wholly unrecorded in the pages—unless the absence of reflection were to be taken as a sign of wisdom.

These diaries came to mind when I reflected on the questions of work among the lake fishermen. Why did the fishermen record some aspects of the fishing with such detail and, as a check survey indicated, with such accuracy, when they were so sloppy about other details, such as the time it took to repair nets? Were they concerned only with the relative profitability of fishing, as Dominique and others had suggested? Suddenly I realized that the very lack of self-consciousness of the diaries could be their most attractive feature. A reader of Western diaries follows the writer's efforts to bring personal experience into clear view; a reader of these altiplano diaries could use them as a point of entry into the inarticulate and inarticulable world of daily life. Here was my chance to look closely at the diaries and draw significant information from them: I could search for the ways in which they described work. What assumptions led the diary-keepers to select certain words (commonplace ones, to be sure, but important ones nonetheless) when other words were available to them? Why did the diary-keepers arrange items in one order rather than another? I realized the tedious and repetitive nature of the entries might assist in answering these questions, that their very lack of adornment might make the basic patterns stand out more clearly.

I found the box containing the diaries perched atop a tall bookcase along with old final exams that students had not picked up and that university regulations required me to keep for three years. I began by studying the word *work*. It appears no fewer than 1,035 times in the 5,754 entries that make up the diaries, both as a noun *(trabajo)* and in the various forms of the verb *(trabajar)*. In only four of these cases was I unable to find some concrete activity to which the word referred. On occasion, the verb *trabajar*, "to work," appears with a direct object: *trabajar la escuela*, "to work the schoolhouse," refers to building the schoolhouse. More often, the word *work*, whether as a verb or a noun, is linked to another, more specific verb. Sometimes this linkage occurs because the activity was interrupted for a meal:

> On Wednesday morning we woke up and soon the whole family had breakfast. We went to the village fields in Hachuta to harvest *oca* [a root crop] and at 12 noon we had our midday meal. In the afternoon we continued this *trabajo,* we gathered two donkey-loads of *oca* and then we rested at 4 in the afternoon. At home I listened to the news broadcast on the radio station San Gabriel, my wife prepared supper, we ate supper and then we went to sleep.

On other occasions, the details of arranging for additional hands led to the use of the word *work:* "On Monday we went to Bacoma to harvest maize and to carry out this *trabajo,* I hired three families and a helper, well we worked all day long. That day daughter stayed home to care for the animals."

It might not seem very unusual for someone in the altiplano to describe building a schoolhouse or harvesting crops as "work." Nonetheless, a careful review does show cultural patterns in the ways the diary-keepers used the word *work*—patterns that can account for the gaps Hilda noticed on the catch survey forms, and that suggest the villagers focused attention on aspects of work different from the profitability that Dominique thought was central.

In all instances, activities described as "work" required effort—usually physical strength, though sometimes manual skill or mental concentration. And they all involved the making or obtaining of a tangible object. I was pleased to see that fishing counted as work—though only on one occasion, when a diary-keeper went with a hook and line to a nearby river. Agriculture accounted for 554 of the 1,031 cases identified as work, a bit over half. Under this broad rubric were many agricultural tasks, such as sorting seed, preparing fertilizer, plowing, planting, weeding, harvesting, and processing crops. There were 368 examples of construction work: building houses, schools, bridges, churches, roads, and tanks, and making parts of buildings (such as adobe bricks and doors). This high proportion of cases of construction reflects the greater attention accorded to such work, since the writers detailed the large work groups

A group of men building a house of adobe bricks. Photograph by Ben Orlove.

formed for construction. Craft activities, mostly sewing and embroidery, accounted for seventy-one cases—a disproportionately low percentage, since these activities took up a good deal of time and yielded a significant portion of the income of several households. The diary-keeping itself was listed as work twenty-four times, and there were six miscellaneous instances of work.

In a set of ten or a hundred uses of the word *work*, an activity might not appear simply by chance. Similarly, it seems unlikely that the omission of an item from the total of more than a thousand cases would be a statistical fluke. The diaries excluded some activities that would be considered "work" in a Western framework. For example, although domesticated animals are mentioned frequently, their routine care was not usually counted as work; even though it entailed effort, it did not produce a tangible, long-lasting object. Taking animals to pasture, a routine chore usually carried out by women and children, appears as *trabajo* only seven times. Cooking and child care, largely (though not exclusively) carried out by women, were never counted as work. It seemed to be actual meal preparation that was excluded, since the processing of crops—winnowing barley, husking corn, taking beans out of dried pods—could be described as work. Other activities associated with maintaining the household were omitted as well, particularly buying and selling in markets, which is largely women's work.

Though this definition of work does exclude many activities carried out by women, it also omits others that are often done by men, particularly repairing tools and other household items. The diary-keepers often mentioned village assemblies and visits to offices, in which both men and women were present and men dominated the discussion. However, they never counted conversation or meetings as work, because, again, they did not entail effort and they yielded no concrete product. On only one occasion was a lawyer described as "working": when he produced a document. In the office visits that led up to this document, however he was not described as working, even though the diary-keeper had to pay him.

This use of *trabajo* clarifies the gaps that Hilda detected in the information the fishermen provided. When the fishermen filled out the catch survey forms, they left out the information they did not count as *trabajo*, even though we had asked about it. Thus they failed to record the amount of time they spent repairing nets, because they did not consider that work. They often omitted the time they spent walking from their houses to their boats for the same reason. The diaries, in their indication of the definition of the word *help*, also provided some insight into why the fishermen recorded scant detail on the formation of their crews. *Ayuda*, the word for *help*, is nearly as common in the diaries as *trabajo*. It appears 701 times, both as noun and as verb. It is discussed in detail because an individual who receives help often is obligated to repay this assistance. Agriculture predominates once again, with 451 entries. Construction and crafts are present, though less frequently: ninety-one and twenty-six times, respectively. (There are no references to helping with diary entries. The diary-keepers, all chosen from the pool of men who were literate and had a working knowledge of Spanish, did not require assistance for this task.) Previously unlisted activities appear in the category of help. Taking animals to pasture, listed only seven times in the 1,035 cases of work, is mentioned as help forty-six times. Entirely absent from *trabajo*, domestic chores appear as *ayuda*: sixty-two instances of cooking, nine of carrying water, two of washing clothes, and one case of taking out the garbage *(echar la basura)*. Interestingly, child care still remains invisible: though someone might have carried another's child on her back, or kept an eye on a toddler playing in front of a house, it was never mentioned. Other activities listed as *ayuda* are all instances of some purposive activity with a concrete goal that required effort: carrying fertilizer, training a newly purchased bull to plow, helping someone look for a lost bicycle. (Entirely absent from the notion of *ayuda* are the forms of emotional help that many westerners describe in their diaries: helping someone get over a failed relationship, or helping them decide what kind of job to look for.) It is not surprising, then, that the fishermen were lax in their recording of the data on crew size that Dominique and I were so interested in. To economists, the young men and boys who came along on the boat would be crew members. To the villagers, not only were such people not engaged in *trabajo*, they were not even giving *ayuda*, since they were not taking part in the purposive activity of rowing. At most, they went to *acompañar* the fisherman, to keep him company.

The diaries clarified the unevenness with which the fishermen recorded information on the forms for the catch survey. By conducting other surveys, Dominique was able to fill the gaps in the data that he required for his dissertation. However, the diaries raised another, larger issue, not merely on obtaining data but on interpreting it: How central is profit to the fishermen? When villagers decide whether to fish, do they look primarily at the hourly returns, or do other factors assume more importance?

The diaries show that the fishermen observed closely the three economic components that are needed to evaluate the returns to fishing and to other activities—such as agriculture, livestock raising, and crafts— much as Dominique and I had. They kept track of the products of their efforts, they described the raw materials and tools they needed for these activities, and they noted the time that they spent doing them. However, the diary entries do not describe these three components only in monetary terms. Of the seven diary-keepers, only one, Pedro Maquera, mentioned prices consistently: "My wife has taken care of the animals and also has worked threshing barley, this day she has gathered about 3 *arrobas* a value of 105 *pesos*."

The other six mentioned the volume, not the monetary value, of crops or the craft items that they produced. If they distinguished between different kinds of crops, they indicated the crops' use in the household rather than their price. Julio Constantino Maquera is representative of the other six: "Today Wednesday, my wife winnowed two donkey-loads of barley, she also gathered half a donkey load of unripe barley for the pigs, and saved some ears of grain for the oxen." He specified the volume and the use of the grain, but not its price.

Prices were mentioned more often when something was sold. Such sales represent only a fraction of the total output of village households, who consumed much of the food, and used many of the goods, that they produced. Justo Yanarico described one Sunday soon after he was selected for a year's term as an official in his village:

> Today we get up very early, my wife prepares the meal, I take the cows out of the corral to feed them oat straw and afterwards I take them to the river so that they can drink. Then I tie them with ropes to a stake. Afterwards together with my wife we go to the fair in the town of Escoma to sell three *cerditos* [little pigs]. Each little pig we sold for 200 *pesos* very cheap two little pigs we sold for 200 *pesos* each and the other for 150 *pesos*. At three in the afternoon all the agricultural unions in the area met, in this meeting we took our posts, the top officer was installed in the swearing-in ceremony. After the meeting we bought four bottles of beer, a carton of cigarettes and liquor in all I spent 100 *pesos*.

This account suggests that Justo decided to sell some animals because he knew that he would be expected to provide beer, liquor, and cigarettes to other people after the swearing-in ceremony. This particular day might not otherwise have been a good time to sell; he repeats that the piglets are little and mentions that the price was very cheap. After selling the first two piglets, he and his wife had obtained the cash that he would need to spend later that day. At that point, unable to receive their asking price of 200 *pesos* for the third piglet, they accepted an even lower price. From what I can infer from the other entries in his diaries, I would guess that Justo did not want to show up at the ceremony with a piglet in tow, presumably the runt of the litter. Whatever the reason, though, two things seem clear: he was familiar with the prices that his goods might receive, and profitability was only one of several criteria that he used to make economic decisions.

The villagers kept track even less of their labor time. The diary-keepers could find the precise time if they wished, since many of the men wore watches, and most households owned radios. However, there are few references to specific times in the diaries. Julio Constantino noted specific hours most frequently:

> We get up at 6 A.M. my wife prepares 3 cups of hot thickened tea for breakfast and then she makes a soup from ½ pound of potatoes, ¼ pound of *chuño* [dried potatoes], onion, meat and seasonings, after this soup, I stay in my house to embroider a costume for the Moreno dancer, my wife takes the cattle, she is also harvesting peas for fodder, she gathered two donkey-loads, my mother was with the sheep and pigs, at 12 we eat the cold lunch together at my house among six people, after 12 my wife piles up potatoes about three donkey-loads and then she covers them with the leaves of the potato plants, at 6 in the afternoon we bring the animals to their respective corrals, my wife prepares supper while I am sewing, at 10 at night we have supper and soon, praying to the Lord, we rest.

Though he mentions the specific time on five occasions in this entry, he recorded only routine household activities: the meals and bringing the animals to their corrals. He did not tally the hours for the activities that counted as work—embroidering, harvesting peas, piling potatoes. The other diary-keepers, who recorded the hour only infrequently, also did not tally working hours. They mentioned the time when they left their homes for trips and when they returned, and they recorded the hour when village assemblies or other meetings took place, but not the time when they started or finished working.

The diary-keepers, relatively unconcerned with the precise length of working time, instead paid close attention to its position in a sequence of activities. They all seemed to have had an implicit template. The most routine activities, the ones that Western diary-keepers tend not to record, are presented in precise and tedious detail. The diary-keeper and his family awaken. They eat a meal. They work or carry out other chores. They eat another meal. They return to their work and chores. They eat another meal and rest (or, in the only variations on the pattern, they rest first and then eat another meal). They go to sleep.

This daily sequence fits into a sequence of days in the week and weeks in the year. The ordinary weekdays of labor alternated with days of rest, during which the diary-keepers performed little heavy labor in the fields—Sundays for the Catholics, Saturdays for the Seventh-Day Adventists. They worked even less, or not at all, on the days of major celebrations—village festivals, national holidays, life-cycle events such as first haircuttings, weddings, and funerals. Even on days when they did not work, though, they reported on the days in the same sequence, indicating the activities that fit into the work slot and describing the greater amount of food and drink that they consumed. Though some might interpret this simple repetition as a great lack of imagination, there are underlying reasons for this choice of structure.

The regular sequence of work, meals, and sleep points to the importance of human strength in the villagers' understanding of their bodies. Work uses up the strength that meals and sleep restore. Generally, this view is only implicit in the diaries, but it does surface on occasion. It appears in the discussion of illness. When Justo Yanarico became ill, he noted the first day that he was so ill he had to go to a nearby town for medical treatment. On the second day, he wrote, "I continue to be ill," and noted he was "barely able to give fodder to the cows." On the third day, he wrote, "I am already a little bit better . . . but I wasn't able to work either, I only watched the cows and fed them." On the following day he made the final reference to the illness: "today I woke up better than yesterday" and described the work for that day: carrying potatoes home from a spot by the river where they were being prepared for storage. He never mentioned any pain or discomfort, or any emotional concern on his part or his wife's.

The diary-keepers had a particular way of describing their work time. Rather than tallying hours spent in activity, they showed that they filled their work time with work. These intervals between the first and last meal on the workday were all accounted for. The highest priority was to work in fields and in building houses, though other work was acceptable. If they did not work, they indicated their reason for not working. They did not present themselves as having a certain number of tasks they had to accomplish, but rather as having a certain amount of time to allocate to their tasks. They stressed the uniformity rather than the variability of the work that they carried out in these intervals. Very few descriptions indicate that a particular task required a particular skill or an especially high level of effort; rather, they stress the constancy of the effort expended in work.

The diary-keepers used certain words to indicate this emphasis on the steadiness of work. The verb *dedicar*, cognate with the English word *dedicate*, appears 296 times. It suggests a seriousness of intent, a resistance to distraction, and a concern with completing a task. Almost three-quarters of the occurrences of *dedicar* (221) are tied directly to the activities that count as *trabajo*, and most of the rest (68) are linked to washing clothes, bathing, marketing, and cooking. Only seven of the cases apply to what could be called leisure activities: three cases of resting, two of strolling *(paseo)*, and two of drinking. The verb *ocupar*, to be occupied, implies a continuity of effort and an avoidance of interruption; of its 130 appearances, 114 refer to *trabajo* and 16 to other chores.

In other words, the diary-keepers were aware of work, of the things produced by work, of the time and effort spent in work. They paid keen attention to price, though they did not direct this attention to all goods. Since they did not tally their working hours, they did not pay as close attention to the relative profitability of different activities, as Dominique would have suggested.

The few direct references to fishing in the diaries show this particular orientation to time. Justo Yanarico wrote:

> On Monday and Tuesday I went all day to the Río Suches to fish with a fishhook for silverside and trout, in a day I caught about 30 silverside with 2 hooks. These days we still have time because the fields aren't ready to harvest, what we planted is not yet ripe. My wife took over caring for the cows she gives them some grass to eat and a little barley then she takes them to the river so that they can drink water. My children as usual take the sheep and pigs to graze in the places that aren't planted,

but always looking for the places with grass so that they can feed, in the afternoon they return with all these little animals [i.e., non-cattle]. This is the activity of today and yesterday.

Another entry about fishing also shows these concerns to fill weekday time between the first and last meal with productive activity, and to give agriculture and livestock-raising priority over other activities:

Today Tuesday I also went to the river to fish bringing my fishhook, because all the *trabajo* of the harvest is finished, so I dedicate myself to fishing, on this day I caught 28 silverside. My wife has gone to help my father harvest barley all day, this field is near the house, also she takes the cows with her so that they can graze in the same place where she is working. As always, my oldest daughter takes the sheep and pigs to graze and when it gets late she drives them back. My son Alfredo goes to his school. This is the activity of all day Tuesday.

The accounts of work in the diaries are much like the accounts that I heard from fishermen. Fishing appeals especially to men in households with smaller fields and fewer animals, and hence with time that might otherwise go unoccupied. By fishing, the men could spend time working rather than remaining idle. It has the particularly appealing feature of flexibility, since trips can often be as short as a couple of hours. A fisherman can set his nets one afternoon after coming back from the fields and before eating dinner. Leaving just after breakfast the next day or the day after, he can check his nets in the morning and still be back in time to help a relative build his house. In the busy seasons of the agricultural calendar, he can get up *bien temprano*, very early, to fit fishing in with the field preparation, or planting, weeding, or harvesting. People who work as laborers for a daily wage, or as petty traders bringing goods to market, must be absent for a full day or perhaps longer. Their working hours are imposed by their employers or by the market schedule, so that they do not have the flexibility that comes with fishing.

The catch surveys document this intertwining of fishing and agriculture. Dominique and I had noted that there were no slow or busy seasons for the fishermen. The average number of trips per fisherman per month fluctuated between the narrow limits of 19.2 to 21.6. This steadiness is also shown by the most common type of trip, the double trip, in which a fisherman rows out late in the afternoon to set his nets, returns home, and then rows out again in the morning to retrieve the nets and bring them back to shore. In check trips, the fishermen leave the nets out in the lake for days at a time, rowing out occasionally to remove the fish that have been caught and then setting the nets back in the water. These trips require the least amount of time, though they also yield the lowest amount of fish. They are concentrated at two times of the year, the planting season between October and December, and the harvest months of March and April. In these months, the fishermen have less free time and less flexibility in scheduling. Their longest and highest-yielding trips are the overnight trips, in which they row out with their nets, set them, and stay out all night, coming back only the next day. These trips are most common between May and August, the slowest season of the agricultural year, when it is easiest for fishermen to be absent for longer periods.

These concepts of work contrast with the bioeconomic models, in which time is a homogeneous resource, an amount of hours to be allocated to generate the greatest profit. The notion of time in these models makes sense in part because our language is filled with metaphors of time as a resource. We can save it, spend it, and waste it; in short, we use it. From this perspective, technology consists of labor-saving devices, or more precisely, labor-intensifying devices. Individuals and firms invest capital in tools or machines so that they can produce more efficiently, with a higher amount of output in each unit of time. For the villagers, though, time comes in varied forms. The different kinds of time complement each other to compose a whole. In their way of speaking, work, meals, and sleep form the cycle of days and establish the balance of strength in the human body. Similarly, the busy and slow seasons of the agricultural year shape the rhythms of activities. In this view, boats and nets are labor-absorbing devices. Villagers invest capital in them so that they can work during the parts of the day that are working time. It is idleness, rather than inefficiency, that they avoid.

For the villagers, work is not just an efficient and profitable way to use time. It is more than a means to the end of generating income. The most valued sorts of work are agriculture and construction, the kinds of work that most fully demonstrate the qualities of effort and productivity that distinguish work from nonwork. They meet the most fundamental human needs, the needs for food and shelter. Moreover, by making food and houses, agriculture and construction allow the villagers to eat and to sleep, the complements of work. This conception of work helps explain why fishermen continue to farm their fields, even though that activity generates less income than fishing. It also suggests why many other men in the lakeshore villages do not leave agriculture for fishing.

This conception of work, moreover, offers a view of the village control of fishing grounds that complements Dominique's account of TURFs. Neither space nor time is a resource to be used, its value determined by the income it can generate. The villagers seek to fill in appropriate ways their workable spaces—fields, pastures, and for the lakeshore villages, fishing grounds—much as they seek to fill their work time with activities that meet their understanding of work. To understand these workable spaces, these village fishing territories, I now turn not to the catch surveys and diaries, both from the same period in the 1970s and 1980s, but to the longer sweep of history.

δ Fish

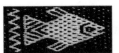A few miles east of the city of Puno is the Isla Foroba. Despite its name, it is a peninsula at most times. Only when the lake is unusually high does it become an island, separated from the shore by a hundred meters of water. On this small piece of land is a two-story building with storerooms and offices for the Titicaca National Reserve, a government-run protected area. This building also houses a small museum whose two rooms contain a large map and a collection of five or six stuffed birds, as well as a wheelbarrow and some shovels that are not kept in the storerooms. A few times a year, zoology students from the university in Puno take one of the urban bus lines out to the last stop and walk the short distance to the museum. The university budget is too small to pay for the rental of a boat for a field trip to these birds' habitat, just a kilometer or so away in the extensive reed-filled sections of the lake, so the students must learn to iden-

tify the local species from these stuffed specimens. Other than the students, the museum receives very few visitors. A representative of the regional tourism office or a consultant to some international development agency might be taken out to it in a chauffeur-driven car, but most of the time, its doors remain locked.

Though the museum has changed little in the last twenty years, one can imagine it much larger, since smaller lakes, such as Lake Geneva in Switzerland and Lake Biwa in Japan, have much more ambitious local museums. Let us envisage a visit to this museum after its expansion and improvement. Surely it houses an exhibit of the native fish of Lake Titicaca. The exhibit does not need to be very large, since the extreme isolation of the lake has meant that few fish have ever been able to reach it. The exhibit contains maps that show the altiplano is connected neither to the great river systems of the Amazon and the Río de la Plata, which drain into the Atlantic, nor to the more numerous smaller watersheds on the Pacific side. High mountain chains to the east and the west block any connection to the ocean. Lake Titicaca drains through the Río Desaguadero to another lake, Poopó, whose waters in turn flow into an arid plain in the southern altiplano. Whatever water enters this lower section does not remain, but evaporates, adding another layer to the deposits that form a vast salt flat, the Salar de Coipasa. The native fish of Lake Titicaca are the descendents of the few fish that had found their way into this isolated set of lakes and rivers—most likely when lowland fish were lifted to high elevations with the rise of the Andes.

The exhibit shows that this remote lake has held only twenty-six native species of fish. Two of them are closely related species of catfish in the genus *Trichomycterus,* found in other parts of the Andes as well. The other twenty-four are all species of a genus, *Orestias,* that belongs to the pupfish family *Cyprinodontidae,* a large group of fish, most of them fairly small and living in surface waters, that includes some species that inhabit small hot springs in the deserts of the southwestern United States. Of these twenty-four *Orestias,* two—*Orestias agassii,* a kind of carachi, and *Orestias pentlandii,* the boga—are distributed throughout the altiplano and beyond, north to Cuzco; the range of the former extends south as well through much of Bolivia and into Chile. The other twenty-two are found nowhere in the world except Lake Titicaca and the streams that flow into it.

These fish are an example of what evolutionary biologists call a fish flock, a set of species that has evolved in a single lake. Several researchers have used anatomical and biochemical methods to study the development of the *Orestias* fish flock in Lake Titicaca and have resolved that the original carachi, a medium-size fish that eats insects and crustaceans, was the ancestor of all of these species. Within the flock are some species that resemble the carachi, and some that are quite different: a long, large-headed fish-eating predator; several tiny, slim fish whose large eyes allow them to detect their prey, microscopic plankton, well below the surface; a chunky, thick-headed fish that lives exclusively on snails and other mollusks, which it plucks from water plants with its upturned jaws and then crushes with additional teeth that it has evolved inside its throat. These remarkable changes have taken place in the relatively short evolutionary period of the last three million years. As shifts in the regional climate have caused the level of the lake to rise or fall by tens of meters, parts of Lake Titicaca and other lakes in the altiplano have been alternately isolated, favoring the formation of new species, and then reconnected, permitting the introduction of new species back into Titicaca. Other mechanisms appear to have been at work as well, as specialists who study this phenomenon of fish flocks have suggested.

The museum's native fish exhibit closes with a display that underscores the importance of Lake Titicaca to science. A world map shows that such fish flocks are found only in Lake Titicaca and a dozen or so ancient lakes around the world—the Caspian Sea, Lake Biwa, Lake Baikal in Siberia, Lake Lanao in the Philippines, and Lakes Tanganyika, Malawi, and Victoria in Africa.

What exhibits about the people of Lake Titicaca complement the ones about its natural history? What comes to mind is a set of displays in the Hall of the History of the Lake Titicaca Fishermen. The first room treats all of prehistory. It opens with the arrival of hunter-gatherers in the altiplano around 6000 B.C. and continues with the rise of small chiefdoms and the development and collapse of the Tiwanaku state, centered just southeast of the lake. It closes with the last centuries before the Span-

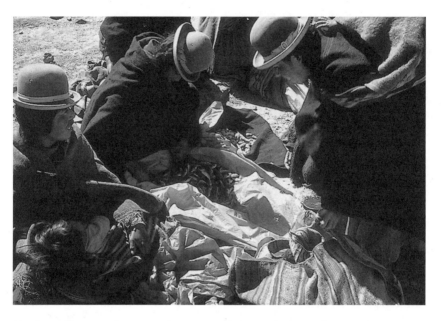

Vendors selling carachi in a marketplace, and their customers. Photograph by Ben Orlove.

ish conquest by tracing the emergence of Aymara-speaking kingdoms around the lake and their incorporation into the Inca empire in the mid-fifteenth century. Despite the complexity of this sequence, the exhibit room is small, since little is known about the undoubtedly varied history of fishing during this lengthy period. Archaeologists have described in detail other aspects of the millennium that preceded the Spanish conquest: the herding of the llamas and alpacas that made this region so rich in prehistory; the extensive systems of raised fields that supported intensive agriculture; the architecture and crafts; the far-reaching trade networks; the urban centers that flourished in certain centuries.

This room devoted to the prehistory of the fishermen, though, contains little more than a few small cases with the bones of fish that archaeologists have found in and around the houses, the oldest of which date back to about 1500 B.C. A few panels contain quotations from Spanish chronicles, whose descriptions of the Inca empire suggest in general terms the importance of fishing in the lake. One or two other panels record the words of the Indian nobles, interviewed by Spanish officials in the decades immediately after the conquest, who spoke of the Urus, a separate ethnic group of people, poorer than the others, who fished, hunted, and gathered plants in the lake. Rather than paying tribute to the Incas, they provided labor and dried fish to the lords of the local ethnic groups.

The next room, which covers the fishermen under Spanish rule, is somewhat larger. Its walls are covered with maps and charts. One map shows the movement of dried fish from specialized fishing villages on the lake to the city of Potosí, six hundred kilometers to the southeast, a silver-mining center that, at its peak of prosperity in the seventeenth century, was the largest city in South America and the center of a trade network that spanned half the continent. This map includes a few details, such as the location of several lakeshore villages that were heavily involved in the trade. This information is sketchy, though, since historians have paid less attention to this shipping of dried fish than to other aspects of the trade to Potosí, such as the movements of wheat from central Bolivia, mules and hides from Argentina, cloth from Ecuador, wine and mercury from Peru, and yerba maté, a kind of herbal tea, from Paraguay.

Other maps and charts in the room trace the size of the populations of Urus. The hypothetical museum curator has based them on the numerous graphs in the work of the French historian Nathan Wachtel, who used Spanish colonial tax records and population censuses to study this group. At the time of this first extensive documentation in the 1570s, the Urus formed sizable clusters not only around Lake Titicaca but also along other rivers and lakes in the altiplano. Recognized as poor, they paid lower taxes than other Indians. Most of them lived off aquatic resources—fish, wild birds, and an abundant and highly productive species of reed known as *totora*—but some of them cultivated fields. By the end of the seventeenth century, their numbers had declined sharply. Wachtel's careful rendering of government records shows that the loss in numbers was not due to demographic causes such as higher death rates in response to epidemics, or to lower birth rates. Nor did military defeat reduce the Uru population significantly. Though a few groups of Uru stalwarts held out against Christianization and Spanish rule longer than did other highland Indians, the last Uru rebellions between 1610 and 1680 were small in numerical terms. The reduction in the number of Urus came instead from changes in identity. Many of them remained in their original areas and adopted the more prestigious Aymara language and identity, while others, who had moved to mining towns and other new centers, mingled and intermarried with other Indian groups and lost their distinctiveness. By the eighteenth century, only a few small groups of Urus remained, concentrated in the altiplano south of Lake Titicaca.

On the door of the third room of this Hall of the History of the Lake Titicaca Fishermen hangs a sign that reads "Under Construction," because very little is known about the fishing in the last decades of Spanish rule and the first decades of Peruvian independence. In 1780, Tupac Amaru, a minor Indian noble from just north of the altiplano, started a rebellion that turned into the largest indigenous uprising in the history of Latin America. With extensive support from local Indians, the rebels occupied the entire altiplano in 1781 and 1782. Hundreds of Spaniards and mestizos were massacred. Many more fled, entirely abandoning the smaller towns and the city of Puno to the rebels. The heavy Spanish repression that followed this rebellion further weakened the regional economy, which had entered a long decline with the exhaustion of the silver ore at Potosí. The altiplano suffered from violence again during the Wars of Independence in the 1810s and 1820s and the fighting among military strongmen in the years that followed, with battles near Ccapia and at other sites. During this period of economic depression, political disorder, and outbreaks of great violence, few records were left about the fishing in the lake, though it is virtually certain that fishing contributed significantly to the local economy and diet. Economic growth and political stability came to Peru in the mid-nineteenth century, with the growth and expansion of new exports and the strengthening of parliamentary government and civil administration. These conditions, in turn, encouraged travel to the altiplano by Peruvians and foreigners alike. These scientists, engineers, writers, and other visitors left extensive documentation that provides material for the next room in this hall, which covers the period from 1870 to about 1930.

The museum curator has organized the fourth room around the theme of material culture. Contemporary balsas are placed side by side with the

Drawing of balsa making by Escolástico Chiripo, a villager from Santa Rosa de Yanaque, 1979 or 1980.

engravings that illustrated many of the travelers' accounts to demonstrate that these craft have remained essentially unchanged. Not only are they of the same size and made of the same totora reeds, but even the regional differences have been retained. The prow and stern are lower and flatter on the balsas from the western side of the lake, higher and more pointed on those from the eastern side.

The principal focus of this room, though, is the collection of fishing gear, the most striking of which is the *wayunaqana*, or large trawl net. As the name suggests, it is indeed huge, consisting of many sheets of fine-meshed net sewn together into a kind of sack eight meters in length, with a mouth that is four meters wide and a meter high. Too large to be displayed in a case, an example of this gear is suspended from the ceiling. A short video demonstrates its operation, because these large trawl nets are still in use, especially in the Lago Pequeño, much as they were in the past. Because they are too big for a lone individual to handle, the net owner must find a helper. Each ties a rope to the mouth of the net. Placing the net and one rope in the owner's balsa, the end of the other rope in the helper's balsa, they carefully pole the balsas in parallel courses out to deeper water, where they release the net behind them. The net owner and his helper, now using their poles as paddles, work steadily to tow the large heavy net through the water. Soon after they release the net, other villagers, as many as a dozen, paddle out in their balsas to search for carachi. Once a concentration of these fish is detected, the net owner, his helper, and the other fishermen form a circle a hundred meters or more in diameter. The other fishermen close in on the fish. By throwing rocks and splashing the water with their poles, they drive the fish toward the advancing pair of balsas and into the net. The fishermen pace themselves carefully, since the fish can escape between the balsas if they move too slowly, and the school will disperse if they are too rapid. Once the fish are driven into the net, the net owner and his helper haul the net onto the owner's balsa. The weight of the net and the fish slow them. By the time they arrive at shore, the other fishermen are already waiting for the division of the catch. One half goes to the net owner, who divides it again between himself and his helper; the other half is split equally among the other fishermen. This sequence may be repeated several times. The net-owner rotates the position of helper among the other fishermen, not choosing anyone for a second turn until the others have had their chance.

The museum curator has developed an audio program for this fourth room. Visitors who enter the room rent portable audiocassette players. As they pass the cases, they use the on-off switch and the numbered keys to select specific objects about which they listen to recorded comments, drawn from the wide range of documents and oral histories that describe this period. The audio guide discusses another aspect of the large trawl net: it is linked to the earliest documented case of village-based fishing

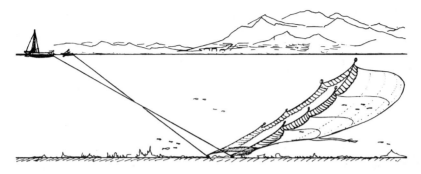

Drawing by Dominique Levieil of the operation of a *wayunaqana* (trawl net).

territories. It quotes from the report of a Peruvian general, Billinghurst, descended from a British visitor and from prominent families in Lima, who became president twice but in 1870, still only a military official, traveled to the altiplano to assess the danger of foreign invasions in this border region. In a deep, self-assured voice, an actor recounts the elaborate ceremonies that this aristocratic officer witnessed near the town of Desaguadero: fishermen from two neighboring villages rowed out into the lake in their balsas, where, to the accompaniment of flutes and drums, they traveled along the invisible line in the water that marked the demarcation between their territories. The recording explains that this report was merely the first of many that described such territories from all parts of the lake.

The other types of gear, smaller than the trawl net, are arrayed around the walls of the room. In one case is displayed a *sajjaña*, or dip net, a heavy wooden pole nearly two meters long with a rectangular wooden frame at one end, from which is suspended a net, often made of llama-wool thread or, more recently, of cotton or nylon. The steps in its use are illustrated by a series of panels or by a video clip, since, like the large trawl nets, the dip nets are still used in a number of villages. A fisherman has only to carry a dip net to the shore, roll his pants up above the knee, and wade into a shallow portion of the lake. (A few women use these dip nets as well; they tuck the bottom of their skirts into their waistbands and then proceed in the same manner.) Once in the lake, the fisherman slides the frame and net of the dip net along the bottom and then lifts it up. This final movement is the most tiring. The poles are by necessity quite long, since a short pole will not allow the fisherman to sneak up on his prey, but the length of the poles makes them heavy and awkward to balance. A lucky thrust brings some carachi. The fisherman then scoops the fish out, puts them in a small sack at his waist, takes a step, and repeats the sequence of motions. After a series of steps, the fisherman returns to shore, empties the sack onto a cloth on the ground, and then enters the lake one more time. Again and again he repeats this sequence, until the size of the heap satisfies him or time has run out. Then he ties the ends of the cloth together, bends down, swings the cloth over his back, and walks home, holding the pole of the dip net in one hand and resting the net over his shoulder.

For this type of gear, the most common around the lake, the audio guide offers an account of the fish trade. Here, the quote is from David Forbes, rendered in a cultured English accent, befitting a scientific traveler who would present his findings to a scholarly society. His report, coincidentally also from 1870, describes how fish were sold fresh in local markets, as well as dried and taken to markets throughout the altiplano and outside the basin to the upper reaches of the tributaries of the Amazon and to the narrow canyons of the arid desert of the Pacific Coast.

The *majjaña,* or fish harpoons, are arrayed in a case or simply mounted on the wall: wooden poles as long as three meters, to which three or four shafts made of hardened wood or of metal were attached, often with a thin braid of human hair. An old photograph has been selected to illustrate its use, rather than a video clip, both because these spears are much less frequently employed at present, and because the curator decided that a photograph would be appropriate to indicate the motionlessness of the spear holder. A fisherman would wade into the lake or pole his balsa out until he reached a spot in which to wait for a catfish to appear. He would then lift the heavy spear to the level of his shoulder and stand utterly motionless. Sensitive to any vibration in the water, an approaching catfish would flee if the fisherman moved his legs or even if he shifted his arm. At most, the fisherman could slowly turn his head while he scanned for the flickers of motion that indicated the arrival of a catfish into the range of the spear. Once it stopped moving, the well-camouflaged fish would be hard to spot. Its smooth, scaleless skin, medium gray in color with small flecks of lighter and darker shades, rendered it almost invisible against the background of mud, reeds, and algae. A throw accurate and strong enough to pierce the fish's thick, slimy skin would yield a great prize, a large fish whose flesh was appreciated for its white color and mild flavor. An unsuccessful throw would require another long, uncomfortable wait, but the fishermen could tolerate such failures with equanimity. Even if the day's effort yielded only one fish, it might be large enough to make a pot of soup that would feed a family. If there were additional ones to spare, the fisherman's wife would hurry to the houses of neighbors or relatives to barter the extras for potatoes or grain.

Another case in the room displays the *haqonta,* or scoop net. For this type of gear, the museum curator has included not only the tools themselves but also a scale-model display in order to explain its complex pattern of use. Each year, toward the middle of the rainy season, as the lake waters rose, fishermen would make long mats by tying reeds to a rope twenty meters or so in length. A fisherman would anchor one end of the rope under water at the edge of a large bed of reeds and the other end at some distance from the edge. The untied ends of the reeds would float to the surface and create a fence, called a *qhencha,* through which fish could not swim. The fish that swam along the edge of the reed bed in search of small crustaceans or aquatic insects would be forced to go around the outer edge of the fence. It would be at this point, just at the end of the fence, that the fisherman would wait in his balsa and sweep up passing fish with the scoop net, a net placed on a conical frame a meter or two in height and in diameter, and attached to a pole several meters in length. This tool could yield a variety of species, not only carachi but also umantu and boga.

The last and most lovely of the old types of fishing gear is a kind of basket trap called the *qollancha.* It appears on one of the most popular postcards in the museum gift shop. A circular wooden frame a meter or so in diameter serves as the base for two pieces of open basketwork. Each section is a simple geometric form. The inner layer is a cone, open only at the apex; this cone is covered by a hemispherical outer layer with no gaps

Qollancha, or basket trap. Photograph by Ben Orlove.

at all. In the museum, a *qollancha* might be set against a dark background, with a bright spotlight shining on it to reveal the delicate twining and lashing of the open basketwork, made from the thin, tough stalks of grasses that grow on the hillsides above the lake. (These grasses are also used for the cords that attach the rock weights to one end of the *qollancha* frame to hold it vertical in the water, and for the ropes that hold two *qollanchas*—they are always used in pairs—to the balsa that drags them through the water.)

Diagrams explain the complex design of this trap, which is used exclusively to catch ispi, the name used for several species of fish about three centimeters in length. With their silvery color, their slim, streamlined bodies, and their large eyes, the ispi look like tiny sardines or anchovies. One diagram shows how the ispi enter the circular mouth of the *qollancha* as it is dragged slowly through the water: they swim through the top of the cone into the space between the cone and the hemisphere, from which they are unable to escape.

A second diagram traces the life cycle of the ispi. Like sardines and anchovies, they graze on plankton, the microscopic plants and animals that form the base of the food chain in the open waters of lakes and oceans. Their eyes are large enough to allow them to see their minute prey, even when they are in poorly lit waters well below the surface. In Lake Titicaca, the ispi are the most numerous of all fish species and make up a significant proportion of the fish biomass. However, they are difficult to catch. They usually remain out in the middle of the lake at depths of twenty to fifty meters. At some point during the year, they form large schools—another way that they resemble sardines and anchovies—and come to shore to spawn in shallow waters. They seem to prefer clear water, choosing rocky bottoms without much vegetation rather than the muddier beds of reeds and algae, and avoiding the more turbid waters when stream flow is high, late in the rainy season and early in the dry season.

Here, the audio guide presents the voice of Dionisio Puma, a fisherman from Azirune. He tells how he learned to use the *qollancha* from his father and grandfather. Dionisio explains that ispi are particularly good fish to catch, since their small size makes them easy to dry. However, they are also tricky fish. The schools remain in the shallows only for a short time, they do not return to the same spot each year, and they can arrive any time from July to December. During these months, the fishermen keep an eye out for unusual movements of aquatic birds and for patches of smoother water in an area with waves. Once a school has been spotted, the fishermen do not go out immediately, since the ispi flee to deep water if they see the fishermen or hear loud noises. Rather, the fishermen meet at the shore at night. Each trawling a pair of *qollanchas*, they row their balsas out, keeping them in a straight line. When they come close to the fish, they form a circle and enclose the school. They move in slowly, to assure that each fisherman gets a share of the fish and that as few fish escape as possible.

Dionisio continues with his explanation of the difficulties of such night fishing. The fishermen must keep an even distance from one another. A fisherman who becomes separated from the others could get lost in the dark and drift far ashore or even capsize. If he falls out of his balsa, he could grab its bow or stern and try to climb back on, but that is a far more daunting task on a cold, dark night than during the day. Separated from the group, the fishermen believe, he would also be more likely to encounter a *qatari,* or sea serpent. These beings act more freely at night and are prone to attack isolated individuals more than members of groups. Dionisio closes his account with the sounds that fishermen make to remain in touch with one another. Unwilling to speak or shout, since noise would drive off the ispi, they whistle to each other, so that, Dionisio says, "hearing us, the ispi will think that we are just songbirds, flying over the water."

At this point, at the end of the fourth room, the audio guide provides an overview of the full range of gear. Speaking directly for the first time, the curator stresses the similarities of these objects, despite their great diversity in form and patterns of use. They were all made of local materials: the reeds and grasses that grew in abundance, the scantier wood, combined in some cases with llama wool and human hair. They all displayed close knowledge of the location and movement of particular fish species. They required a great deal of patience and precision, though the specific combination of these qualities varied: the close coordination of partners and careful sequence of turn-taking with the large trawl net; the repeated movements of the dip net; the motionless attentiveness of the thrower of the fish-harpoon; the long waits for fish to swim to the scoop net; the balletic precision of the *qollancha*-fishermen, shifted from a line to a circle, whistling to one another in the dark.

This patience and sustained effort stemmed from the villagers' capacity for hard work—echoing the theme so evident in the *diarios campesinos*—and from another source as well: the relative poverty of the fishermen. They were among the poorest of the villagers in the late nineteenth and early twentieth centuries. Owning fewer fields and animals than most, they had to seek other sources of food. The lake, available to all members of the lakeshore communities, provided them with sustenance. The fish helped feed their families and gave them something to barter or sell so that they could augment their meager livelihood.

And then the curator explains that this fourth room, for 1870 through 1930, centered on fishing gear, is the last one in the hall of the History of

Lake Titicaca Fishermen. The 1930s, we are told, mark the boundary between the past, enshrined in the museum, and the contemporary period.
The curator bids the visitor farewell and suggests that we close our visit
with a stop at the museum café. Let us decide that it is still early enough
in the afternoon that the sun has not set behind Cerro Azoguini, to the
west of Isla Foroba, and that we can sit on the deck as we sip our tea and
watch the coots paddle in the shallow waters of the lake.

The curator was correct: two events in the 1930s affected the fisheries
with particular strength. Still remembered by the oldest living villagers,
familiar to all as the stories told by parents and grandparents, these
events left marks on the fisheries that remain evident today. The first of
these was a drought, the longest and most severe of the century. For more
than a decade, little rain fell on the lake or fed the rivers that emptied into
it. The lake level dropped nearly five meters between 1932 and 1943,
when it reached its lowest point on record. To the lakeshore villagers, this
drought underscored the critical nature of the lake and its fish to their
well-being. This point struck me with particular force one afternoon
when I was walking with Saturnino Quispe to his village, Carina, on the
shores of the Chucuito Peninsula, facing the open water of the Lago
Grande. There was no regular transport service to Carina, so we walked
from the spot on the road where we had been dropped off by the bus that
lumbered from town to town along the main dirt road on the south side
of the lake. For several kilometers we followed a track between the fields
and adobe houses of the village closest to the road. We then left the flatlands near the lake to climb up a low ridge. As we reached the top of the
ridge, the expanse of the Bahía de Puno came into view. We paused and
took in the scene. Facing northwest, I squinted into the mid-afternoon
sun. The low houses of the city of Puno clustered along the shore, and
from a point to the right of the center of town, a pier stretched far out into
the water. I looked over the broad sweep of the hill-bounded bay. Off to
the right, a vast sheet of dark blue, its surface sparkling with innumer-
able points of reflected sunlight, stretched to the steep rocky flanks of the
Capachica Peninsula. A mottled pattern of green, yellow, and brown
patches of the reedbeds filled the shallow waters to the left.

Eager to demonstrate to Saturnino my familiarity with the landscape,

I indicated a few points of light at the edge of the reedbeds. Look, I told him, those are the roofs in K'api. I used the local name for these settlements, which are known to the townspeople and to tourists as Urus, the floating islands. Saturnino nodded in agreement. "Our grandparents tell us," he began, using the phrase often evoked to describe events in the village to which an entire generation was eyewitness, and which they passed on to the next. This simple phrase asserted that Saturnino and the other people his age had all heard this from the eyewitnesses: The lake dried up, he continued, and people could walk from here to K'api. Their feet would not even get wet, he said. I understood his emphasis on this point. Villagers around the lake regularly wade through streams that come down from the hills to the lake; in regions such as this, where low peninsulas stretch into the lake, they also cross stretches of a hundred meters or more to reach fields on hills that are cut off from the shore in years when the lake is high. Accustomed to walking through chilly water up to their calves and knees and even to their thighs, the villagers were astonished twice, first when they could reach the K'api villages at all, and a second time when the lake fell even further so that they could keep their feet dry.

The lake dropped over several years, Saturnino continued. The rains that came each year were not enough to bring it back to the level to which it had fallen in the previous dry season. At first the villagers were excited at the new lands that were exposed, rich with the muck from the bottom of the lake. A few people got good harvests of barley when they planted in the moist soils right at the edge of the lake. But there was not enough rain for crops. People ate through the potatoes that they had stored. They had to sell off their animals. But those who lived on the shores of the lake were in a favored position. At least there were still fish in the lake— carachi, umantu, boga, and catfish—that could be used for soup, and they could stretch their meals with the stems and rhizomes of the totora. Though they sorely missed their staple potatoes, and they did not relish turning totora from an occasional food item into a staple, they recognized that they did not face as extreme a hunger as the villagers farther from the lake.

Many other sources confirm the existence of the drought: records of the lake level recorded at the dock in Puno, rainfall data from weather stations, the bands of snow deposited each year on glaciers high in the cordilleras around the lake. However, drought is not only a climatological phenomenon, but a part of human experience as well. For the lakeshore villagers, the rains were capricious, but the lake offered reliable sustenance. Though the lake had a destructive side, in some years rising into fields and drowning crops before they could be harvested, it was a great boon, their unfailing bulwark against starvation in hard years. They might suffer from a *yarqa wata,* a hunger year, but not as severely as those who lived farther from its shore.

The value of the lake was even clearer, I knew, because the drought came at the time of the Great Depression, a shift in the global economy that had its impact even in the remote Peruvian altiplano. With the collapse of world prices for many raw materials, fewer villagers from the altiplano could find employment in the plantations and mines of southern Peru. These wages, which had formed one element of the village economy, were reduced at the same time that city dwellers had less money to spend on potatoes, grains, meat, and cheese from the altiplano. These shifts turned the lakeshore villagers back toward a subsistence economy and made the steady supply of fish from the lake even more important.

The second shift that the 1930s brought to the lake fisheries was the introduction of a new species, and its consequences have lasted longer than the effects of the drought. The rains finally returned, but the trout have not left. As with the drought, the effects of the introduced species became noticeable only after several years. In 1935, the Peruvian and Bolivian governments agreed to establish a commission to study the lake fisheries and promote their industrial development. As things turned out, this commission consisted of a single individual: M. C. James, an American fisheries specialist who came to Lake Titicaca in 1936. Noting that the native fish were mostly small and bony, he suggested introducing larger fish that he thought would provide more abundant and higher-quality catches. He recommended lake trout and two kinds of whitefish as the first species to introduce, since these deep-water fish could prey upon the ispi. If they did not establish themselves in the lake, James suggested trying river trout species, though he thought these shallow-water species might not adapt as easily. Another American fisheries expert, A. J. Smyth, arrived in 1938 to carry out James's suggestions. He helped set up the fish hatchery that James had proposed as a source of fingerlings to stock the lake. It was opened in Chucuito, near Puno, in 1940. Of James's five recommended species, only one, the rainbow trout, succeeded in establishing itself in the lake.

Dominique and I had several long conversations about James and his fateful recommendation. Something about his proposal did not sit well with us. We knew that this suggestion, carried out in the following years, transformed the lake's ecosystem profoundly and irrevocably. It was not that Dominique and I thought these changes brought unmitigated disaster. In fact, we were among the few people to question it at all. The trout are a popular item in restaurants, the basis of many development projects, the raison d'être of the region's famed hatchery in Chucuito, and above all, an important source of income. The lakeside villagers like the trout, which is easy to catch and easy to sell. For the scientists at IMARPE and the officials in the Ministry of Fisheries, trout also represent an expansion of work, another fish to study and to regulate.

It is virtually impossible to imagine the subsequent expansion of the fishery without the presence of the new species. It is equally difficult to deny that this expansion brought a measure of prosperity to the region, one of the poorest in all of Latin America—a prosperity, moreover, that has lasted for decades, reached a large number of families, and has had a record less spotted with corruption than most. One could even say that this introduction caused relatively little environmental damage, compared to the devastation wrought on native species by the introduction of the Nile perch into Lake Victoria, the goby into Lake Lanao, and similar cases throughout the world. Numerous extinctions in these lakes and others have led contemporary fisheries specialists to recognize the seriousness of introducing a new species into an ecosystem. It is difficult to anticipate the many consequences that can ensue, both for the native fish species and for the people whose lives and livelihoods are bound up with them. A new species might prey directly on the existing fish populations, or harm them by eating their food supplies. Granted this danger, it is remarkable that there has been only one documented extinction of a native species of fish in Lake Titicaca, *Orestias cuvieri,* the umantu, no specimen of which has been collected since 1937. Its disappearance was almost certainly caused by the trout, a faster and more voracious predator, which competed with it for food and may have eaten it directly.

The umantu was the largest of the *Orestias* and the only one that ate other fish. Its carachi ancestor, a small, lumpy, slow-moving fish, took on an odd task when it shifted its diet from tiny prey, such as insects, crustaceans, and zooplankton, to other fish. Current estimates suggest that it began to evolve about three million years ago and that it took two million years for the numerous changes in the formation of a new species to be completed. In this time, its body doubled in length. Its head and mouth grew even larger in proportion to its body, so that it could grab and hold its prey. Its teeth became longer and sharper and moved farther forward in its mouth. Though it was far from being built like a barracuda, it was a bit sleeker than its carachi ancestor. Its tail became less stumpy and began to develop the pointed tips characteristic of many fast swimmers.

The former abundance of the umantu suggests that it was a successful hunter. The scientific travelers, from S. W. Garman in the 1870s through Gibson in the 1930s, reported seeing them frequently. Since its shape did not lend it to the sustained pursuit of prey, it probably hung in place and darted when a smaller fish came close, much as a pike does. It might well have spent a good deal of time in the totora beds or in the algae that grew on the lake bottom, rather than cruising the open waters. These ideas are speculations, though. If researchers wish to study the anatomy of the fish, they can examine the hundred or so individual umantu that are preserved in jars on museum storeroom shelves in London, Paris, Leiden, Washington, Cambridge, Chicago, and San Francisco. They can make only conjectures, however, if they want to describe its behavior.

In our discussions of the transformations of the lake fisheries, Dominique and I acknowledged that other lakes had lost a much larger proportion of their native fish species than had Titicaca. Nonetheless, it was a source of regret for us to know that we would never see a living example of this ancient species of which the oldest fishermen spoke so often. We also recognized there might well have been another kind of extinction—a cultural extinction of indigenous fishing. With the introduction of the commercially viable trout, numerous types of fishing gear and the complex patterns of local knowledge and belief could have been replaced by modern technology and science. Money-based exchanges of commercial sale could have replaced the elaborate set of customary ties that linked fishermen, their wives, and other female kin with their barter-exchange partners in their villages, throughout the altiplano, and beyond. When cash supplants foodstuffs as a medium of exchange, the kilogram usually replaces the indigenous units of weight and measure. Most seriously, local customary law could have been eliminated. New commercial fishermen might have tried to catch trout in areas from which they had been excluded by local custom at the same time that government agencies, which had paid little attention to the small-scale native fisheries, began to regulate the expanding commercial fisheries. As a result, village fishing territories could have been replaced by a system of licenses and permits in which government agencies, rather than the villagers, determined fishing rights. Dominique and I knew of some African lake fisheries that had disappeared in such a fashion. The boats and the gear of the fishermen, like the umantu, are now preserved in museums, their knowledge and customs recorded in old volumes on library shelves and in the stories told in villages, but their way of life has vanished.

In addition to the biological and cultural extinctions, there was one more threat: the economic extinction of fishing. The entire occupation could decline or disappear. New species can attract more fishermen and encourage investment in boats and gear. The profits from the sales of the new fish can lead to an expansion for a year or two or even longer. Such bonanzas face their limits, though, when the new species become depleted. Historians of fisheries have documented many cases of such cycles of boom and bust.

But neither the cultural nor the economic extinction came to pass. In much the same way that only a fraction of the fish species were lost when a new species entered the lake, only a few of the elements of the indigenous fishing culture disappeared as new technologies and forms of behavior were introduced. Wooden rowboats now outnumber reed balsas by about two to one, but they have not eliminated the traditional craft. The nylon gill net drove out a few types of fishing gear once it became established, notably the harpoon and the fish fence associated with the scoop net, but others—the dip net, the large trawl net, and the *qollan-cha*—have remained. Barter remains an important component of fish marketing. Most important, the customary regulation of fishing grounds remains in force; the new fish species and forms of technology have not erased the lines that mark the boundaries of the village fishing territories. Like the carachi, the ispi, and the boga, then, many elements of the indigenous fishing culture—the tools, the knowledge, and the forms of regulation—have survived.

It would have been unrealistic to expect that a fisheries expert in the 1930s would have been concerned about these possible biological, cultural, and economic extinctions. Charged with optimism about innovation and progress, fisheries biology rested on precisely such introductions to expand fish catches. An entire set of technologies had developed around introductions. Engineers had designed hatcheries to produce eggs and fingerlings in mass quantities, and they constructed tank-trucks to carry the fingerlings to streams, rivers, and lakes where they could be stocked. Introductions had already been carried out in other, more advanced Latin American countries, especially Chile and Argentina, and even in another part of Peru, the central highlands closer to the capital city of Lima. Moreover, M. C. James was the assistant chief of the Fish Culture Section of the United States Bureau of Fisheries. He would have been predisposed to suggesting the introduction of new species, especially one from the United States.

Even by the standards of the time, though, the introduction of trout into Lake Titicaca was a slapdash affair. The government commission hired James to spend six months in the altiplano so that he could study the lake in detail. Such a study implied the need for extensive travel to the deep open waters of the main basin of the Lago Grande, as well as to the smaller, shallower basins of the Bahía de Puno and the Lago Pequeño; visits to the lake's vast reedbeds; and travels through the rivers that fed into the lake. But although James received payment for the full period, he stayed only a month. His report, eighteen pages long, was briefer than many had expected. Nor were his arguments very sophisticated. Lake Titicaca reminded him of the Great Lakes of the United States and Canada, so he recommended bringing in the fish that were found there. Yet even a cursory glance would have revealed major differences. The rivers that flow into Lake Titicaca are much smaller than the ones that empty into the Great Lakes. The pattern of rainy and dry seasons in the altiplano, typical of tropical regions, differs sharply from the temperate-zone seasons of the Great Lakes. James also failed to examine the social and economic dimensions of the fisheries. Completely unaware of village control of fishing grounds, he stated that the fishermen are "disorganized and individualistic." He proposed "continuous patrolling by a large number of boats" to make sure that the fishermen would follow his suggested restrictions on gear, fishing season, and size of fish that were caught.

Made with haste and inattention to local conditions, James's suggestions were implemented with casual disregard. Smyth oversaw the construction of a fish hatchery at the site that James indicated at Chucuito, near Puno, but did not follow his other recommendations closely. A. J. Smyth raised fifty thousand lake-trout fingerlings from a shipment of fish eggs, but they did not survive long in the lake. He lost one set of whitefish eggs and never obtained any more. He also tried the river species to which James had assigned a lower priority. The brown trout that he released in 1939 formed a few small populations in tributaries of the Río Ilave. The introduction of the rainbow trout in 1941 progressed further. Conditions in the lake seemed close to ideal for this species. The water remains cool throughout the year, with no major fluctuations in temperature. The levels of dissolved oxygen were high, and there were no pollution problems. Food, moreover, was abundant—a variety of insects, crustaceans, other invertebrates, and small fish. The first group of rainbow trout multiplied rapidly. Smyth finally had succeeded.

It is only in the paucity of spawning grounds that the altiplano is less than wholly appropriate for rainbow trout. Though the trout in Titicaca, like those in many other lakes, spend most of their adult life in lakes, they must swim up rivers to find appropriate spawning grounds: shallow gravel beds with cool, fast-flowing water. But the seasonal and irregular rainfall in the altiplano often leaves rivers without sufficient water for the trout. The rivers flow most rapidly late in the rainy season, in February and March, and begin to fall soon after the rains end. By June and July, the most important spawning season, only the largest rivers have sufficient water, and even these may be too low during dry years. As stream flow decreases, the water temperature increases beyond an optimum level and the oxygen content falls. In conditions such as these, only a small proportion of the fertilized eggs ever hatch, and the fish fry die off at a high rate. Moreover, only certain portions of these rivers are suitable for spawning. The streams that descend from the high cordilleras join to form rivers that meander across plains before emptying into the lake. The trout must swim upstream for long distances to reach their spawning areas in gravel-bottomed zones.

Local people still tell the stories of the first trout that appeared in their fishing grounds. Pedro Castillo described this event in his village of Piata. When he was a boy in the 1940s, his father, Ignacio, was one of ten men who built a long *qhencha*. They had established an order among themselves: each day, a different partner would take his turn to row his balsa out to the end of the fish fence and wait with a scoop net. He would give that day's catch to his wife, who would cook, barter, or sell the fish. The first fisherman who brought up a trout was so startled by the unfamiliar sharp-mouthed creature that he threw it back in. A few days passed in which the fishermen caught only the accustomed carachi, boga, and umantu. When Ignacio took his turn, another trout appeared in the scoop net. Though it flopped more than the native fish, Ignacio managed to keep it in his balsa as he paddled back to shore. When he landed, other villagers gathered to inspect the huge fish. Ignacio could have claimed it under the customary terms of the partnership, but he offered to share it with all the members in his group. It was long enough to divide into ten equal slices. The trout's strangeness was revealed a second time when Ignacio began to cut it. Its flesh was pinkish in color, unlike the white flesh of the native fish. Some villagers warned of the dangers of eating it, since it resembled the color of rotten meat. Once again, Ignacio remained undaunted by the caution of others. He asked his wife to cook the still unnamed fish. It proved to have a pleasant, mild taste and an agreeably firm texture, and above all, it caused no harm. The fishermen kept all the trout that they caught after that, and told neighboring villages of the arrival of this new fish. They soon learned its name, *trucha*, or trout, and noticed the rapid growth of its numbers.

Town residents also got wind of the new fish. Many of them had heard of the hatchery in Chucuito. Fishermen and other vendors began to sell trout in urban markets. The new fish became popular in La Paz around 1950. Demand in that city grew even more after the revolution of 1952, when supplies of beef were reduced after a cut in trade with Argentina, which was unsympathetic to the new government. By the mid-1950s, the residents of Arequipa, Cuzco, and other cities in southern Peru ate trout regularly.

The growth of the trout population and the increased demand for this fish led to a shift in technology. The village fishermen found that the trout were too fast to catch with a spear and were strong enough to rip the woolen fibers of the traditional scoop nets and trawl nets. Searching for alternatives, some of them purchased hooks and lines, but they found that with this equipment they could catch only a few trout on each fishing trip. Some fishermen who had migrated from villages on the west side of the lake to the Pacific Coast had seen gill nets in operation in ocean fish-eries. In structure gill nets are something like the nets used for tennis or volleyball, since they are long rectangles divided into many squares. However, they are larger and much longer, usually a hundred meters long and three meters high, and they are made of nylon, a much thinner fiber. Gill nets trap fish, which cannot see the thin, transparent fibers. If a small fish swims into the net, it will pass through the squares of the mesh. But if the fish is large, its gill-covers will become tangled in the net. Unable to move forward or back, the fish remains where it is; it can sur-vive for hours or even a day or two, until the fisherman returns and hauls in the net.

The villagers brought these gill nets back to the altiplano and tried them out in the Río Ilave. Their successful experiments were widely copied throughout the lake. The fishermen found that the nylon was not only stronger than wool or cotton, but that it dried quickly, rarely tore, and lasted a long time. Though gill nets would have been too expensive for fishermen to buy in the 1940s, the new income from the sale of trout brought the nets within their budgets. Moreover, fishermen were already accustomed to joint ownership and use of gear. They formed small groups, pooled their money, and sent a representative to buy a net that they would then cut into equal pieces, smaller and more manageable than the original net. The fishermen experimented with the gill nets, setting them at different depths and distances from shore. They tried stretching them tight and leaving them slack. Virtually every heavy object was used at one time or another as a weight, every light object as a float. Closely watching the results of their experiments—and, whenever possible, the results of the experiments of others—the fishermen developed patterns of use in keeping with the changing seasons and the changing level of the lake from year to year.

Some fishermen who had switched from native gear to gill nets also replaced their reed balsas with wooden boats, which had been used since the late nineteenth century as ferries to carry passengers across the Straits of Tiquina. The wooden boats could hold more nets, and they allowed the fishermen to travel faster. The first fishermen used the same oars and sails as they did on reed balsas. As incomes rose, some fishermen purchased outboard motors. Artisans built the wooden boats in small workshops—one could hardly call them boatyards—in villages such as Huatajata, on the shores of the lake. For lumber, they turned to the mills in the forests in the upper reaches of the Amazon Basin; for labor, they hired their immediate relatives and their fellow villagers, who had learned the craft by watching them work; for models, they scaled down the ferries and came up with a standard pattern.

Dominique and I both found these boats appealing, with their simple, clean lines. On my own, I would not have made any but the most rudimentary inquiries about the prices of the boats and the number of years they lasted. Dominique, though, had spent several summers sailing off the coast of Brittany. Familiar with all sorts of small watercraft, he was fascinated with the wooden fishing boats. He spoke at length with builders and fishermen and took a number of measurements, finding that the boats were roughly the same size and design. All built by hand, all made to accommodate particular features of the wooden boards the boatwright had obtained, they did have minor differences, but rarely did one vary by more than a meter from a length of five and a half meters, or by a quarter of a meter from a width of a meter and a half. The shape, too, was always the same, a pointed, slightly upturned bow and a flat stern. At most they might vary in the size of the small front and back decks, in

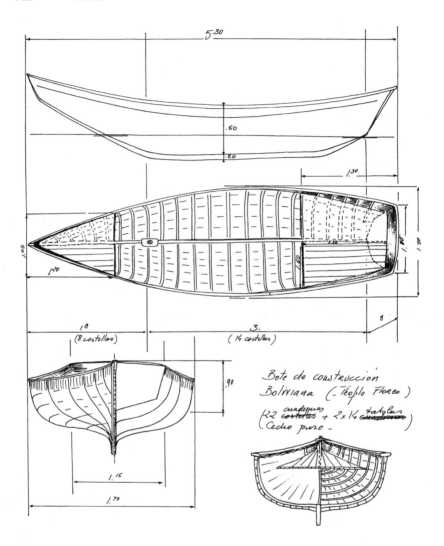

Drawing by Dominique Levieil of the construction of the wooden boats.

the presence or absence of flooring. We had seen enough old boats and photographs of boats to know that this pattern had held from the first wooden fishing boats in the 1950s to the present.

Dominique was puzzled by this striking lack of change. The fishermen had adopted new gear and experimented with it in many ways. Why, he wondered, didn't they seek any shift in the size and design of their boats? When he asked boatwrights and fishermen this question, they too were puzzled. The idea of changing the boats evidently had not occurred to them. They assured him that the boats were quite good. Perhaps other kinds of boats would work well in France, they told him, but this is the way that we make boats here on the lake.

These answers did not satisfy Dominique. The question, he realized, was not just a matter of personal curiosity, but rather an integral part of the history of the fisheries. The practice that each village had of restricting fishing rights to its local inhabitants kept a limit on the total number of fishermen in the lake. If the fishermen had shifted to much larger boats, they might have increased their catch beyond the limits that the lake ecosystem could support. After talking in some detail to Cirilo Cutipa and Pedro Castillo, Dominique was confident that he understood the uniformity in the size of the boats. Smaller boats would not be as stable and could not carry enough nets and fish; larger boats would be difficult for a single individual to manage if the wind grew strong or died down, or if a motor failed. Fishermen cannot count on finding assistants, since even brothers and sons are often occupied with other work. Hiring other villagers as crew members was out of the question. If they were not already busy with their fields, animals, and other activities, the villagers with enough skill to be worth taking on were already fishing—for themselves, if they owned boats of their own, or for relatives, who would give them a generous share of the catch, if they did not. So no fisherman would buy a boat that he could not row alone.

For the design, though, Dominique remained puzzled. Were the artisans reluctant to put additional time and materials into building a new sort of boat, when demand was adequate for the familiar ones? Perhaps the fishermen were the ones who clung to familiar habits and resisted additional expenses. The uniformity in boat design might simply be another example of the local emphasis on continuity and homogeneity that leads people to dress alike, to eat similar foods, to build the same kind of adobe houses—a characteristic that goes hand in hand with the villagers' concern for steady work, modesty, and lack of ostentation. Dominique and I believed that the answer lay in some combination of these reasons, but we never resolved their relative importance.

Though they did not change their boats, the fishermen experimented with the spatial aspects of their fishing. Seeking out spots to catch trout, they often went farther from shore than they had gone with their balsas and their older types of gear. Many of them took overnight trips in their boats—an act of considerable daring, because none of the fishermen had ever spent a night alone out on the lake far from shore. At most, some had gone out in groups at night to catch ispi with *qollanchas,* and a few had used a scoop net at night, half-dozing in a balsa a few hundred yards from shore and then waking to light a reed torch to attract fish. These solo overnight trips were a complete novelty to them. Such efforts might yield a large catch of trout. However, they also created a considerable risk. More than a quarter of the fishermen Dominique and I interviewed had a relative or neighbor who had drowned, especially in the first years of the trout fishery. Nearly all told stories of their own near-drownings, most of them set well in the past. I knew that they must have recounted these stories many times, yet each telling was vivid, as if the fisherman were experiencing with great immediacy the events that lay years or decades in the past. One told of the night that he spent after a monstrous *qatari,* or sea serpent, got tangled in his nets, tore itself free, and overturned his boat. He managed to clamber part-way onto the boat's slippery bottom and cling there until dawn arrived and another fisherman came to his rescue. More frequently, the danger came from wind and waves. Fishermen were blown far from shore into areas with high waves that would lift and nearly upend their boats, or that would fill them with water till they nearly sank. One fisherman described a storm that came up suddenly and threw him overboard and made it nearly impossible for him to work his way from the side of the boat to the bow, where he somehow managed to pull himself back in.

To avoid being harmed by a *qatari,* a fisherman might utter a brief prayer before setting off from shore or toss a small offering into the lake—some coca leaves or a few crackers and a bit of wine. To anticipate winds, fishermen gradually developed skills in interpreting the patterns that they could see on the water. I was intrigued to note that the fishermen do not classify water as English speakers do, by texture ("smooth," "choppy," "rough"), but rather by color. The lake is usually blue, but it can be white in a dead calm. Wind turns the water green—a dark green if it is a strong wind. Strong winds are also signaled by the appearance of black water in the distance, invariably in the direction from which the wind will start blowing. As the wind dies down, the black water becomes gray before the blue color returns. In areas where rivers empty into the lake, the fishermen note patches of yellow or red water that carry sediment. They infer the direction and strength of wind-driven currents by the intensity of these colors.

In their efforts to anticipate the winds that might drive them off their intended courses, the fishermen draw on local systems for naming winds. Farmers, though less influenced by winds than the fishermen, also seek to anticipate the strength and direction of the winds. A calm day is preferable for thatching a roof with totora reeds, a day of steady winds for threshing grain. Each portion of the lakeshore has a distinct set of winds, known to fishermen and nonfishermen alike. Rather than naming them by the compass direction from which they blow, as English speakers do, the local people name the winds by the places from which they come—the lake itself, or occasionally a high grassland, but most often a prominent hill or mountain that lies in the direction of the wind and that is the source of the wind itself.

I found that the villagers understood me when I asked them, "How many winds are there here?" They would give me a list of winds, usually four or six, but always an even number. I once asked my question about winds to several people in Junsani, near Huancané. The oldest man in the group took it on himself to answer me. Speaking slowly, he named twelve *thaya*, winds, indicating that some came from *kupi*, the "right," and some from *ch'eqa*, the "left." At one point he paused and then removed his hat as he uttered, "Illimani," the tallest peak in the region and the source of the strongest wind. As I talked over the list with the group, I commented that six were from the right, generally from the direction of the eastern cordillera; the six *ch'eqa thaya*, left winds, were from the western cordillera. They were not surprised by this comment. They had never bothered to tally up the winds before, but this balance seemed intuitively obvious to them. It wasn't that the winds came in pairs, they said, but rather that there would have to be the same number from both sides. I tried to

A man with a team of oxen preparing a field for planting late in the dry season. Photograph by Ben Orlove.

probe this matter further, but the conversation did not progress very far. I felt as if I were being rude: they were puzzled by my inability to accept at face value the idea that left and right winds would be equal in number. The only additional point that they added was that the two strongest winds came from the right. This idea clarified things a bit, since I had heard villagers speak on other occasions of the greater strength of the right hand, and of the right ox in a team yoked together to plow. At any rate, I decided, these ways of discussing winds were so widespread and so rooted that they must have been established before the introduction of the trout. The fishermen had a body of knowledge to draw on as they encountered the life-threatening winds far from shore.

Drawing on the new technologies of wooden boats and nylon gill nets, adapting existing knowledge about the color of water and the winds, fishermen continued to seek out trout. Catches rose throughout the 1950s, often reaching levels of excess and wastage. The villagers would sometimes feed trout, a day or two old and beginning to spoil, to their pigs, rather than waste them altogether. They tried to preserve the trout, but they had no success with any of their established techniques of salting, sun-drying, and baking in stone ovens. They took trout to markets or sold them to vendors who would carry them to the larger towns. On some occasions they would receive good prices, but at other times they brought more fish than customers could buy. Older residents of La Paz tell stories of such oversupply. Unsold at the end of the day, not worth carrying back to the lakeshore villages, the fish would be left in the urban markets, to be eaten by beggars and dogs, or simply to be thrown into a ravine along with other trash.

Many people had noticed that the supply of trout exceeded the demand. Some buyers tried to bring trout to more distant cities on the coast in Peru, or farther south in the altiplano in Bolivia. Transportation was the obstacle that they were unable to resolve. Because of the poor mountain roads, trucks could not reach these cities before the trout had deteriorated and became unmarketable. It was almost inevitable that some entrepreneur would try to make a profit by finding new means of bringing the excess fish to other, more distant markets.

This entrepreneur was Burt Hamilton, a Canadian engineer who had arrived in the altiplano in 1946. He worked as an engineer in a mine on the Bolivian side of the lake until the 1952 revolution, then shifted to another mine in Peru near the lake. Around 1960 he formed a corporation, the Compañía Pesquera Puno, with two local wealthy Peruvians, the owner of the largest hardware store in Puno and the rector of the local university. They pooled their resources to obtain the thirty thousand dollars or so necessary to open a cannery. On a plot of land that they purchased in the nearby town of Chucuito, close to the lake and to a road, they built a dock and installed sinks, worktables, can-sealing machines, and autoclaves to heat and sterilize the cans. When they opened in 1961, they fished on the lake with boats that they had purchased, but they soon found it cheaper and more reliable to buy fish directly from local fishermen. The cannery gave nylon gill nets to the fishermen on credit and lent them money to purchase wooden boats and, in some cases, outboard motors. To increase their supplies, Hamilton and his partners drew on their local contacts to arrange for instruction for the fishermen, few of whom had used this new gear. More than 150 villagers took a training course at a School for Indian Fishermen (Escuela de Pescadores Indígenas) that was set up through the fisheries branch of the local Ministry of Agriculture office.

The cannery soon developed a fixed working pattern. The fishermen checked their nets early in the morning and brought the fish to pre-arranged points on the local roads. They were met by one of the pickup trucks that Hamilton and his associates had purchased. By late morning or early afternoon, the fish were being processed. There were about twenty-five workers, divided more or less equally between men, who cleaned and gutted the fish, and women, who cut large fillets and placed them in cans. A few male workers sealed the cans, cooked them in the autoclave, let them cool, and placed labels on them. Almost all of the canned trout was exported to Europe and the United States. A small fraction remained in Peru, where it was marketed in Lima and in mining camps.

Hamilton and his partners quickly regained their initial investment and operated at a level of considerable profit. The costs in materials and in labor were low, and the sales were steady. They were able to process more than a hundred metric tons of trout in their first year. Their success led to the creation of several competing firms, all with the same pattern of purchasing trout directly from fishermen, with the same processing technology, and with the same foreign markets. Four canneries opened in the next three years. By 1964, each portion of the lake had a cannery: one in the Bahía de Puno, three in the Lago Grande, and one in the Bolivian portion of the Lago Pequeño.

The expansion of the canneries placed great pressure on the customary system of village fishing territories. The money the fishermen earned gave them incentive to fish more frequently and at greater distances from shore; it also allowed more of them to purchase boats and nets. Most of the traditional types of fishing gear, such as the harpoon, dip net, and scoop net, were restricted to use in the shallow waters close to shore. However, the gill nets could be deployed in the deeper waters farther from shore, where trout were often found. Once the fishermen learned to use the wooden boats with confidence, they often traveled to these areas and in many cases simply incorporated them into their fishing territories. The fishing territory of a village still consisted of the portions of the lake adjacent to its lands, but now extended farther into the lake.

In other cases, fishermen moved out of their customary village territories to invade the richer fishing grounds of other villages near the mouths of rivers, especially in the months when the trout moved upstream to spawn. These incursions provoked tense standoffs, still recalled decades later. Pedro Castillo linked his story of the discovery of trout in his village of Piata, for example, to his sense of entitlement to fish for trout in grounds belonging to the neighboring village of Cohasía, close to the mouth of the Río Ramis. Nonetheless, even the most hard-pressed villages were able to retain control of their fishing grounds. Though some fishermen might probe the territories of other villages, they were in unanimous agreement on the urgency of excluding outsiders, and they received strong support on this point from villagers who did not fish. It was easy to chase away the outsiders who came close to shore. A few larger skirmishes took place farther away in deeper water. Even in this distant area, however, villagers could protect their territories by fouling or stealing outsiders' nets or by making—and occasionally carrying out—threats of physical violence. They maintained their territories out to a distance of several kilometers. Only the deepest waters of the lake farthest from shore, generally with poorer fishing, remained open to outsiders.

With a supply from fishermen all around the lake, the production of the canneries rose steadily in the first years.[1] The 1964 total catch, 292 metric tons, was nearly three times the 1961 figure. These were times of prosperity for the fishermen. In the first decades of the century, fishing had been the recourse of the villagers who owned few fields and small flocks. At that time, they were among the poorest of the villagers. The sale of trout to the canneries brought them higher incomes that allowed them to purchase not only boats and nets, but also medicine, education, and the simple amenities of village life—a well-crafted wooden door in a frame to re-

1. The production levels and other economic statistics for the canneries are available in electronic form at http://www.des.ucdavis.edu/faculty/Orlove/book/appendices/canneries.xls.

place the blankets or hides at the entrance to their house; more elaborate celebrations for village festivals and for household ceremonies such as weddings or a child's ritual first haircutting; perhaps even a bicycle so that they could ride, rather than walk, to market.

By the time that the last canneries were opening in 1964, their owners were noticing the first signs of trouble. Accustomed to fairly constant prices, they began to pay the fishermen more for trout. They could explain away this increase as the result of growing competition, since some fishermen now had a choice of canneries to which they could sell trout. Eager to obtain fish that might be sold instead to their competitors, the canneries sent their trucks out more frequently and offered higher prices to the fishermen who supplied them. In 1965, the first and largest cannery, faced with increased competition, had a 7 percent decline in volume, and its share of the market fell below 50 percent. Nonetheless, the newer canneries expanded, and the total catch climbed to 409 metric tons. However, the sharp price rises in some months—8 percent in January 1965, 12 percent in October 1965—were a source of concern.

By 1966 the crisis was clear. Even as prices continued to rise, the trucks returned to the canneries with fewer fish. The total amount of fish that the canneries purchased began to decline. This quantity fell by 15 percent to 345 metric tons in 1966. A general awareness of the trout crisis spread through the altiplano, but the responses were weak and ineffectual. In order to maintain the trout population, the hatchery in Chucuito increased its operations. It released about 150,000 fry in its 1965–66 season and 700,000 fry, a record, in the following season, but even that did not alleviate the problem.

The government attributed the decline to overfishing—a reasonable explanation at the time, since the number of wooden boats had increased steadily during the 1960s. In response, government officials tried to reduce the level of catch. The naval base in Puno became involved in fisheries for the first time. In 1967, it demanded that fishermen register their boats, though it had previously registered only the few large commercial boats, such as the steamers that carried freight across to Bolivia. Had this measure been carried out fully, it could have led to direct supervision of the lake fisheries by the navy. In fact, the navy could have assumed the level of control that it had in the more commercial sectors of marine fisheries, where it had the right to prohibit fishing boats from leaving the shore without a written statement of permission from a harbor captain. However, the navy did not pursue its demand. It would have been an onerous task to travel out to the 150 or so fishing villages along the lakeshore. Only a fraction of the fishermen registered their boats in the next few years.

A second government agency also took measures to restrict the levels of catch in 1967. In that year, the fisheries branch of the Ministry of Agriculture passed, but could not enforce, regulations that prohibited the use of small-mesh nets that would catch young trout. It also forbade the capture of trout in rivers and streams, but this measure too was largely ignored. The agency did succeed in closing the canneries during the peak months of the spawning season. As with the large boats at port, these few, highly visible facilities were easier to regulate. This measure reduced fishing to some extent during the period of the trout's greatest vulnerability, when large masses of them concentrated at the mouths of the largest rivers before swimming upstream. However, some fish were sold in local markets, and others were carried to Bolivia.

The total catch fell to two hundred metric tons in 1967, the last year when the catch exceeded a hundred metric tons. The canneries began to close. By 1968, only the first cannery, the Compañía Pesquera Puno, continued to process trout. It closed in the following year, ending cannery operations in the altiplano eight years after they had begun.

In precipitating the decline of the trout fisheries and the rise of regulation, though, heavy fishing by the villagers was only one factor. As is so often the case in the history of fisheries and indeed in all environmental history, a number of causes were at work. Though the intense pressure doubtless had an impact on the trout population, two other factors also shaped the course of the fisheries: the introduction of a second fish species into the lake, and a coup in 1968 by a quirky group of populist army officers that reshaped state policy in fisheries, as in many other sectors.

The second fish, the silverside, is not as beautiful as the rainbow trout, with its sleek curves and speckled tones. It is a striking fish nonetheless, most memorable for the stripe that runs from its gills to its tail and that

Equipment in an abandoned fish cannery, Vilquechico.
Photograph by Ben Orlove.

has given the fish its name. The silvery tone and well-defined edges of this line contrast sharply with the darker gray scales above it and the pale belly below. On a recently caught silverside, gill covers flapping as it lies on the bottom of a boat, the stripe jumps to view, accentuating the length and narrowness of the fish. On a silverside in the water, one may see no more than a few flashes of the metallic glint of this stripe before the fish swims out of sight.

The silverside entered the altiplano at the opposite end from the trout. It was introduced into Lake Poopó, south of Lake Titicaca, by the Oruro Sport Fishing Club in the late 1940s. The members of this club, wealthy men from the Bolivian city of Oruro who prided themselves on their imported fishing rods, wanted to have a fish that would be more of a challenge to catch than the slower native fish, which they found too easy to pull out of the water. They discovered a likely candidate in the silverside, a muscular fish from the estuaries and rivers of southern Brazil, Uruguay, and adjacent portions of Argentina. It was able to survive and reproduce in Lake Poopó even though the waters of the lake are much colder and more saline than the fish's native habitat.

The silverside spread slowly through the waters of the altiplano. Traveling up the Río Desaguadero, it reached Lake Titicaca in 1955 or 1956 and built up its population in the Lago Pequeño. There are no records to show when it first passed through the Straits of Tiquina, but it was still rare in many portions of the Lago Grande in the early 1960s. The first silverside were caught in the Bahía de Puno in 1966. In other words, its expansion overlapped considerably with the development and decline of the trout canneries.

The silverside concentrate close to shore and remain in shallow water, rarely venturing more than 10 meters below the surface. These are the regions of the lake that most resemble their native rivers and estuaries. They may prefer the warmer temperatures close to the surface. Their vision, limited by their relatively small eyes, might make it difficult for them to find prey and avoid predators in the darker waters at greater depths. The silverside compete with the trout for food. Both eat plankton when they are smallest, insects and crustaceans when they grow a bit, and other fish when they mature. The silverside is a more voracious predator, since it starts to eat other fish when it is still quite small. As biological reports on the silverside began to appear in the mid-1970s, government officials began to recognize that this second introduced fish also contributed to the decline of the trout populations and the collapse of the canneries.

As with the trout, reproduction is the principal difficulty the silverside face in Lake Titicaca. In their native habitat, females spawn only when water temperatures are relatively warm. Lake Titicaca is so much colder than these low-elevation estuaries and rivers that the average surface temperature, even in the warmest month of year, is too low to permit spawning. The female silverside must search out sheltered bays and other spots where temperatures rise. In cooler years, many females sometimes do not spawn at all. Their bodies retain the eggs. In some cases, their ovaries close up, fill with liquid, and form hernias that push through the muscles lining their abdominal wall. Less able to swim and more prone to infection, such fish lead short lives. However, the females who find proper spawning conditions produce large numbers of offspring, whose effective feeding and growth have led the population of silverside to expand.

The villagers had no initial reticence to eating the silverside, as they had with the trout. They found its flesh acceptable in flavor, and it began to appear in fish and potato soup, a common dish in the countryside and one that is well adapted to the clay pots and dung-fueled adobe stoves found in rural kitchens throughout the altiplano. These fuels, stoves, and cooking implements are all part of the subsistence and barter economy of the countryside, as are the potatoes, the other key ingredient in the soup. Though villagers found that they could use silverside for this soup as they had used trout, they still preferred carachi. Unlike the bland silverside, the native carachi imparts a strong, distinctive flavor. Moreover, the carachi is less prone to falling apart after cooking. By contrast, the silverside became more popular than the carachi with most townspeople. Longer, flatter, and less lumpy in shape, it lends itself well to frying, a common means of cooking in urban areas. Townspeople, much more heavily dependent on the cash economy, rely on purchased fuels such as gas and kerosene, purchased stoves that require such fuels, and purchased cooking implements such as metal skillets. Their diet rests on purchased ingredients such as oil in which to fry fish and rice over which to serve it.

Fishermen experimented with different methods to catch this new species, so strongly in demand in towns and somewhat accepted in rural areas. They substituted nets of a smaller mesh size and found that they could obtain higher catches of silverside by placing the nets closer to the surface than they did for trout. Some of them rigged up cords that connected the tops and bottoms of nets to form pockets, which seemed to trap this new fish effectively. This innovation spread widely around the lake.

Eventually, the silverside replaced the trout—at least in part—not only in the lake itself, but in the nets that fishermen placed in the water, in the goods that vendors displayed in markets, and in meals that women cooked. Caught in great abundance, it afforded the fishermen incomes

View of the weekly marketplace in Huata. Photograph by Ben Orlove.

comparable to the levels they had enjoyed in the 1960s, when the canneries were operating. The fishermen and their female relatives were able to bring these fish to people who would buy them, because roads were improving in the altiplano and marketplaces in towns and rural areas were expanding. However, the silverside could not substitute for trout in the canneries. Since the price was lower for fresh silverside than for fresh trout, it seemed likely that the price for canned silverside would be correspondingly lower. Moreover, silverside are often caught when they are smaller than trout, so they would be an awkward size for processing—too little to can in fillets or chunks, like trout, but too big to can whole, like sardines.

In the late 1960s, a force as significant as the silverside entered the altiplano: the military government that took power in 1968. The officers who led the coup initiated a populist program of economic development and state-led political participation. They hoped that these measures would redress the extreme inequalities they saw as the root of left-wing mobilizations in several parts of the country. Their major programs in the high-lands expropriated privately owned haciendas and foreign-owned mines, so they did not address the lakeshore region directly. Through a series of odd coincidences, however, several measures of this new government did affect the fishermen. The military officers quickly nationalized the large marine fisheries in order to distribute the earnings of this prosperous sector more widely throughout the country. To support that effort on the coast, a new Ministry of Fisheries was created in 1968 from the for-mer fisheries service of the Ministry of Agriculture. Soon after, a regional office of the Ministry of Fisheries was opened in Puno, which was di-rected to supervise the lake fishermen with the assistance of the IMARPE laboratory.

The navy's presence on the lake grew in these years as well. Since army officers had led the 1968 coup, they directed resources to the other branches of the military to forestall any rivalry. The navy base in Puno expanded, as did the much smaller navy stations in Moho, Juli, and Des-aguadero. By the end of the 1970s, more than a hundred government employees in civilian and military agencies were charged with some as-pect of regulating and developing the lake fisheries.

Among the most active of these personnel were the navy officials, who undertook the registration of the fishermen and their boats with alacrity. I was puzzled by their sustained efforts, since I could see no pressing rea-son for them to trouble themselves with these matters. Registration con-tinued well after there was any chance of salvaging the trout canneries. It was carried out for years before the Ministry of Fisheries began to un-dertake specific development projects with the fishermen. Nor did there seem to be any military motive for the navy to register the fishermen and their boats. Though the border with Bolivia ran through the lake, rela-tions between the two countries were cordial. The line that separated the Peruvian and Bolivian waters was a peaceful one, unlike the tense fron-tier zone with Ecuador.

During the week in 1981 that I went down to the navy base near the dock in Puno every morning, carrying the letter of presentation that per-mitted me to enter military grounds and the notebook into which I copied data from hundreds of registration forms, my puzzlement gradually abated. The navy officials registered boats and fishermen on Lake Titicaca, I realized, because they were accustomed to such registrations of marine fishermen on the Pacific Coast, and because it just seemed to them like the most natural thing to do. These navy officials, who arrived in increasing numbers after the military coup, were doing what government employees do in many settings: inspecting and registering local activities. The lack of registration struck them as sloppy, a kind of disorder that should be rectified. The officials with whom I spoke mentioned their wish to obtain information about the fishermen who traveled on the waters they were supposed to control. They also knew that their superiors in Lima wanted reports on local conditions, preferably ones filled with numbers, tables, and accounts of official documents.

The data that I collected in 1981, and on later visits in 1983 and 1995, allowed me to trace the course of this registration of boats. It had begun in 1967 and continued at a low level for several years, and then picked up after the navy base expanded in Puno, around 1971. An average of more than a hundred boats were registered each year between 1973 and 1978. By 1981, when the registration had tapered off, about 56 percent of the fishing boats were registered. The fishermen had ambivalent feelings about registration. By and large, it struck them as a nuisance. The fees of about five dollars, though low by the standards of more prosperous countries, placed a significant drain on the limited cash reserves of the fishermen's households. The trip to Puno, the one place where boats could be registered, also represented an expense, especially for the fishermen who lived some distance from the city. The fishermen were concerned as well that these fees might increase or be replaced by some form of taxation. In theory, they had to come to Puno once a year to renew their registration, though few kept it up for more than a year or two.

In addition, there was something faintly ridiculous about the process of registering a boat. The fishermen were required to list the length, width, and depth of their boats in tenths of meters. To them, the boats did not differ much. They were built according to a single plan, all roughly the same size. At most, a fisherman might speak of a boat in such terms as "large" or "small." Moreover, once again imposing the model of the marine fisheries on the lake fishermen, the navy listed boats by name. If a fisherman bought a boat from another fisherman and wished to trans-fer the registration rather than pay the higher initial registration fees, he needed to indicate the name under which the boat had first been regis-tered. Such practices were alien to the fishermen, who simply referred to boats by their owner's name. When pressed, some fishermen named boats for their villages, for favorite saints, or for soccer players. Some of the names, though, were imposed by bored navy officials, and a few were in-sulting, such as *Lodo de Titicaca*, "Titicaca mud," or, worse, inauspicious, like *Aguacerito*, which means a sudden heavy rain shower.

The registration of boats did have one great advantage. It protected the fishermen from navy officials and policemen. A fisherman who could not present his boat registration certificate might have to pay a fine or a bribe, or risk having his boat impounded until he could do so. In a few spots, the fishermen rebelled against the registration requirement. The fishermen near Moho, the most remote and smallest navy station on the north shore of the lake, noticed that the base—little more than a building with a small dock and motorboat—was often left under the supervision of only two sailors, without any officer. One afternoon when the officers were away, the two sailors took their boat out on patrol. Near the village of Umuchi, they were surrounded by a group of more than two dozen fishermen, who quickly overpowered them. The fishermen drained the gasoline from the engine and stripped the sailors. The naked sailors man-aged to row their boat back to the dock by the next morning. Not sur-prisingly, Moho and the adjacent district of Vilquechico had the lowest rates of boat registration in the entire lake.

By contrast, fishermen in the districts of Pomata, Yunguyo, and Ze-pita, on the south shore of the lake, were far more likely to register their boats. The principal advantage for them was protection from the Boli-vian navy. Bolivia has been a landlocked country since Chile defeated it in 1880 and occupied its coastal provinces. As a sign of its unwillingness to concede that this lack of a seacoast is permanent, Bolivia has been com-mitted to maintaining a navy ever since, in the form of a sizable corps of officers and sailors and a few boats on Lake Titicaca and some eastern rivers. This navy grew in importance under the military dictator Hugo Banzer Suárez, in power from 1971 to 1978. In those years, the officers at the two largest Bolivian naval bases on the lake, in Copacabana and Tiquina, would often detain Peruvian fishing boats that previously had moved readily back and forth across the border that cut through the Bahía de Copacabana and snaked between the numerous small islands in the Lago Pequeño. Charged with violating Bolivia's national sovereignty, the Peruvian fishermen were sometimes detained for a few days at one of the Bolivian bases, where they would perform manual labor. The safest way to avoid this was to have their boats registered and painted with the red and white stripes of the Peruvian flag.

In 1970, the navy took its efforts at registration in a new direction. It started issuing licenses to fishermen.[2] The fishermen opposed this move more than the registering of boats, since the fishing licenses were enforced not only on the lake and at the shore, but elsewhere on land as well. Policemen would detain a fisherman who was returning home with his catch and demand to see his license. Often the policeman only wanted a few fish—trout, if there were any; silverside, catfish, or boga if there were not. Since there are several dozen police stations around the lake, many more than there are navy stations, this petty interference was quite frequent.

The fishermen also opposed the fishing licenses because they threatened the autonomy of their villages—far more severely than did boat registration. The two forms of registration might appear to be similar, since the government based both on the same principle—the notion that Lake Titicaca belonged not to the villages, but to the Peruvian nation as a whole. However, the registration of fishermen cut far more deeply into customary village rules than did the registration of boats. The only people who registered their boats were the lakeshore fishermen who followed the well-established system of village fishing territories. By contrast, a fisherman who received a fishing license might cross the boundary between villages and claim that the license gave him the right to do

---

2. Data that show the spatial and temporal distribution of boat and fishing licenses are available in electronic form at http://www.des.ucdavis.edu/faculty/Orlove/book/appendices/fish_licenses.xls, and at http://www.des.ucdavis.edu/faculty/Orlove/book/appendices/boat_licenses.xls.

so. It was even possible that the navy would issue licenses to fishermen who did not even come from lakeshore villages.

Faced with harassment by the police and the attack on their customary fishing territories, most villagers strongly opposed the fishing licenses, obtaining them only when pressed. The fishermen who lived in the villages closest to the provincial capitals were more than twice as likely to have a license as those who lived farther away, presumably because the police stations were larger in those towns. In a few cases, though, fishermen whose villages had small or unproductive fishing grounds obtained licenses in the hope that they could encroach on the grounds of neighboring villages: their rivalry with neighboring villages led them to participate in this registration, even though it undercut village autonomy. Fishermen from the relatively crowded waters on the western side of the Capachica Peninsula moved to fishing grounds off the tip of the peninsula and up its eastern side. Similarly, fishermen from the villages immediately to the southeast of the city of Puno traveled some distance to the richer fishing grounds near the large totora beds to the north. At the opposite end of the lake, fishermen from densely settled portions of the Lago Pequeño, especially the village of Amaquilla and the Vilurcuni Peninsula, began trespassing into the territories of other villages on the mainland.

These incursions were met with severe opposition. As in the period of conflict at the time of the canneries, other villagers supported the fishermen in the protection of their territories against such invasions. To the villagers who earned a livelihood from their fields and flocks, these fishing territories were not merely a source of income to some of their neighbors—they were an integral part of the village commons, a key element of their collective patrimony, which prior generations had protected and which they would guard as well. The villagers maintained their ultimate line of defense by preventing outsiders from landing boats on their shores. The totora beds found near several contested areas also proved unassailable. Even the most daring outsiders were reluctant to enter another village's totora beds. The local inhabitants knew the narrow channels well and could surprise the invaders, who could not flee easily. When pressed, the villagers resorted to violence in defending their territories. The fishermen in the Bahía de Puno attacked outsiders with the long, heavy wooden poles that they used to push their boats through the reed beds. The fishermen in the Lago Pequeño used slingshots, capable of hurling a stone at high speed for distances of more than a hundred meters.

Such opposition limited the incursions into fishing territories and ended the only positive incentive that fishermen had to seek fishing licenses. At considerable effort, the navy registered more than five hundred fishermen between 1970 and 1972, but the levels dropped off after that. Very few fishermen were registered after the mid-1980s, and the program was officially dropped in 1991. Only 33 percent of all fishermen ever got fishing licenses, a smaller proportion than the 56 percent who registered boats in the program that had at least some advantages for them. The village fishing territories thus survived the second major threat to their existence.

In addition to registering fishermen and their boats, the government officials intervened in the fisheries by promoting schemes to expand the production of trout. Despite the collapse of the canneries, these officials continued to view trout as the principal route to success for the lake fisheries. One major reason for this belief was that the trout hatchery at Chucuito was too large to close. No director of the regional office of the Ministry of Fisheries would entertain the notion that the largest facility under his supervision did little more than waste government funds. The hatchery also had broad support among other government agencies and the prominent families in town, who enjoyed occasional trout dinners served at the hatchery; they would have taken any suggestion of shutting the hatchery down as an insult. Regional pride also was involved. Since similar hatcheries operated in northern and central highland Peru, officials in the southern highlands felt they were entitled to one as well. This governmental focus on the trout also may have been a mild form of snobbery, or even discrimination, against the native species, especially the ispi and carachi. The ministry officials would have had to overcome the habits and prejudices of their background as educated urban people to acquire a taste for those native fish, which were small, bony, strong-flavored, and closely associated with the presumably inferior indigenous villagers. In their minds, development was a process of bringing the highlands into the modern Peruvian nation and into the cosmopolitan world of international trade. As imported fish, trout fit easily into this vision, despite the economic and technical obstacles to expanding trout production in the altiplano. The hatchery continued to produce fingerlings year after year and release them in the lake and its tributaries, as well as in some lakes high in the cordilleras.

The Ministry of Fisheries set up two kinds of trout aquaculture projects in the altiplano. The first, stream-based trout farms in the 1970s, closed after a few years. The second, lake-based floating cages for raising trout, began in the late 1970s, peaked in the early 1980s, and has continued at a low level to the present. Though government agencies obtained support for these projects by promising to involve lakeshore villages, they did not follow through with those promises. The limited benefits of the projects accrued principally to private firms and state enterprises that set up trout farms and floating cages, rather than to the villages that also tried their hand at aquaculture. Thus, the projects reinforced two basic notions that the fishermen had formed in earlier decades: that the government was not a source of direct help to the fishermen, and that their accustomed form of fishing—capture of fish in open waters, and sale through customary village markets—remained the most effective.

The first of the aquaculture projects, the stream-based trout farms, consisted of large concrete-lined pits, filled with water from a stream or river, in which trout fingerlings from the hatchery in Chucuito could be raised. In the 1970s the Ministry of Fisheries supervised the construction of twenty or so trout farms, six of them in lakeshore villages. In 1975, the peak year, the output of all the farms totaled eight metric tons. Though none of these projects lasted very long, several of them did run long enough to recover their initial expenses and to generate a profit. These more successful ones were on government enterprises such as technical schools or agrarian cooperatives. The village projects, often on poorly chosen sites with streams that did not provide enough water during the dry season, closed in 1975 and 1976. For a few years, villagers kept the tanks full and brought their cattle and sheep to drink there during the dry season. Even this use, though, required more cleaning and maintenance than was worthwhile, so the tanks became stagnant, scum-filled ponds in the rainy season, empty pits in the dry season, and reminders of failure in both. With greater access to capital and to government advice, the other trout farms lasted a few years longer. By the late 1970s, though, the Peruvian economy was suffering the effects of an international debt crisis. The Ministry of Fisheries was unable to support the trout farms. The last one closed around 1983.

In the late 1970s, as the trout farms began to run into difficulties, the Ministry of Fisheries shifted to a second type of project: aquaculture in floating cages. As their name suggests, these projects are structures— a framework of rods covered with nets—that are suspended by floats at the surface of a body of water. Fingerlings are placed in the cages, provided with feed, and harvested when they are grown. The fish are taken fresh to markets in La Paz, Puno, and Juliaca or sold directly to restaurants in those cities. Because they are in Lake Titicaca itself rather than in artificial tanks, the water conditions in these cages are more optimal than those in the trout farms. Between 1977 and 1997, about forty cage culture projects opened along the Peruvian shores of Lake Titicaca, and another five or six in Bolivia. Few of them remained in operation for longer than two years. The total production has fluctuated widely from year to year. The highest production, around 350 metric tons in 1981, was close to the level of the canneries at their peak years, though still less than 5 percent of the total catch in the lake. There was a second, smaller peak of 140 metric tons in 1989. After dropping a bit, the production returned to about 120 tons in 1999.

The first cages were managed directly by the Ministry of Fisheries; the national university in Puno and four private firms soon opened cages of their own. These operations, though successful on technical grounds, were not profitable. Trout, adapted to eating live prey, have delicate digestive systems. They can be raised on commercial feed, but they require a special type made of pellets that are more uniform in size and higher in protein than feed for poultry or domestic livestock—and it is prohibitively expensive, even though trout process it efficiently, converting about two kilograms of commercial feed into one kilogram of trout. Other cage operators experimented with grinding up ispi to feed to the trout. The ispi were cheaper than commercial food, but the trout required more of it. It took four kilograms of ground ispi to produce a kilogram of trout. The retail price of trout at the time was barely sufficient to cover the cost of feed, and it left no margin for wages, marketing costs, or equipment maintenance.

Moreover, the private firms faced opposition from the lakeshore villages. The Ministry of Fisheries, which supervised aquaculture as a kind of food production, issued the private firms formal concessions, registered with the Peruvian navy, that gave them the exclusive right to use certain portions of the lake. These agreements conflicted directly with the villagers' firm belief that they owned the parts of the lake close to shore. The villagers explained to the ministry officials and to the private firms that they should have been the ones to issue such concessions and, moreover, that they should receive compensation for use of their waters. When the cage operators tried to keep the villagers from fishing close to the cages, their opposition increased. Additional problems arose in the village of Huincalla, in the southeastern portion of the Bahía de Puno, when villagers noticed heavy, though localized, pollution near the cages run by a private firm. Uneaten food and wastes from the trout farm contributed to heavy growth of algae along the beaches where the villagers landed their boats and washed their clothes.

The villagers, who had maintained their territories against incursions from other fishermen when the trout canneries were in operation and the fishing licenses were required, certainly were not going to tolerate the cage culture projects, which were much more alien to their ways of life. The private firms were unable to prevent them from taking reprisals against this usurpation of their territory. The cages were built of simple materials that were easy targets for petty vandalism. On a number of occasions, their mesh panels were cut open, allowing the trout to swim away. More frequently, a few villagers would take trout from the cages. These fish would be widely distributed and quickly eaten, leaving no evidence that could point to the individuals who had removed the fish. (Sometimes the villagers were more brazen. In one famous incident, around 1981, the manager of a floating cage project near Juli looked for sheets of corrugated iron that had been stored at the project site for the

Two men sewing old fishing nets together to make a floating cage. Photograph by Ben Orlove.

construction of a shed. He found that they had been installed as the roof of a new village school building.) The firms could not protect their investments against such attacks. With steady boat traffic from fishermen and totora-cutters, the waters near the cages could not be patrolled day and night. If the firms brought navy officials and policemen to investigate, the villagers would deny any knowledge of the acts and pass the blame on to other villages.

In some cases, external financing allowed villages to set up their own floating cages. International agencies provided funding to villages after an El Niño–related drought in 1982–83 and, to a lesser extent, to a regional development program that operated from 1988 to 1990. These funds paid for the initial investments in materials to build a cage, acquire the first set of fingerlings, and amass a feed supply for the first few months of production. Like the private projects, though, few of these village cages survived for more than a year or two. Though they did not face vandalism and petty theft, they ran into the same cost squeeze: the price of trout could not cover the expenses for feed, even if supplemented by locally caught ispi. They also faced difficulties in obtaining new supplies of fingerlings. The shipments would arrive late, with some underfed and ill individuals, or would come poorly sorted by size, so that the larger fingerlings would have eaten the smaller ones.

By the late 1990s, only a few cage culture projects were running in the lake. The Japanese International Cooperation Agency still maintains a large demonstration project in Bolivia. Situated near the large navy base in Tiquina, it has not suffered from vandalism, and it is heavily subsidized by its sponsor. On the Peruvian side of the lake, four projects are run by villages on the west side of the Chucuito Peninsula, in a favored location. Since the projects are close to the hatchery in Chucuito, the villagers running them can supervise the shipment of fingerlings. Their proximity to the city of Puno has allowed them to establish long-lasting ties with restaurants that cater to tourists. With trout caught in open waters in decline since 1990, restaurant owners welcome these steady supplies. By timing the harvest of trout for the times of highest demand, the villagers receive higher prices and have lower wastage than other, less successful cage culture projects.

Though the fisheries appeared stable at the end of the twentieth century, they may be vulnerable to two major threats, both potentially more serious than the introduction of the trout and the silverside. The first is the risk of contamination from oil drilling at Pirín, between Pusi and Taraco on the northwest shores of the Lago Grande. Drilling had taken place here around 1915. The initial yields, though modest, attracted some attention, but the fields were not developed, because World War I disrupted international trade, and other oil fields in more accessible portions of Peru were discovered soon after. A concession granted to a Russian consortium in this area in 1997 was the first serious activity in decades. The Russians hired private guards who did not allow outsiders, or even local villagers, to enter the concession. Rumors abounded in this atmosphere of secrecy: the exploratory drilling leaked lubricants and industrial chemicals into the lake; they would soon reach layers of groundwater that had heavy salt content, which, if they ran into the lake, would

increase the mineral content of the waters and lead to the decline or disappearance of plant and animal populations. These rumors were corrob-
orated by photographs circulated around Puno and elsewhere, allegedly
taken by individuals who had sneaked in past the guards. Though none
of the photos unambiguously documented extensive damage, they were
cause for serious concern. Several showed petroleum and drilling mud
spilling out of wells into ravines and across fields. Others depicted fields
and meadows that contained large white patches where saline groundwater had spread and then evaporated.

The second threat also involves a large corporation. Several biologists
who work for government agencies in Puno have spoken of proposals
to divert water from the Río Huenque and other streams in the western
cordillera. Rather than flowing into the Río Ilave and then into the lake,
the water would pass through a tunnel dug through the cordillera and
into the arid western slopes of the Andes. This diversion would remove
more than half the water of the Río Ilave, the river with the second-largest
flow into the lake. The total reduction in water input might be as much
as 8 percent. The consequences would be disastrous—a permanent drop
in the level of the lake and an increase in the salinity of the water. The totora beds and the waterfowl that live in them would be greatly reduced.
The biologists have stated that the proposals for this project emphasize the importance of providing water to the city of Moquegua, whose
growth has been limited by its small local water supply, but that the real
beneficiary would be the Southern Peru Copper Corporation. This firm
is widely known for its recalcitrance in addressing the extensive pollution around its mines and processing plants. It wants to divert the tributaries of Lake Titicaca in order to obtain cheap water for its coastal ore-
concentration plant, rather than installing equipment to conserve water
or to desalinize seawater. As with the petroleum exploration, the critical
details have been kept out of view, in this case in the planning sessions
for the dams and canals required to divert the water.

These petroleum and mining corporations may well open a new, grim
chapter in the history of the lake and altiplano. At present, the petroleum
drilling has not progressed very far. Facing economic turmoil in Russia
and low petroleum prices worldwide, the consortium withdrew from

Peru after a few years. No other firms have undertaken activities there. Nonetheless, Perupetro continues to promote the Titicaca deposits in its information catalog. Similarly, the plans for water diversions from the Río Ilave drainage have not proceeded very far, in part because of low prices for copper on the world market and because of the financial difficulties of the Southern Peru Copper Corporation and ASARCO, the holding company that controls it. However, the mining company still plans to expand its capacity to process ore at its facilities on the coast. Late in 1999, Grupo México, a Mexican mining conglomerate, purchased ASARCO and may well provide financing for these projects.

In the meantime, at least, few shifts have occurred in the fisheries in the decades between the close of the canneries and the end of the twentieth century. The fishermen catch a somewhat different mix of species: carachi still predominates, though silverside has replaced trout as the second most important species. The technology is quite stable. The most recent boat surveys, from the 1990s, show that wooden boats make up 64 percent of the fishing vessels, an increase of less than 10 percent since the early 1970s. Balsas still account for 36 percent of the fishing vessels. Similarly, nylon gill nets are the most common type of fishing gear, but several traditional types, such as the large trawl net, the dip net, and the basket trap, are still used. Despite the government's regulations and its allocation of fishing rights to others, the customary rules remain in force, allowing only lakeshore villagers access to fishing grounds.

Change has not come in these years from the efforts of government agencies to regulate and develop fisheries. In the areas where the navy received the support of local fishermen, it was able to register a significant number of boats. The licensing of fishermen, more strongly opposed by the villagers, had less success and was terminated more quickly. With few exceptions, the trout farms and cage culture projects closed after facing severe technical and economic problems. Only two changes in the fisheries can be noted for this period, neither of them very large. The first is a limited expansion of the operation of the fisheries. As recent studies by international development programs show, the number of fishermen has increased from the 3,000 or so in the late 1970s to between 3,750 and 4,000 in the late 1990s, a growth rate of 0.88 percent per year, well below the overall growth rate of population in the region. The total catch has risen more slowly, from 8,100 to 8,500 metric tons per year, less than 0.5 percent per year. This figure is still well within the limits of sustainability, as suggested by the fact that this catch constitutes less than 10 percent of the total biomass of fish in the lake, recently estimated by echo-sounding at 91,000 metric tons. The village-based system of fishing rights is a major restraint on any growth, since it places such strong limits on the access to fishing.

The second change, a shift in fish marketing, is in some sense not a change at all. Lake Titicaca fish have been shipped to different areas in different periods: to mining towns in the Spanish colonial period, to valleys in the Amazon and along the Pacific Coast in the nineteenth century, and even to foreign countries in the 1960s, when the canneries were in operation. It is not surprising, then, that fishermen in the last quarter of the twentieth century sought new markets. Some bring their fish directly to urban customers, as in the case of the cage culture projects run by villages on the Chucuito Peninsula, which supply urban restaurants with fresh trout. Other fish vendors began to seek out new markets in the 1990s. One group of vendors from the northwest side of the lake gathers at the main bridge over the Río Ramis to purchase silverside from the fishermen's wives. They pack the fish in wooden crates and take them by truck to the city of Arequipa. Farther south, three men from a village near Acora use a motorcycle that they jointly purchased to carry silverside from their village to the town of Moquegua, near the coast, where the price of fish is three times as high as in the altiplano. They take turns embarking on this long, uncomfortable ride. The trips generate enough money for them to pay off the loans for the motorcycle and to earn a steady income.

Dominique and I learned about the fishermen's interest in other forms of marketing as well. When the catch surveys were operating smoothly, we decided to conduct an economic survey in which we would interview fishermen about their investments in equipment. We tried to include every item that we could think of: boats, balsas, outboard motors, oars, sails, nets, each of the types of native gear. As we discussed what items to include, Dominique remembered that he had seen, out near Moho, a kind of cage that a fisherman had made. Taking old sticks, the fisherman built a cylindrical frame about thirty-five centimeters in diameter and a meter in length. He sewed old, fine-meshed nets over the entire frame, leaving one end partially open. He could place freshly caught fish inside this frame, tie up the open end with cord, and then set the fish and frame in the lake. He tied a string with a small float to it, so that he could locate it again in the lake, and after he had accumulated two or three days' catch, his wife would take the fish to a nearby market. Not only could she go to market less frequently this way, but she could also count on receiving the higher price for fresh fish (as opposed to dried). Someone else in the village had made a device like this, the fisherman said, and he'd decided to copy it.

Dominique and I wanted to include this device in our fishing economic survey, but we did not know what to call it. The fisherman had not given Dominique a name for it, nor had Cirilo or Pedro or anyone else around the IMARPE office ever heard of it. Pressed for time, we simply called it *una bolsa para guardar peces vivos*, a sack for storing live fish. When we tested out the questionnaire, the other fishermen asked us to explain what we meant by this term. They were delighted with the idea. Several of them said that they would be able to sell carachi live rather than drying them, thus getting a better price, and would also save the considerable effort that went into gutting and salting fish and protecting them from dogs and chickens when they were placed out to dry. When Cirilo went around to give the questionnaire to other fishermen, he got the same response. On our travels later that year and in subsequent years, we found these *bolsas* in a number of villages. Though they would have made their way around the lake without our assistance, our inquiries probably accelerated the process.

At several points Dominique and I had wondered how we might return the results of our overlapping research projects to the local communities whose support and cooperation had been essential to us. We felt some responsibility toward them and hoped that we would have something more concrete to show for our efforts than the general claim that our research might somehow inform government policy in ways that would benefit them. We did not know which of our research results would be of use to the villagers, or how we might communicate these findings to them. The irony of the *bolsas* thus amused us: the fishermen were quite capable of recognizing what was useful to them, and taking it when they wanted it. The research that interested them the most was not what came out of the surveys and interviews that Dominique and I had conducted; rather, it was the experimentation through which the fisherman near Moho had developed the *bolsa*.

6 Reeds

More than 150 villages line the shores of Lake Titicaca. No two have identical landscapes. Much as a quick look is sufficient to recognize the face of a friend whom one meets unexpectedly when walking down a street in a strange town, so too a traveler around the lake needs only a single glimpse to recognize a familiar village that comes suddenly into view when riding in a boat on a new route around an island or when crossing the crest of a ridge for the first time. It is enough to see the clusters of adobe houses, set in the recesses of the hills that rise up suddenly from the flat farmlands by the lake, in order to know that this village is Yanaque. The mind does not need to pause and reflect in order to distinguish it from Socca, with its broad bands of scattered houses and fields, separated by low, shrub-filled streambeds that run from the peninsula's high rocky spine to the lakeshore. Nor would one ever confuse Yanaque, even

for an instant, with Piata, set in a narrow valley flanked with groves of eucalyptus trees and the stone walls of sheep corrals. As with human faces, each village acquires its distinctiveness from a specific combination of common features. If the features of human faces are eyes and noses and mouths, foreheads and cheeks and chins, those of the lakeshore villages are hills, plains, and the shoreline; pastures and fields; houses and paths; and one thing more: the beds of reeds that grow in the shallow waters of the lake.

These beds are at once unvarying and endlessly diverse. Since all that can be seen in them is a single species, *Scirpus tatora*, known in Spanish as *totora*, in Quechua and Aymara as *t'utura*, these beds are uniform. This homogeneity is unusual, because most wetlands throughout the world contain a variety of plant species that grow above the surface, each restricted to a band of water of a particular depth. (Like other wetlands, the reedbeds of Lake Titicaca also contain plants that are entirely submerged below the surface of the water.) The totora is homogeneous in another way as well. Only one portion of the plant is visible: its stems. Carrying out photosynthesis through these stems, totora plants lack discernible leaves. Nor do these plants have the flowers and seeds that make other reeds, such as cattails and papyrus, so distinctive. Reproducing chiefly by sprouting on the rhizomes that spread in the muck at the lake bottom, totora plants grow for several years before they can form flower heads, and even those are small and inconspicuous. Many individual plants never form flowers at all. Few other ecosystems present so basic a geometry: a totora bed is nothing more than a vast array of cylinders that rise from the surface of the lake.

And yet the beds of this single species take on a great range of forms. Varying in width and shape, they are a kind of map of the lake bottom, since they indicate the zones that are between two and five meters deep, where the totora grows most successfully. The beds are commonly a few hundred meters wide, though they are narrower where the lake bottom drops off sharply, and in shallow areas they may be as much as ten kilometers wide. Beds often form crescents that mimic and accentuate the curve of a bay, thickening in the broad, shallow regions at the middle, and narrowing at the steeper zones at the edges. In other areas, the reeds

A boy harvesting totora with a scythe in the Bahía de
Puno. Photograph by Ben Orlove.

are entirely absent. Where hillsides plunge down to the depths, the bottom is often so rocky and exposed to severe waves that the totora cannot
take root and grow.

The totora also varies in thickness and height, since the villagers harvest reeds from the beds. Ordinarily done in rectangular sections, harvesting is often spread over a number of months, and the totora may
be left to regrow for a year or more. As a result, a single bed may look like
an enormous patchwork quilt composed of pieces of fabric of varying

textures and colors: the intense green nubs of newly emerging plants; the dark greens of the mature plants, whose firm stalks may be as tall as three or four meters; the lighter beige and straw tones of the oldest stems, dried by long exposure to wind and frost. As if to sew these patches together with pale blue satin ribbons, narrow watery paths run between them. Sheltered by the high reeds, the water in these channels remains calm and reflects the sky, even when winds stir the open waters of the lake into a deep blue.

If the fishing in the lake brings to mind the possibility of a museum, the harvesting of totora seems like a kind of living history exhibit. It might appear even more authentic than the sort of display in which costumed local residents re-create daily life in a colonial New England settlement or in a fort on the western frontier, since the past is reenacted all around the shores of the lake, rather than in specific locations. The reeds themselves are certainly the same species that has been present for centuries. But it is not the vegetation alone that gives this sense of great continuity. A tour promoter who wished to set up a living-history exhibit about traditional plant use in the altiplano could simply bring visitors to the shore of the lake during totora-planting season. There, the visitors could watch as the villagers pole their balsas into areas where the totora is densest. They pull entire plants from the muck at the bottom of the lake, making sure to get a significant mass of roots and rhizomes, and poke around the base of plants that do not come out easily, in order to loosen them. When they have enough plants, the villagers carry them to the planting zones. They wade into the water and use spades to open up spots in which they root the plants. If they wish to plant in water too deep to stand in, they go out in balsas. Once they reach the zone of appropriate depth, they use poles to push the clumps of roots and rhizomes into the lake bottom, or drop into the water clumps that are weighted down with stones.

Although villagers are reticent to discuss some aspects of their lives with outsiders, they speak readily about the totora planting, a point of great pride among those who live right on the lakeshore. They describe the depth to which they wade out as "half a leg" deep, what English-speakers would call knee-deep. This depth can also be measured as four handbreadths or as "half an arm"—the distance from the elbow to the tip of the extended middle finger, a term for which the English equivalent, the cubit, is now an odd and archaic word, hardly part of everyday conversation.

The usual time to plant is in September or October. The villagers explain that if they plant earlier, the lake could continue to fall, and the sun would dry the new plants when they are freshly sprouted and vulnerable. If they plant later, they face the risk that early rains might increase the sediments in the waters at the shore, causing young plants to rot. Heavy rains could make the lake rise quickly, so that new plants would become detached and float to the surface.

To an interested visitor, the villagers could offer a fuller explanation of this planting season. They would point out that the lake rises and falls once a year. (This pattern has often made me think of tides, since the twelve-month cycle of the lake's level is as strong a rhythm for the villagers as the twelve-and-a-half-hour cycle of the tides is for people who live by the sea.) The lake is at its minimum in the month of December, early in the rainy season, and rises steadily from December through March, the months of heaviest rain. Though the rains taper off in April, the lake rises in that month because the rivers that descend from the cordilleras are still full. The lake reaches its peak, about seventy centimeters higher than its minimum, late in April and falls steadily during the dry season, which lasts until October. At this time there is virtually no rainfall, and even the largest rivers drop sharply. In these months of cloudless skies, dry air, and strong winds, water evaporates from the surface. The first rainstorms of October and November are not enough to overcome this loss, so that the lake continues to fall until the rains pick up again in December.

Though the timing of this rise and fall changes little from year to year, the amount can vary greatly—much as a heavy storm can cause tides to rise well above their normal levels. After a season of heavy rains or of rivers swollen by massive snowmelt in the cordilleras, the lake can rise by a meter or more, while a warm, windy dry season can make it fall a good deal. Though totora plants can grow on their own from buds that sprout from rhizomes in the muck and from seeds that are carried by wind and waves to the shores, the reedbeds take a long time to reestablish themselves once they have been dried out in times of low water or drowned when the lake is high. The villagers keep a close eye on fluctuations in lake level and adjust their totora planting accordingly. By planting in September and October, they are able to monitor the lake level when the dry season is advanced enough to permit a precise estimate of the minimum level that the lake will reach. If the lake has been unusually high, they plant totora at the deep offshore end of the totora beds, to compensate for the plants that drown at the outer edge. When the lake is unusually low, they plant at the shallow onshore end, since the loss of totora occurs from plants that have dried out at the inner edge. (In years of very low lake levels, the villagers also burn off patches of dead totora. This burning, which usually takes place in July and August, when the lake is roughly midway between its maximum and minimum, clears out the dense thatch so that new plants can grow.) It is in these dry years that villagers plant most intensively, knowing that without their efforts the totora will not come back as fully in years of higher water.

Any visitors who miss the planting season can have the sense of seeing a living history exhibit if they arrive on Palm Sunday, which usually falls in April. On this date, villagers make their annual visit to the boundaries of their reedbeds. Many of them carry a special kind of weapon called a *liwi*. It consists of three rocks, each tightly wrapped in leather. Three handmade ropes, woven of llama wool or horsehair, connect these rocks into the shape of a Y. A man can grasp one rock in his right hand and swing the other two over his head so that it acquires a good deal of momentum, and then release it at his target with great accuracy. (This weapon has been widely distributed in South America since pre-Columbian times. Its Argentine version, known as the *bolas*, was adopted by the gauchos, or cowboys, of the pampas.)

On the morning of Palm Sunday, groups of men from neighboring villages set forth from shore in balsas. They assemble out in the lake close to the boundary between their respective reedbeds. Organizing themselves into small groups, they hunt coots and other waterfowl with the *liwi*. The competition at times is friendly, though it can be accompanied by a certain amount of animosity as they shout insults to each other.

Drawing by Escolástico Chiripo, a villager from Santa Rosa de Yanaque, of the annual Palm Sunday hunt of waterfowl, 1979 or 1980.

Fights occasionally break out, though most villagers are eager to return to shore and to prepare for the feasting that always follows this hunt.

Should the visitor miss this festival, there is still a good deal to see any time between March and June, late in the rainy and early in the dry season. This is the peak of the harvest season. The main tool for harvesting is a simple one, a long pole to which a knife has been tied at one end. A villager can use the knifeless end to push a boat or raft through the channels out to a plot of reeds. Standing at one end, with feet firmly planted, he or she—both males and females carry out this work—inverts the pole, which now serves as a scythe. The villager thrusts it into the water and swings it to slice off several reeds. These actions require some strength, considerable coordination, and a good sense of balance. Moreover, they must be performed rapidly, or else the blade will just push the reeds, rather than cut them. For the sweep of the knife to cut a number of reeds, the lower hand on the pole must describe a slightly larger curve than the upper. An experienced cutter also puts some strength of the back and abdominal muscles into the operation by rotating the shoulders and twisting the waist. The lower body plays a part as well: at the same moment that the cutter swings the scythe, he or she must bend the knees—kept slightly flexed to permit this action—in order to compensate for the tendency of the sudden jerk of the heavy tool to make the balsa rock excessively. This work requires not only strength and skill but also patience, since the cutter must repeat the motions again and again, stopping only to retrieve the felled reeds that float on the surface and to propel the balsa through the water to a new spot. Depending on the quantity that has been harvested, the reeds can be loaded into the balsa or massed into a raft of floating reeds that can be tied to it.

The sense of witnessing living history continues even in the months after the totora has been harvested. During the dry season, the villagers lay out the totora on meadows and on the stubble of recently harvested fields. Broad fans of totora stems are a common sight along the lakeshore in these months. Other than drying, the reeds require little processing, since there are no leaves to strip off the stems. Though the totora loses a great deal of its weight as it dries, it does not shrink in volume. The pithy tissues of the inner portion of the stem turn into a firm mass, quite like Styrofoam, while the outer layers of cells retain their tautness. When pressure is applied to dried reeds, they can bend, but it is difficult to break them, or even to split the outer layer of cells. This strength is a second advantage of the absence of leaves: totora lacks the remnant bud-scars that weaken the species of reed that do have leaves.

The villagers make good use of these light, strong, water-repellent stems. If tied at one end, bundles of reeds can be used, like shingles, to thatch roofs. If tied at both ends, the bundles can be lashed together to form rectangular mats, which often serve as mattresses. These mats are so strong that they can be rolled into vertical cylinders for storing grain or potatoes. Small bundles of reeds can be gathered into large cigar-shaped bundles, three or four meters long and a bit under a meter wide; four of these large bundles can be tied with rope to make a balsa.

Visitors who hope to find the past alive in the present would be de-

Man in one of the final stages of balsa making—tightening the cord that holds the reeds together. Photograph by Ben Orlove.

lighted by the bustle of activity at a roofing party, in which a few men venture out onto the framework of poles and sticks to arrange the reeds and tie them down with twine—itself another craft item, made from the tough bunchgrasses that grow on hillsides. They would also be charmed by the slower, steadier efforts of a balsa maker, who passes twine around the bundles and laboriously tightens it, pressing one foot against the balsa and pulling up with a simple wooden hook, until the reeds are bound so tightly that no water can enter. These visitors, though, would be most impressed by another use of the reeds, the construction of floating islands. Some villagers have cut reeds in the large totora beds in the Bahía de Puno and made them into enormous mats, hundreds of square meters in area and a meter or so thick. Once or twice a year, they place freshly cut reeds on the top surface of these islands, to compensate for the gradual rotting of the waterlogged reeds on the bottom. The one-room houses on the floating islands are identical in shape to the rectangular, gable-roofed houses on land, with the single striking difference that they too are made from reed mats. Several hundred households live in a dozen or so communities on the floating islands.

Tourists who travel from the city of Puno to the islands can feel a strong sense of living history. As they step off the motorboats onto the slightly springy surface of the islands, they may feel as if they are stepping out of the present into a remote, unchanged past. But is it fair to perceive the islands as a piece of the past, floating in a lake of the present? There is no reason to take seriously the notion, encouraged by some tour guides, that the residents of the islands are the last living descendants of the Urus, a hunting and gathering people who fled centuries ago to these remote swamps to escape the successive conquests of the altiplano by the Tiwanaku, Inca, and Spanish empires. The floating islands and the communities built on them are relatively recent, by Andean standards at least; they are the product of a movement of land-based villagers from Coata and Huata on the shores of the Bahía de Puno late in the nineteenth century. However, there is equally no reason to deny that the islands reflect a long and continuous history of involvement with the lake, a history that demonstrates an intimate knowledge of the lake and a thorough exploration of the possibilities that it offers. It is a history of livelihood rather than a living history—a history that is alive, that changes and responds. In this kind of history, the living draw on their memory of earlier generations, rather than attempting to impersonate them for an audience.

This history of livelihood has many chapters. The establishment of the floating islands was one such in the nineteenth century; the poorly recorded earlier decades of that century may well contain others. In the twentieth century, two major chapters may be recognized. The first is the development, in the latter half of the century, of a new use for totora, one that has provided a source of cash income that does not require migration from the altiplano. This new use—the simple practice of feeding green totora to cattle—allows many villagers to purchase calves late in the rainy season and to fatten them up for sale during the dry season, at a time when other sources of fodder are scarce.

Through the late 1930s, villagers primarily harvested the dry yellow stems of the mature totora, which they used for thatch, mats, and balsas. They ate fresh green shoots of young totora plants on the occasions when

Two men harvesting lakeweed in the Bahía de Puno. Photograph by Dominique
Levieil.

they lacked potatoes and grains. Such times of scarcity could come in the
rainy season before the first crop harvests came in, or in years of famine,
especially during the long drought of the 1940s. Villagers never harvested the green totora for cattle fodder, though they occasionally fed
green totora stalks to donkeys and mules when grasses, crop residues,
and other fodder were scarce. By the early 1960s, the use of green totora
as cattle fodder had become the plant's most widespread use. No longer
a novelty, this practice now seemed entirely routine. About sixty-five
hundred households harvested totora for cattle fodder in the early 1960s.
The number was close to thirteen thousand in the early 1980s and
twenty-two thousand in the mid-1990s.

The practice was linked to the increase in demand for meat in southern Peru after the recovery from the Great Depression. Once the drought
of the 1930s and 1940s had ended, traders who supplied the cities in that
region with meat were eager to purchase animals. They traveled to cattle
fairs that have been held in the altiplano since the eighteenth century and

to the new markets that opened in the livestock-producing areas in the 1940s and 1950s. Hearing word that these buyers were offering high prices, the villagers tried to find ways to raise more cattle. The principal obstacle that they faced was the scarcity of fodder during the dry season, once the grasses and other plants that grew during the rainy season were no longer available. Their supplies of dried barley stalks and other crop residues were limited, and they were reluctant to plant alfalfa rather than food crops in their fields, so they began to experiment with alternatives. Some gathered large quantities of lakeweed, the plants that grew entirely submerged in the water. Though the cattle ate it with relish, its high water content made it heavy and difficult to harvest and carry to shore. Others considered totora. Since it grew in the lake, it remained green throughout the dry season. However, many cattle refused to eat it.

Cirilo discussed this problem when he described at length a trip that he took to a cattle fair in the mid-1950s, when he was a young man.

There are cattle that don't recognize totora as a kind of fodder. They are the ones that had never eaten it from when they were calves till they were two or three years old. They have grown up eating grass. In the high pastures where they graze, there are small ponds where a kind of lakeweed grows, and they eat that too.

Then someone will travel from the shores of Lake Titicaca where there's totora, and travels to the *alturas,* the high country, to buy cattle in May or June. Then he takes the cattle from the *qhatu,* the market, to the village. First he gives them totora, and they don't want to eat it, because they don't recognize it, they only recognize grass. So he gives them lakeweed and they eat that.

Now there are two things that we can do with this cattle that don't know totora. We cut up the totora that is mixed with lakeweed. The cattle remember the lakeweed in the ponds in the high pastures where they used to graze, and then, when the cattle eat the lakeweed, they are also eating totora with it. But if the cattle don't know either lakeweed or totora, there is something else we can do. We mix green barley stalks with green totora, both of these in pieces of the same length. Then they eat the barley stalks together with the totora, as if it were just barley stalks. It's another way to get them used to totora.

Once I went to Rosaspata with my uncle and two cousins. We went during the Feast of Pentecost. It's a huge fair. They bring cattle to Rosas-

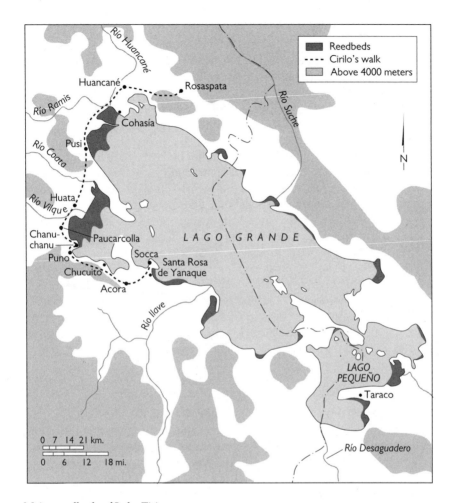

Major reedbeds of Lake Titicaca.

pata from many places, even from the *yungas*, the low eastern valleys of Bolivia. It is only in the month of June. At those times then they bring cattle that aren't familiar with totora. So then I bought two bulls, really big ones. My uncle bought six cattle. And we brought them back, the four of us. Each of us had a team. We drove them along, walking right behind them all the way to our village. We went along on a path that took us directly, from a little above the Río Ramis past the Pampa de Moro, and Huata, and Paucarcolla and Puno.

As we were passing near the shores of Lake Titicaca near [Río] Ramis, I bought a *pichu* of totora [a *pichu* is the amount of totora that can be encircled in both arms and held tightly against the chest] to give to the cattle while we were walking on the path. None of the cattle wanted to eat it, even though they were hungry. So then when we had stopped to rest, we put the cattle in a line like this. [Cirilo sweeps his arm and dips his hand repeatedly to indicate each bull in its position in line.] So then we gave a little totora to each one. Among these, one bull, one of my uncle's, begins to eat a little. So then the other bulls, they are looking at that one, and they lift up a little like this. [Cirilo lowers his head, opens and closes his mouth to imitate a bull picking up some fodder, and lifts his head.] They tried it and then just left it. They wouldn't keep eating it. So then I could have killed myself from anger. *Por gusto,* in vain, I had bought the totora and carried it on my back. A *pichu* of totora is heavy, after all. I didn't want to throw it away. So we waited a while longer. We left it for the cattle, we put some for each one. Another bull of my uncle's had eaten a bit, but mine didn't want to eat a single stalk of totora. So we continued the journey, leaving some totora, throwing some down.

And then, Huata. We slept in Huata, it was already late by the time we got there. But there wasn't any totora in Huata, so we bought barley straw. Oh, did they eat a lot! Wah! [Cirilo pauses after this interjection, and then returns to the story.] Now in Huata we slept in the house of people we knew. These are the people who always put us up. Their family were compadres of our grandfathers.

So the next day in the morning, around three in the morning, we started traveling toward Puno. Then we came to the Pampa de Illpa, the place that is also called Moro, where there was a cooperative during the time of the Agrarian Reform. [Cirilo refers to the program of the first phase of the military government from 1968 to 1975.] Illpa is higher up, Moropampa is below. We saw that there was a lot of grass. It belonged to the *hacendado*, the landowner, that used to be there. So we took advantage of the situation and grazed the cattle in the middle of the *hacendado*'s pasture. Then after two hours we continued our journey to Puno. Around noon we had gotten near Paucarcolla. Then, around the time that it is now, late in the afternoon, we were near Chanu Chanu. We stayed there. The people who put us up would cut totora. They were cutting totora from K'api. We tried buying one *pichu* for all the cattle. Some of them wanted to eat it. They ate one, two, three stalks of totora, eating it like that. We left the cattle staked down, like this. [Cirilo makes a gesture of pounding a stake into the ground.]

The next day, we could see from the way that the totora was tossed around that some of the cattle had woken up at night and eaten it, and others had not. We continued the journey around three in the morning to Socca. We arrived there around five in the afternoon. There we gave them the totora since they were hungry, but they didn't want it. So we mixed together some barley that was still partly green with pieces of totora cut to the same length as the barley. When we woke up early the next day, we saw that the cattle had eaten the barley and the totora. They had set aside about a third of the totora that we had mixed in. That day, we did the same thing in the morning. They ate that mixture more readily. In this way, little by little, they became accustomed to totora, and they came to know totora. Within a week we gave them unmixed totora. At our house we had cows that ate unmixed totora. Watching them, the new cattle also learned how to eat.

That's how they learned. This was the year 1954 or 1955. The return journey lasted five days. From Rosaspata to Huancané, one day; from Huancané to [Río] Ramis, the second day; from Ramis to Huata, one day; from Huata to Puno, one day also; from Puno to Socca, another day. To go there it took us one day, traveling in a truck. It's very far.

This story is something that I saw directly. It's real. It's not a quotation of what other people said. Each year I would go to Rosaspata to bring cattle. But I haven't gone for the last ten years or so, because the cattle there are very expensive now. They don't bring them from the *yungas* in Bolivia, because Peruvian money has fallen in value. It's pretty expensive to buy cattle there, and it isn't worthwhile for us.

Cirilo's account offers a view of a time only a decade or so after the first use of green totora as cattle fodder. He suggests a number of parallels between himself and the cattle that he purchased. Both Cirilo and his cattle travel to a new portion of the altiplano. They remember their homes: Cirilo recalls the totora-eating cattle in his lakeshore village; the cattle he buys wait for the grasses and the lakeweed that they knew in their native *alturas*. At first, they face unpleasant sensations (anger and hunger, respectively), provoked in part because their memories are imperfect guides for action in these new circumstances. Through observation and experiment, they gradually change their habits. Cirilo learns a new way of feeding cattle, and the cattle learn to eat a new kind of fodder. Within a week or so they become accustomed to one another. These bovine immigrants fit into their new home, and Cirilo knows how to draw on the animals of a new portion of the altiplano.

Such experiments, repeated around the lake, led to a major change in the use of totora. A report published in 1959 showed that a complex commercial network had sprung up to take advantage of this new fodder. Cattle, raised in the high pasture zone near the cordilleras or trucked into the altiplano from the neighboring highland department of Cuzco, were sold at the large weekly cattle fairs in Taraco and Paucarcolla. Purchased by villagers from the area around Chucuito and Taraco, they were fattened on totora and sold in weekly fairs in Ilave and elsewhere, and shipped by truck to Arequipa, Tacna, and smaller coastal cities. This shift from the use of yellow totora for crafts to green totora for fodder led to an increase in the total amount that the villagers harvested.

Despite this increase, the patterns of ownership of totora have changed only slightly. A few of the villages on the Bahía de Puno have such an abundance of totora, with beds that cover thousands of hectares, that they allow residents to harvest anywhere within the village territory. In most villages, however, totora plots are much like agricultural fields. Rectangular in shape, they can be divided into equal shares at the time of inheritance from parents. They are occasionally sold to relatives or neighbors within the village. It is somewhat more frequent to rent totora beds to people from nearby villages, since the size of the reedbeds varies greatly from one village to the next. Prospective renters from a community with little or no totora would travel to one of the areas with large totora beds. They would return to the same village for a number of years and, in some cases, to the villages where their parents had traveled to cut totora. There has been a shift in the payment of rent, however. Through the 1950s and 1960s, renters usually gave potatoes and grain and offered additional gifts of coca leaf and alcohol. In more recent decades, cash payments have become more frequent. Individuals can also purchase totora in markets, but most prefer rental arrangements. It costs less to obtain totora that way, and the supply is surer, since the ties can last for many years.

Though the increased harvest of green totora did not change patterns of ownership, it led to increasing disputes over totora theft. Individuals would accuse residents of the same village or of neighboring villages of entering their totora plots and cutting their reeds. The villages held meetings to discuss the problem. As at all such assemblies, the adults gathered at a central plaza or schoolhouse or other meeting place. The men would form a semicircle, standing or sitting on benches, and the women would sit on the ground nearby. The men would dominate the conversation, though women would occasionally break in and offer their comments. A number of villages decided to add a totora guard (*vigilante del lago*) to the list of community offices. Familiar with the patterns of ownership of plots, these guards would travel through the reedbeds to watch for incursions and theft. Like other such positions, the guard would have a yearlong term of office.

To make this work less burdensome and more efficient, the villages established rules for the timing of harvest. They closed the reedbeds to cutting altogether in the middle of the rainy season, since they had learned that totora does not resprout well if it is harvested when the water is most turbid. They also selected certain days for harvest, usually two each week. Each village tried to choose days different from those its neighbors. If one allowed harvesting on Mondays and Thursdays, the neighboring villages would choose Tuesdays and Fridays, or Wednesdays and Saturdays. This pattern reduced the number of days that the totora guard had to work. It also spread around the effort of defending territory, since all villagers, aware of the days when their neighbors would harvest, would be prepared to look out for trespassers who came across the channels that mark the boundaries between village beds. It took some effort for villages to agree on harvesting days. They tried to avoid the days when major markets are held. Religious arguments were often raised as well: most villagers preferred not to harvest on Sundays, but Seventh-Day Adventists, who are numerous in some sections, do no work at all on Saturdays. Villagers wanted to select days convenient for them, rather than for their neighbors. Nonetheless, the advantages of linking the schedule for totora harvest were evident to all. The dates, since they were established, have rarely changed.

If this use of totora as fodder is a chapter in the history of the villagers and their livelihoods, it shows striking parallels with another such chapter, the expansion of the fishing in the lake after the introduction of trout and the shift to wooden boats and nylon nets. In both cases, villagers increased their production of foodstuffs as demand grew in markets. And in both cases, the village control over the lake increased, rather than decreased, as the boundaries of village fishing territories expanded farther from shore and as new rules defined totora harvest periods more precisely.

In many other parts of the world, such commercialization has led to a breakdown of local control. The lakeshore villagers are distinctive in their extreme touchiness about incursions of outsiders into their territory and in their eagerness to preserve the resources in the lake, as a protection against hunger in times of drought, as a source of income, and as a legacy for the generations that will follow them. Their tenacity stems as well from their determination to remember the efforts of earlier generations to maintain this control.

The histories of totora harvest and of fishing show another parallel, the success of the lakeshore villagers in keeping the government at bay. In this regard as well, this pattern in Lake Titicaca stands out in contrast to many other regions around the world in which state agencies regulate economically valuable resources. Though the Titicaca villagers seek out the support of the state in certain areas—they welcome schoolhouses and health clinics, and they treasure the official documents that indicate their status as recognized peasant communities—they strive to retain control of their territories and the resources that they contain. In the case of the reedbeds, the government attempted to establish a system of management in the name of conservation, much as the navy registered boats and fishermen as part of its efforts to patrol and develop the waters under its jurisdiction. The Titicaca National Reserve is at the center of this chapter of the history of totora.

Much as the growth of the Titicaca fisheries is part of a global story of the commercialization of food production, so too the Titicaca National Reserve is only one case of a worldwide trend toward the expansion of protected areas that are set aside to preserve habitat for endangered species. Governments on every continent established such protected areas in the 1970s and 1980s. In the case of Peru, this timing coincided with the rise to power of the military government that was so important in the fisheries as well. This government, which took power in 1968, was more

receptive than earlier ones to lobbying by Peruvian scientists and activists and by international environmental movements that wanted to
protect the country's great biological diversity. In 1975, the military government established the National Forestry Center (Centro Nacional Forestal). This agency, commonly known by its acronym, CENFOR, was a
subministerial branch within the Department of Forestry and Wildlife of
the Ministry of Agriculture and Food. It was assigned the responsibility
to regularize and consolidate the management of natural plant and wildlife resources through a system of national parks and reserves in the tropical forests of the Amazon and in other regions. The government was well
aware that Titicaca is by far the largest lake in Peru and indeed in all the
Andes, and CENFOR officials were familiar with its enormous reedbeds
and its large and diverse populations of waterfowl. It was virtually inevitable that the government would decide to set up a protected area
around Lake Titicaca.

In 1976, the government opened a regional office of CENFOR in Puno.
Word of the establishment of CENFOR already had spread from official
circles to the countryside, creating great concern on the part of the villagers. A number of them knew that a wealthy storekeeper in Puno had
considered setting up a paper factory that would use the reeds for raw
material, and they feared that the government might take over the reedbeds for this purpose. Others believed that new taxes might be imposed,
or simply distrusted new government programs. Some villagers feared
that recently promulgated regulations over water use—the new *Ley de
Aguas*—might harm them. These worries increased as CENFOR representatives visited villages and traveled out on the lake.

As with the efforts of the navy and the Ministry of Fisheries to license
boats and fishermen, these visits by CENFOR met with different responses along different portions of the lake. The first region to act was the
western part of the Río Ilave delta. This area, one of the earliest to become
involved in fattening cattle, and one with large concentrations of mat
makers, was particularly dependent on totora for its economy. Afraid
that they would lose control of the reedbeds, villages in the districts of
Acora and Ilave discussed the matter in assemblies in 1975–76. They decided to form an organization, which they named the Totora Defense

League (Liga de Defensa de la Totora). They coordinated their meetings even more closely than they had in the previous decades when they had met to establish harvest days for totora. Eighteen villages held assemblies in which they formed communal committees *(comités comunales)* and chose delegates to the league. The committees raised funds by collecting fees from every household in the villages to support the trips of league delegates to Puno and to Lima. On these trips, the delegates visited the offices of the navy, the Ministry of Agriculture, and the Ministry of the Interior. They presented *memoriales,* long documents arguing that CENFOR should not administer the totora beds, but should leave them in the hands of the villages. The presentation of these *memoriales* reminded villagers of other trips that delegates had made over the decades to Lima: in the 1920s to request the construction of rural schoolhouses, in the 1940s to guarantee village control over the lands that had been exposed when the lake fell during the severe drought. Though government officials at first rebuffed them, the villagers persisted. Representatives from the league met with the Minister of Agriculture during his visit to the department of Puno in September 1976, a month of growing political tensions throughout the Peruvian countryside and in the department of Puno. Six months later, in March 1977, the ministry issued interim regulations that guaranteed the peasants in the western Ilave delta the right to continue harvesting totora as they always had. The concession greatly heartened the villagers in this region.

The efforts of the Totora Defense League overlapped with work carried out by CENFOR in 1977 and 1978. CENFOR officials conducted research to establish the boundaries of the proposed reserve and to determine the precise status of this new entity. There was some debate over whether the appropriate "conservation unit" status was the stricter "national park," under which resource extraction would be prohibited entirely, or the more permissive "national reserve," under which extraction would be allowed, but regulated. Pressure from the league seems to have been a major influence in the decision to draw the boundaries so that the Ilave delta was excluded, and in the choice of "reserve" status over the "park" alternative. One step down from national parks, national reserves are the equivalent of national monuments in the United States.

In 1978, the government set up the Titicaca National Reserve through Supreme Decree 185–78-AA. This decree states the government's decision to act on the basis of studies that CENFOR and the Puno offices of the Ministry of Agriculture had conducted; it makes no reference to the Totora Defense League. It established the reserve "in order to guarantee the conservation of natural resources and landscapes and the socioeconomic development of neighboring populations through the rational utilization of the flora and wildlife and the promotion of local tourism." The first and longest article indicates the boundaries of the reserve in its two portions, the first and smaller Ramis Sector in the Ramis delta, and the second, larger Puno Sector in the Bahía de Puno. The next four articles charge CENFOR and the regional office of the Ministry of Agriculture with the development and administration of the reserve. In addition, these articles discuss the inhabitants of the floating islands in the Bahía de Puno, who were given special status as the only people who lived within the borders of the reserve. The decree recognized their right to maintain their "customary agricultural activities and livestock raising." At the same time that the government issued this decree, it made maps that indicated the reserve and its *hitos*, or boundary points. Rather than following the curves of the outer edge of the totora beds, the boundary consisted of straight lines connecting these *hitos*. Thus it placed within the reserve a strip of open water beyond the reeds. The separation between the reserve and the rest of the lake, defined so precisely on the maps, was invisible on the lake itself.

This decree raises a question: was there an urgent need to establish new mechanisms to guarantee the conservation of "natural resources and landscapes"? Though it is difficult to argue with the notion that protecting unusual ecosystems is a prudent move, the reedbeds of Lake Titicaca appear to be less vulnerable than many such ecosystems. This point can be supported by an examination of the maps that document the location and area of the reedbeds since the beginning of the twentieth century. The plants are easy to map, since they jut out of the waters of the lake so visibly and since they grow unmixed with other plants, in what ecologists call "single-species stands." The French naturalist Maurice Neveu-Lemaire made the first detailed map in 1903. When it is compared with the surveys conducted by the Peruvian Military Geographical Institute in 1927, the aerial photographs made in 1955 by the Peruvian Cartographic Service, and more recent satellite images, the stability of the beds is apparent. Between 1927 and 1965, for example, there was a decrease of a few square kilometers of reeds off the northwest tip of the Chucuito Peninsula and an increase of a slightly larger area to its southwest. Overall, however, the area of the major reedbeds in the Bahía de Puno, the Lago Pequeño, and nearby river deltas has changed very little. Moreover, the density of totora also appears to be stable.

CENFOR's reports on the fauna of the lake focus on the aquatic birds as the target of their conservation efforts. This emphasis is understandable, since the lake is rich in waterfowl. (Many land birds also feed and nest near the shores and in the totora.) Nearly all these waterfowl, though, are widely distributed, since birds can fly to the lake from other areas, unlike the fish, blocked from entering the altiplano by the cordilleras. Of the forty-odd species of aquatic birds, CENFOR listed twenty-six as being of particular importance. Of those, twenty-five have distributions that extend north into central Peru and south into Chile—the reverse of the pattern of the fish species, nearly all of which are restricted to the lake. Some of these waterfowl are migrants, traveling as far south as Patagonia and even to North America in their annual movements.

The one endemic bird species, found only in Titicaca and the nearby Lago Umayo, is *Rollandia microptera,* the short-winged grebe. Like other grebes, it has large feet with broad, lobed toes set far back on its body, allowing it to swim and dive effectively. (The scientific name of the grebe family, *Podicipedidae,* derives from Latin roots that mean "rump-footed.") This species shares with most other grebes a long, narrow bill and head, a slim neck, and an elongated body. Propelled under water by its powerful feet, it resembles a streamlined torpedo that homes in on the fish, insects, and crustaceans that make up its diet.

This bird has a characteristic highly atypical among waterfowl: it has lost the ability to fly. Many other grebe species take flight only a few times a year, when they move between their nesting areas in stands of aquatic vegetation and the areas where they feed in other seasons. The ancestors of the short-winged grebe remained in the altiplano lakes, where they found abundant food throughout the year within swimming distance of their favored nesting sites in the totora beds. Moreover, they faced little danger from predators. Like other grebes, they could escape their pursuers by diving. Once under water, they could hold their breath for a long period and easily shift direction, enabling them to elude capture.

By abandoning flight altogether, the short-winged grebe has traveled further down the path of specializing as a diver than most other grebes. It has become larger than other grebes, an advantage in this cool climate, since it loses heat more slowly than smaller birds. Its bones grew denser as well, conferring strength and allowing the grebe to submerge itself more quickly. These changes favor the short-winged grebe, though they would handicap a flying bird that must minimize weight.

Once the ancestors of the short-winged grebe settled in Lake Titicaca, they did not need to take to the air in order to obtain food, to raise their young, or to avoid predators. Thus they faced no evolutionary pressure to preserve their ability to fly. Over time, their wings decreased in relative size. This change gave them the characteristic for which they are named: microptera, or tiny-winged. This bird can now only flap its wings and skitter along the surface of the lake when it is startled—a graceless, though efficient, movement that the local villagers find amusing, as do I.

Though they are unusual as a flightless waterfowl, these grebes are not scarce. They are protected by the effectiveness of their ability to avoid capture, by the size of the beds of totora in which they breed—and by the preferences of the lakeshore villagers, who target the giant coot (*Fulica gigantea*) on the infrequent occasions when they hunt waterfowl. The large, plump coots make better eating than the smaller, stringier grebes. Moreover, despite their ability to fly, coots are easier targets for hunters than grebes. They are less wary, and they form large flocks that allow groups of villagers to hunt them. Since this single endemic species remains abundant, there seems to have been little need for CENFOR to set up regulations to protect it. Like the other aquatic birds and the reedbeds, this species has coexisted stably with human populations around Lake Titicaca for centuries. So, although it was a sensible and cautious act to seek protection for an ecosystem as distinctive as the Titicaca reedbeds, the government overstated its case when it claimed that it needed to introduce new regulations to conserve the flora and fauna. It also further alienated the local villagers, who under other circumstances might well have supported the reserve.

Once the reserve was established in 1978, events unfolded very differently in its two sections, Ramis Sector and Puno Sector. Villagers opposed the reserve forcefully in the Ramis Sector. Some of them followed the model of presenting *memoriales* that had worked successfully in the western Ilave delta. In December 1978, villagers in the districts of Taraco and Huancané held assemblies and formed the Totora Defense Front (Frente de Defensa de la Totora), which peasants from the neighboring district of Pusi joined in 1980. Some of its founding members had contacts with the Totora League in the western Ilave delta and with the left-wing Peruvian Peasant Confederation, one of the main organizations of the political opposition in the southern highlands and throughout the country. The front sent *memoriales* similar to those of the league to government officials in Puno, demanding the suspension of the decree that established the reserve. These efforts did not bear fruit, and the Totora Defense Front lapsed into inactivity in the early 1980s.

A more diffuse but effective form of opposition in Ramis Sector was the consistently antagonistic stance toward the presence of government agencies. Starting in 1979 and continuing through the 1980s, the villagers drove government officials out of their communities by threatening to beat them, and in some cases, by surrounding their vehicles and throwing stones at them. These confrontations, more than the presentation of *memoriales,* have kept CENFOR from attempting to enforce its jurisdiction over this region.

These disparate violent encounters were spontaneous and brief. An example from 1983 is representative: One morning early in the year, the IMARPE driver, Victoriano, brought the agency's Land Cruiser from its garage to the laboratory in Puno, where he picked up the IMARPE biologists Eufracio Bustamante and Hugo Treviño. (Victoriano's wife, Hilda, who had prepared the results of the fishermen surveys for entry into the computer, was still working at IMARPE at the time. She occasionally accompanied him on trips, but remained at the Puno office that day to as-

Eufracio examining a sample of aquatic invertebrates along the upper stretches of the Río Ramis. Photograph by Ben Orlove.

sist Eufracio's secretary in typing reports.) They anticipated a routine trip from Puno to take water samples at different parts of the lakeshore, and set off on the main road around the north shore of the lake. After they crossed the bridge over the Río Ramis, they turned onto a dirt road that they had taken on other occasions. Though the roads in the Ramis delta often became impassable in the rainy season, this road, running parallel to the river on the side of a ridge, was firmer. Victoriano drove to the end of the ridge, close to the point where the river emptied into the lake. Eufracio and Hugo got out and walked out toward the shore, while Victoriano remained with the jeep. They had planned to measure the distance from the road, clearly marked on maps, to the lake; to note the plant species growing in the shallow water at the shore; and to collect water samples in small plastic bottles. They walked a hundred meters or so to a spot where Eufracio stopped to jot down a few notes, while Hugo continued on toward the lake.

A villager from the local community of Cohasía had noticed their jeep driving down the dirt road and followed on foot. When he saw that they had approached the lake and begun writing in their notebooks, he called out to other villagers. A small crowd quickly formed. Some of them gathered around Eufracio and shouted at him. One raised his hand to his cheek and made the gesture of pressing the eye out of its socket. Others repeated this gesture. A second group of men picked up stones from the base of the ridge and threw them at Hugo. None of them hit him, though several came close. Severely frightened, Eufracio began to talk to the villagers. The ones who had been throwing stones at Hugo came over to listen to the discussion. Seeking the relative safety of the jeep, Hugo ran back to the road.

It took a long time for any mutual understanding to be reached. Victoriano, who had learned Aymara when growing up in a Spanish-speaking landowning family west of Puno, was able to translate. The people from Cohasía had thought that Eufracio and Hugo were preparing to measure the beds of totora that grew offshore so that they could impose a tax on the reeds. They had heard that CENFOR required the villagers around the Bahía de Puno to pay fees in order to receive permission to cut totora. The IMARPE scientists explained that they had nothing to do with that and were not even examining the totora. Their only objective, they said, was to collect water samples and make notes about the vegetation; by gathering such information in different places and at different times, they could understand the consequences of shifts in the lake level. These claims somewhat mollified the villagers, who finally let them return to their vehicle. Several accompanied the jeep as Victoriano slowly drove to the edge of the village lands.

It seems to me that this encounter, with its threats of violence, is also a kind of living history, though not the sort that tourists might wish to see. It does not evoke a bucolic harmony of villager and landscape; instead, it reenacts the skirmishes between an alien occupying force and a subjugated but defiant people. For the villagers of Cohasía, the unexpected presence of government officials on their lands brought to mind earlier periods of interference, stretching back several decades to the confiscation of fishing nets by policemen, and perhaps even further into the past to other forms of taxation and expropriation. The IMARPE biologists may have recalled the stories of Indian uprisings throughout the history of the altiplano since the Spanish conquest; indeed, such stories surfaced occasionally in routine conversation at the IMARPE laboratory in Puno.

Like other living-history performances, this event was repeated again and again. There have been dozens of similar incidents in the Ramis Sector since the reserve was established. Another case, a bit to the south of Cohasía, involved a French staff member of a project, funded by overseas development money, that promoted bilingual education in Spanish and Aymara for schoolchildren. One afternoon, she walked to a picturesque spot, a rock that overlooked the lake not far from the schoolhouse where she worked. She had sat down and begun to write postcards when the president of the village approached her. He told her that she was writing too much. He was not satisfied by her explanation that she was merely writing personal notes to her friends, and he stood over her until she got up and left the rock. Soon after, she shifted her work to another village. As on the occasion when the villagers had challenged the IMARPE staff, the president was particularly incensed at seeing an outsider who was writing, and his anger took the form of physical intimidation and expulsion from the territory of the village. Such intimidation can be very direct. The suggestion that villagers would be willing to put out someone's eye seems a particularly vivid rejection of the government's claim that it has the right to observe and regulate local resources. As Eufracio's nervous recounting of that gesture indicated, the threat also suggested that villagers do not need special weapons to attack outsiders. They can simply use their hands.

Hilaria Quispe, a villager from Pusi, also suggested this ready availability of means to defend local territories when she described a confrontation with CENFOR staff. She had been apprehended when a couple of CENFOR employees had made a sweep through the reedbeds, checking boats and balsas for waterfowl eggs that villagers had collected. Hilaria had had the misfortune to be caught on one of these infrequent trips. Even at its peak of activity in the early 1980s, CENFOR did not send out regular patrols through the reedbeds, since it was expensive for them to rent boats and since villagers rarely set out in search of eggs. It takes a fair amount of time and effort to find the nests, hidden in dense regions of totora. The villagers do not gather enough of them even to have a quantity to bring to market; they take only a few for their own consumption or to trade with neighbors for grains and potatoes.

Hilaria described her anger at the guards who had taken the dozen or so coot eggs that she had collected. "They take the eggs away from us," she said. "What are we going to feed our children with?" She paused for a moment and continued, "We are making sure we have our poles with us." She paused again, for a longer interval, and then looked up and nodded her head to indicate that she saw that her point had sunk in. It was clear that she was referring to the poles of eucalyptus wood, like the one she had in her hand. Most households in the lakeshore villages have at least one of these poles, five or six centimeters thick and two or three meters long. They are the most common means of pushing a boat or balsa through shallow water, though many households also have a set of smaller wooden oars.

The poles serve other purposes as well. With a knife tied to one end, they can make a scythe for harvesting reeds, as already discussed. Propped up against a wall, they can support nets that are drying in the sun. They can be used as flails, pounded on piles of harvested barley to separate the grains from the stalks. And, as Hilaria suggested, they make effective weapons. Though their length and weight make them awkward to use in long fights, they can deliver a powerful blow. A direct strike would be enough to break an arm or even to crush a skull. The most important feature of these poles as weapons, however, is that they are not exclusively weapons. They share this quality with pitchforks and slingshots and the other classic weapons of peasant rebels. They might not succeed in direct battle against firearms, but they possess great advantages over firearms because they are readily available and it is impossible for the government to prohibit them, or even to license or register them. Much as the ordinary work implements can become weapons in the defense of village autonomy, so too the villagers themselves can become soldiers, and the complex web of channels through the reedbeds could become fortifications.

I am not sure of the exact nature of the threat that Hilaria had made.

Would she have been willing to hit a CENFOR guard and possibly kill him, or would she have just shoved him hard enough so that he would have fallen, fully clothed, into the chilly waters of the lake? She might have been suggesting that she would merely swing the long pole so that he would have to duck. Even if she would do nothing more than raise the pole to intimidate the CENFOR guard, though, he would be frightened enough to turn and flee. Hilaria certainly had heard of the other incidents when villagers had chased officials out of their territories. It seems to me that she knew the effectiveness of her threat lay in its imprecision. The villagers were willing to offer a mild response to a minor challenge to their control of their territories and to act with great violence if this control were seriously menaced. The specific government agencies and the laws could vary, but the villagers sustained their simple claim that they have the right to provide for the next generation through the food they produce in their territory.

Violent encounters like the ones in the Ramis Sector were not repeated in the other portion of the reserve, the Puno Sector. CENFOR had some apparent initial success there in establishing new patterns of resource management and in obtaining the acquiescence of the villagers to its laws and regulations. This sector, in the Bahía de Puno, was the area where CENFOR made the most intense effort at control. It is close to the capital city of Puno, where the regional naval base is situated and where other government offices are concentrated. CENFOR officials traveled through the Puno Sector in the late 1970s. They held meetings at which they asked village leaders to apply to them for the status of *calificación*, a qualification that consisted of registering adult men as household heads, listing their livestock holdings, and recording their production of craft items from totora. CENFOR said it would not issue contracts to members of communities that had not undergone this registration. Most villages in the area received the CENFOR staff openly. The inhabitants of the floating islands gave them a particularly warm welcome, since their settlements had a special status under the decree that had established the reserve: in the eyes of the national lawmakers, they were residents who actually lived within the reserve, rather than "neighboring populations" who lived on or near its boundaries. However, a few villages refused to meet with CENFOR. These included Yapura and Perca, both of which had long traditions of obtaining totora from the area within the reserve because of the small size of their own totora beds and their proximity to the ones in the reserve.

By 1980, CENFOR had begun issuing annual contracts for totora cutting in the Puno Sector. Organized initially to control the vast expanses of the Amazonian forests, this agency had no established procedures for regulating plants so different from trees, in a region so unlike the warm, humid lowlands. In a striking example of the unwillingness of bureaucrats to recognize regional variation, CENFOR did not create a new type of contract for the villagers who wanted to harvest a few tens of square meters of totora. Instead, it offered them permission to "extract forest resources other than timber in extensions of less than 10,000 hectares." These contracts stipulated the amount of totora that an "extractor" was permitted to cut, the precise location of the portion of the reserve where this cutting would take place, and the fee that would be charged.

These contracts offered a set of tricky possibilities. First, they gave many people who did not own totora plots a chance, at least in theory, to harvest totora directly instead of getting permission from village owners to cut totora in their plots. Formerly, only the inhabitants of lakeshore villages had harvested totora, but the law extended this right to all Peruvian citizens; of particular importance were peasants who did not live on the lakeshore, traders, and wealthy cattle owners. Second, the contracts raised concerns about the fees CENFOR would charge and the sanctions that forest rangers (*guardias forestales*) based in Puno would place on individuals or villages who did not comply with the law. Finally, since the law asserted that the state had sovereignty over the totora beds, it challenged one of the fundamental principles of the social and political life of villages: their right to manage their territories. It insinuated that the government's right came from the nature of the totora as a wild plant that would be "extracted," whereas the villagers spoke of it as a cultivated plant that they harvested.

The pressure from CENFOR and the concern over sanctions led several dozen villages around the Bahía de Puno to obtain such contracts in the early 1980s. Even in seeking these contracts, though, the villagers demonstrated their concern for retaining control of the reeds. To apply for a contract, a set of villagers filled out a form that contained eight clauses. CENFOR officials were particularly concerned about two portions of the form: the third clause, in which the applicants indicated the specific location and the total area of the section that they would cut and sketched a map of this section, and the fourth clause, in which applicants indicated the total amount of reeds that they would remove. The government officials pressured the villagers to quantify this total in cubic meters or in kilograms, since those were units the officials could measure and verify. However, the villagers kept reporting the amount in *pichus*, their customary measure. Villagers know that three standard reed mats can be made from a *pichu*, and that a balsa of standard size requires thirty *pichus*. Villagers who cut large amounts of totora arrange for donkeys to carry the reeds from shore. To calculate the number of animals they will need, they convert *pichus* to *cargas*, as donkey loads are known. The conversion rate seems to be fixed within particular regions: five *pichus* per *carga* around Chucuito and Acora, four near Huancané. (This difference might indicate variation in the size of the *pichu*, or the strength of the donkeys, or the length and steepness of the path from the lakeshore to the houses.)

Like many customary units of measurement, the *pichu* adopts the human body as a frame of reference and hence is imprecise. Though such units have been used for millennia, they have been replaced in recent centuries by more precise and standardized measures. Market economies have often led buyers and sellers to press for exact weights and measures—an impulse strongly supported by governments that wish to regulate and tax such transactions. By coordinating inputs and outputs, industrial technology also encourages the standardization of measurement. These processes, found throughout the world, play out in a distinct way in the altiplano. Industrial technology is largely absent in the rural economy, so there is often no need for precise measurement. It is enough to know, for example, that totora is planted in water "half a leg" deep. Nor have market economies fully imposed such standardization, especially granted the wish of rural people to keep the state at bay. In many marketplaces, women sell or barter carachi and ispi in amounts of three or four or sell them by the *huk'a*, the mounded double-handful. To bring a scale for weighing would be to invite officials to inspect the scales and charge a fee. Similarly, a mat weaver can accept some variation in the volume of a *pichu*, since mats—made at home by hand, rather than by machine in a factory, and traded for foodstuffs or sold in small open-air markets—can also vary a bit in size.

The managers of the reserve could not fit *pichus* easily into their bureaucratic procedures. It made enforcement more difficult. The officials who detained villagers with boatloads of totora found it hard to determine whether the amount stipulated in the contract had been exceeded. A quantity in cubic meters would be easy to assess, and some judgment could be made of the tonnage, by weighing a sample. A number of *pichus* is not only harder to define, it also gives the villagers a definite edge over the urban officials in estimating the amount.

Moreover, CENFOR officials would have been embarrassed to send reports to their superiors that detailed the annual harvest of totora from the reserve in so archaic and local a unit as the *pichu*. They would not have been able to justify rates of extraction if they were reported in *pichus* per hectare, rather than metric tons or cubic meters per hectare. The solution upon which they settled was to issue contracts in *pichus* and to multiply the number of *pichus* by some constant to obtain the number in kilograms for their final reports. (They never resolved their own internal debates over whether a *pichu* contained ten or twelve kilograms.) They were concerned nonetheless that an audit of their records would reveal that the contracts had been written in these nonstandard units. Unlike the navy, which had been able to demand that the fishermen measure their boats in metric units, CENFOR—a weaker organization—never reached that degree of control over the totora, an older and more established element in the village economy.

CENFOR was also unable to impose its system of regulation over space. The applications for a contract required the villagers to provide a sketch map of the proposed extraction zone. Dominique and I reviewed a number of these maps. In drawing them, the villagers did not conceal their intention of continuing with customary practices. The sketch maps include houses, paths, and other local features, but never the straight lines of the reserve boundary that figured so prominently in the maps drawn by CENFOR. Many of the sketch maps included the totora beds adjacent to their villages, where the local residents had always cut totora, rather than the more distant zones to which CENFOR wished to direct them. Others prominently displayed the floating islands, suggesting that the villagers would travel to them and ask the inhabitants for permission to harvest their reeds. In this regard, at least, CENFOR officials did not risk any difficulties with their superiors. Though the proposed extraction zones on the sketch maps looked nothing like the neat rectangles on CENFOR maps, the officials in Puno and Lima would have agreed that the crudeness of the sketch maps simply demonstrated the backwardness of the villagers in this remote region. Nonetheless, the CENFOR staff knew that the villagers did not travel to the areas to which they were assigned. Once, when I was discussing totora cutting with the reserve manager, he spoke to me about the villagers. *"Se equivocan,"* he told me plaintively; "They make mistakes."

The manager's statement suggested a hope that these mistakes would become fewer in number. Instead, CENFOR lost rather than gained ground. The agency issued thirty-one contracts in 1980 to villages in eight districts spread all around the Bahía de Puno and on islands out in the Lago Grande. By 1984, the number of contracts had fallen to thirteen, all to villages in the district of Puno itself and the two districts immediately adjacent to it on the main highway. CENFOR granted its last contract in 1986.

The steady opposition of the villagers to the reserve contributed to this decline. Early in the 1980s, some villagers who attempted to enter distant totora beds with no backing other than a CENFOR contract were confronted by the local villagers, who drove them out with poles, the same kind of pole to which Hilaria Quispe had referred. Faced with incidents like these, some villages played under both sets of rules. They obtained contracts from CENFOR but also maintained customary rental agreements from traditional totora owners, such as the inhabitants of the floating islands.

The villagers also learned that there were few negative consequences to cutting totora without a contract. CENFOR managers found it difficult to monitor activities in the reserve. Had they obtained support from the navy and the Ministry of Fisheries, the other government agencies with legal authority over the lake, they might have been able to patrol the open waters of the Bahía de Puno across which villagers carried totora to the Chucuito Peninsula and sections of the Lago Grande. However, neither agency had much interest in adding this policing to its set of responsibilities, given the difficulties that CENFOR had faced in the Ramis Sector.

In the Puno Sector, under the strictest control, the outcome of the conflict between the villagers and the government was the same as elsewhere. By 1986, just over a decade after the CENFOR office had opened in Puno, the villagers had regained full control of the reedbeds. Pressure from the Totora Defense League in the 1970s had kept the western Ilave delta out of the reserve altogether. The intransigence of the villagers in the Ramis Sector in the early 1980s had prevented the reserve officials from visiting that portion regularly. And even in the Puno Sector, next to the only city on the shores of the lake, CENFOR was not strong enough to expand, or even to maintain, its initial toehold.

How did the lakeshore villages come to be so effective in their opposition to the reserve? They had a strong interest in retaining control over the totora, an important part of their economy. They faced a relatively weak opponent, since the national government, confronted with more severe crises elsewhere, provided CENFOR with little support. It is striking that the villagers' opposition took such different forms: an organized campaign against the reserve, with lobbying of government agencies, in the western Río Ilave delta; sustained hostility to all reserve personnel, with many threats (and occasional acts) of violence in the Ramis Sector; passive resistance to the reserve, with some lukewarm cooperation, in the Puno Sector. This variation reflects some differences in timing and location. The villages in the Ilave delta had more opportunity to lobby, because they had begun to act before the reserve was established. It was easier for those in the Ramis Sector to threaten violence, because of their greater distance from Puno and the more hilly topography of the region. Nonetheless, these apparently different cases show an important uniformity: the actions were all spontaneous. This quality contributed to the success of the villagers in undermining the reserve, since the government had no organized counterpart with whom they could negotiate.

The sources of this spontaneity lie in the social and political fabric of the villages. The assemblies that they held provided an opportunity for a thorough public airing of opposition to the reserve. This opposition also gained support, oddly enough, from the distrust with which neighboring villages often view each other. Villagers often try to sneak into one another's territories and are jealous if one gets particular attention from the government in the form of a school or health clinic, so they watch each other closely. In this instance, any village that contemplated developing particularly strong ties with CENFOR knew that it would be roundly criticized by the others, and possibly attacked as well.

Another source of this spontaneity lies in the landscape itself, in the sharpness of the boundary between land and water. Though other government measures might affect different villages to varying degrees, it was clear from the start that the reserve would have strong consequences for the lakeshore villages, and only for those villages. The state intervenes in many ways on land, through ministries that supervise agriculture, education, and transportation. The lake, by contrast, has remained in the hands of the villagers, as earlier conflicts over the regulation of fisheries had demonstrated. In this sense, there was no need for organized movements to create and evoke symbols of unity, so that villages would be drawn into the movement. The lake itself was a powerful reminder of the villagers' enduring efforts to maintain their autonomy.

The landscape figures in the most recent episodes of the reserve. CENFOR's last effort in the Bahía de Puno was to delineate its boundaries in a form that would be visible to all. In 1985 and 1986, the reserve built markers at six of its boundary points, a bit beyond the outer edge of the totora beds. Each of these floating markers consisted of three barrels, welded to a frame that supported a tripod made of metal bars. At the top of the tripod, more than two meters above the surface of the lake, were signs very much like the ones found in national parks in the United States: a rustic piece of wood, painted brown, with letters inscribed in the surface and painted white. The signs bear the name of the reserve. The markers bobbed on the surface, anchored to the lake bottom by heavy masses of concrete. They were intended to separate the portion of the Bahía de Puno that was directly administered by CENFOR from the region under the control of the navy. The effort failed. The barrels were dented, the metal bars bent, and the words of the signs were defaced. Rather than showing the government's management of the reserve, the markers indicate the villagers' control of the lake on both sides of the line that the government tried to draw in the water.

After 1986, the reserve became what many conservation biologists and environmental activists call a "paper park"—a protected area that is depicted on maps and discussed in reports, but is not managed in any way by government officials or scientists. The term conveys the absence of significant activity by CENFOR or its successors (the reserve passed to the Ministry of Agriculture in 1988, to a joint Peruvian-Bolivian regional development program in 1990, and to the National Institute of Natural Resources, an independent Peruvian government agency, in 1992). Indeed, the reserve does exist quite literally on paper, since it is mentioned on the pages of the plans for activities written by government agencies in Puno. The documents give the reserve a kind of existence, to government officials at least. The term also expresses an understanding of the villagers: that projects, written on paper in towns and cities, can spring upon them for good or for bad. Well aware of the power of paper, they have made concerted efforts to defend their territories against it.

7 Paths

It was not on the first or second look through my photographs, but only much later, that I noticed how frequently paths and roads appeared in them. My position as an outsider and my work with the catch surveys led me to travel more than many people do in the altiplano, but the paths and roads, I realized, form an integral part of the landscape for the villagers as well as for a foreign anthropologist. I think of the women who wrap up in a cloth the fish caught by their husbands or sons or brothers, place the bundle on their backs, and set forth from their houses. They walk down paths from the villages to nearby markets, or to roads where they catch trucks that take them to markets. I recall as well Cirilo's account of the five-day journey he took with his uncle and cousins on foot. They walked down a road from the market of Rosaspata in the high grasslands, where they had purchased cattle, to the lake, and then along its shores, travel-

ing each day on paths from one village to another, spending each night at the house of a godparent or other acquaintance, until they reached Socca. The *diarios campesinos* also contain many references to *caminos*, roads and paths, often in the context of the villagers working with picks and shovels to construct and maintain them.

These paths, thousands of kilometers of them, form a network that covers the altiplano: a web of lines on the land. Most of them are barely a meter wide, beaten or trodden by the feet of animals and men and women, and also of children, who, by the age of three or four, trot along uncomplainingly to keep up with the adults, whether for a short walk to a relative's house or a field, or for half a day's hike to a distant pasture or market. Some of the lines are quite literally drawn in the earth by villagers working with picks and shovels. A few of them are broader, as much as five meters wide, and receive the passage of an occasional car or truck. A vehicle might reach a speed as fast as seventy-five kilometers an hour on a straight, unrutted stretch during the dry season. Often, however, they travel at a lower speed to avoid people or animals, or to negotiate sudden turns and potholes. A vehicle might have to stop altogether, for several minutes to let a flock of animals pass or for the driver to talk with villagers who challenge the presence of outsiders on their land, for hours if a wedding party or a group from a village festival happens to be dancing in front of it.

As lines on the land along which people walk, paths have a material existence. Their physicality and their unbreakable association with movement and travel allow them to stand for other, less tangible lines and movement. One can think of metaphorical paths as lines through time rather than space: paths as sequences, not of places, or, more precisely, not only of places, but of the events and phases that mark an individual's life.

My own path has led me back to the altiplano a number of times since my first visits in 1972 and 1975, and my main period of fieldwork there between 1979 and 1981, when Dominique and I collaborated on the catch surveys and other questionnaires. I returned for short visits in 1982 and 1983. My life changed soon after that: I married and had children. I was uncertain whether I would ever return to the places that I had come to know. In 1986, when my wife, Judy, and I arrived in the altiplano for a couple of weeks with our two children, then a toddler and an infant, we flew to La Paz but did not cross from the Bolivian side of the lake into Peru. Political turmoil at that time made Puno dangerous for foreigners as well as for Peruvians. The return from that trip brought another change to my family life. My parents, whose health had been declining, moved from New York to California. With the need to care for them, and with the birth of a third child, in 1989, I did not travel to the altiplano at all. Even my correspondence with the people I knew best began to decline. Cirilo and I wrote to each other a few times a year, and I exchanged Christmas cards and occasional notes with the IMARPE staff.

It was with Dominique that I corresponded most frequently. I followed his career after he completed his Ph.D. in 1987 at the University of British Columbia and began to work for an agency of the French government that set policy for the country's marine fisheries, in conjunction with owners' associations and workers' unions. In one of his letters he described to me a trip that he had made to Brittany, where his family had a country house. He visited a local fishing museum and donated two particularly fine *qollanchas* that he had brought back from Puno. I remember that he had commissioned a fisherman to make these lovely devices, and I had assumed, without asking, that he would keep them in his home. As I recalled our conversations, though, it made sense to me that he would want them to be in a place where many other people would see them, and where they would also serve as a tangible sign of the links that connected him with the altiplano: path markers, in a way, since Brittany was on the route that had led him from Paris to more remote shores in Canada and Peru. It had been during his boyhood summers in Brittany that he discovered his enduring engagement with the sea, his love of sailing, his fascination with the lives of fishermen. These have all continued in his life. He left his first job and now works as a planner who manages socioeconomic research in the fisheries division of the European Union. He works in Brussels and travels often to the coast to sail and to kayak. We have seen each other in recent years, once when an invitation to a conference in the Netherlands allowed me to visit him in Brussels, where the EU offices are located, once when a vacation back to North America brought him to visit me.

In the summer of 1995, the political situation was calm in Peru and Bolivia, and my family responsibilities were less pressing as well. My parents had both died, and my children were older and easier to leave for a while. I planned a trip back to Puno and sent over a dozen letters to the people I knew well, and to more distant acquaintances. As the time for my departure approached, I became concerned that I would not find anyone whom I knew. Cirilo had not replied to the letters I'd written him. I feared that he had been ill, or that the brother-in-law to whose post office box I sent the letters had left Puno. I had not heard from Hugo in more than a year, so I was less surprised by his failure to reply, and by the lack of response from the other people to whom I sent Christmas cards. I knew as well that I could not simply go to the IMARPE laboratory to find Hugo, Eufracio, Hilda, and others. From an American biologist who had traveled to Puno in the early 1990s, I had heard that the IMARPE laboratory had closed during a period when many government offices were reduced, privatized, or terminated.

I flew to La Paz and stayed for several days in Copacabana to adjust myself to the high altitude and to the rhythms of traveling in the altiplano. I visited the cathedral with the famous image of the Virgin, and I joined archaeologists on a trip to hilltop sites. I had a chance to attend a market, and to chat with fishermen who kept their boats on the beach near town. My Aymara phrases and simple sentences still served me well, and my conversational Quechua had somehow survived the intervening years, as I discovered when I was greeted by the one speaker of that language whom I knew in Copacabana, Doña Nieves, a woman from Ayacucho who ran a small restaurant on a side street between the main square and the lake.

A bus dropped me off at the border, and I walked several kilometers to Yunguyo, pleased to have the horizon in front of me dominated by the broad dome of Ccapia, the mountain I had climbed years earlier with Dante and his son Juan. The town of Yunguyo had grown considerably, swollen by refugees who had fled the Shining Path guerrillas and the military counterinsurgency units. Another bus carried me on the new road that circled some of the towns that had been my familiar landmarks, though it did go through Ilave, which was also much larger. I arrived in Puno late in the afternoon. I had dinner in one of my favorite restaurants and strolled around the town. I thought that I would spend the evening reading in my hotel room and set out to look for Cirilo and Hugo the next morning. I had barely walked through the door of the hotel, however, when I found that three people were waiting for me: Cirilo, the former IMARPE biologist René, and someone whom I did not recognize at all. All of them greeted me effusively.

I was surprised to find how much Cirilo had aged in the twelve years since I had last seen him. I knew that he would be past seventy, but I did not expect him to walk slowly, to tire so early in the evening. However, he spoke with great contentment on that evening and on the other occasions when I saw him during my stay. All eight of his children had graduated from high school, and most of them had studied at the local university. Several of them worked as teachers in village schools. With his lifetime of frugal habits, Cirilo had continued to spend little money even after he no longer had the expenses of his children's education. His savings allowed him to open a small store on a plot of land that he had bought in the town of Acora. We went there one day, driven by one of Cirilo's nephews in a car that he had borrowed from a neighbor. The store was stocked with the simplest items—noodles, soap, candles, soda, and aspirin—but it brought in additional income. I knew that the location close to the main road would assure him of a steady flow of customers. He explained that it also made it easy for him and his wife to see other people from Socca and to travel there to assist his children, who now carry out the bulk of the work on his fields, at the time of planting and harvest.

We chatted for a bit and then continued out together to Socca. I saw Cirilo's house, which had recently been painted. I was glad that I had brought some gifts with me, because his relatives had made me a vest of homespun cloth. His wife had prepared some of my favorite foods— carachi soup and *wathiya*, a particular kind of potato baked in an earth oven. A number of his relatives had come to greet me. I was most surprised by Cirilo's youngest son, Osvaldo, whom I remembered as a slim boy barely in his teens. He was now married and had a son of his own, a toddler named Felix, with long, unruly hair. I realized how carefully this visit to Socca had been orchestrated only when I received the invitation to cut Felix's hair; this act would make me a godfather of the boy, a compadre of Osvaldo and his wife, Alejandrina, and a kinsman of sorts to the extended family.

Cirilo's relatives had evidently anticipated a positive response to the request. They had a pair of scissors, and a bowl had been prepared to receive the shorn locks: it contained three tiny round *chuño*, dried potatoes, on top of which was a layer of barley and quinoa grains, which in turn were covered with multicolored confetti. The scissors proved to be dull, so it took some effort for me to cut the hair. The baby cried and wriggled a bit but, to my relief, did not burst out in loud shrieks. When I had cut off half his hair, Cirilo and his relatives asked me quite formally for permission to take turns. Cirilo's wife slipped a coin under the *chuño*, and I also placed some money there. With the haircutting concluded, we toasted one another.

Cirilo, my new compadres, and several other relatives walked to the top of the ridge that forms the spine of Socca. Cirilo pointed out once again the spot he had showed me several times before, the location of the house from which his grandfather had set off to join others in a commission that traveled to Lima. He told me the story once again: the commission had petitioned the Ministry of Education for a schoolhouse in Socca; they were physically beaten by officials from Puno, who thought that Indians should remain illiterate; they continued to Lima and were ultimately successful.

We saw a few fishing boats that were setting out in the late afternoon. The low sun made their sails gleam a brilliant white against the deep blue of the water. Cirilo's uncle Francisco was still living, but he no longer fished; one of his sons had taken his place. Cirilo mentioned that carachi had become scarce, but that silverside were more abundant than ever. I told him that I had heard the same in the villages and markets I had visited in Copacabana. Finally we stood silent for some long moments, and then returned to Cirilo's house. I had made plans to see Cirilo, his son and daughter-in-law, and my new godson in Puno, but I would not travel out to Socca again. I assured the relatives from whom I was taking my leave that I would continue writing when I returned to the United States, and that I would return before another interval of twelve years had passed. I have complied with the first part of the promise, and I fully in-tend to carry through with the second.

On that first evening in Puno, I also made plans with the IMARPE biologist who had come to see me, René Alfaro. He and his wife, Charo, also a biologist, had begun to work at IMARPE toward the end of the catch surveys. They were younger than the other researchers and had more recent scientific training. René had grown up in the neighboring highland department of Cuzco and liked Puno fairly well, but Charo, who is from Lima, found Puno to be cold, isolated, and dull. She had wanted to return to Lima, but, as René explained to me when he came to my hotel room, they had decided to stay. In the course of a long lunch and afternoon visit later that week at their apartment, I heard from them that it was partly Charo who had changed, partly Puno. When the first of the modern apartment blocks was going up a kilometer or so south of town, they put their names in the lottery to have the chance to acquire an apartment there. They were fortunate, they said, and also forward look-ing. The first building was undersubscribed, since few people in Puno would consider living out on the edge of town in an apartment rather than in a house in town. As we sat drinking coffee after lunch, they ges-tured around the living room. The parquet floors, the modern closets, and the abundant electrical outlets were all like Lima, they said. There was heavy competition to buy apartments in the newer blocks in the development.

René's work life also represented a new period in Puno. He had re-mained at IMARPE for a few years, though Charo had left when their two children were born. To make up for the loss of her salary, René took several other jobs as well. He taught at the local university and con-ducted some research for development agencies and nongovernmental organizations. When IMARPE closed, he was able to draw on these sup-plementary jobs to build a new career as a kind of environmental con-sultant. He joined a board that drew up plans for the expansion of Puno's urban water supply and sewage treatment facilities. With some asso-ciates, he hoped to get funding for sustainable development projects around the Bahía de Puno.

We traded news of the other people we knew in common. I told him about Dominique and my biologist colleagues in the United States. He had remained in touch with the other people who had worked at IMARPE. Eufracio, the former director of the laboratory, had taken early retirement and settled back in his hometown in the central highlands. Hugo had received a small settlement when the laboratory closed and was transferred to a lower-level position at an IMARPE facility in the town of Ilo, on the southern coast of Peru. He had difficulties making ends meet in this area, with its higher cost of living, especially since his salary had been reduced. He was looking, with little success, for consulting positions with fishing firms.

The others had remained in Puno. Hilda, the woman who had coded the catch survey data, had finally left her husband, Victoriano. Her secretarial and computer skills were in demand. She had a position of some responsibility in the office that handled the medical records of the regional hospital. It was not easy for her to raise two teenaged children as a single mother, René told me, as Charo nodded in agreement, but the hospital paid her a good salary, and her children were doing well in school. She did not regret leaving the jealous man who had beaten her. Somehow I was not surprised to hear this revelation. I recalled how possessive Victoriano had always been, how reticent and almost ashamed Hilda had seemed in his presence.

We continued through the list of the other scientists and employees at IMARPE, and then I asked René about the fishermen. He had spoken with a mutual acquaintance about Pedro Castillo, the fisherman whom I had visited several times in his village of Piata, out toward Huancané. His life has followed a course similar to Cirilo's, though his investment has been in a truck, rather than a store, and he has remained in his village of Piata, right on the lake, rather than moving to a town. Though not as old as Cirilo, he, too, sounded less vigorous than when I had stayed with him during the period of my main fieldwork. With some frequency his children drive the truck, as it carries passengers, potatoes, fish, and many other goods back and forth from Piata and the neighboring villages to Juliaca. Like Cirilo, he continues to work the fields.

Though I had not recognized the third visitor to my hotel room, I knew that it would be a severe breach of etiquette to admit that I had forgotten his name. I simply told him how good it was of him to come, how glad I was to see him, how fortunate I had been to spend time with him when I had lived in Puno. As I hoped, my nods brought forth from him enough anecdotes for me to recall his name, and, at the same instant, his mailing address: the number for his post office box was a single digit, since his family, one of the most established in Puno, had been among the first to acquire one, many decades ago. Cristósomo Valenzuela had been working at the local branch of the national weather bureau when the biologists from my university and I were most active in fieldwork, in the 1970s and 1980s. He was now on an extended leave at a new, large international program, the Special Lake Titicaca Project (Proyecto Especial Lago Titicaca, or PELT). It was through Cristósomo and his associates at PELT that I was able to trace other paths, not of individuals, but of the lake itself, and of the reeds and the fish.

As I discovered from his explanations and from visits to the offices that PELT had rented, down near the dock and navy base, the program had vast aims indeed: to map out geographical features—soil types, rainfall, roads, vulnerability to landslides, land use, and so on—for the entire altiplano, not merely for Lake Titicaca and the watersheds of the rivers that flow into it, but also for the Río Desaguadero; Lake Poopó, into which it flows; and the salt flats at the lowest, southern end of the basin. The planners argued that this mapping would allow a more rational pattern of resource use. They would divide the entire altiplano into macrozones, which would then be subdivided into microzones, each of which would have its own set of projects, ranked by priority, according to the criteria of efficiency and sustainability. They had some notion of what sorts of projects they might sponsor. For the agricultural sector, they particularly liked a kind of raised field known as *waru-waru*, which had been used extensively in the altiplano in pre-Columbian times, studied by archaeologists more recently, and reintroduced with mixed success in low-lying areas close to the lake: village households worked together to build systems of long, low mounds, which drained wet soils, improved soil fertility, and reduced frost damage to crops.

The planners also were certain that they wanted to improve livestock raising and fishing, though they lacked proposals as concrete as the *waru-*

waru. Did I have any advice, the head of the mapping program asked me, as a professor from the United States? I was taken aback. I could not find words to address what seemed to me the most evident gap: the top-down approach lacked any kind of local participation and involvement. I thought of telling about the history of floating cages and village hatcheries, of the design of the Titicaca National Reserve, but I did not want to reproach them. I promised to send them the articles that I had written in Spanish, and hoped that they might read them and draw some conclusions on their own. Finally, I suggested that they include in their numerous maps one that showed the line that separated Quechua- and Aymara-speaking villages. If they wanted to organize local people into meetings, it would be easier if they could all speak the same native language. This point did not seem to strike them as very important, though they did accept the addresses that I gave them to obtain the information needed for such a map.

Thanks to Cristósomo's introduction to the PELT staff, I was able to borrow and copy a number of reports. I was grateful for these and others in subsequent years, which proved important in writing several chapters of this book. They allowed me to trace the path that the fisheries had taken. The PELT reports confirmed the continuation of the pattern that had developed in the late 1960s and early 1970s with the collapse of the trout canneries. The fishing continued to be carried out by individual households, operating in small wooden boats with nylon gill nets. A new census of fishermen showed that the number had increased slightly to a total of 3,826, continuing the slow growth rate of earlier decades. The catch estimates were less precise and less secure, but they suggest a total catch in the range of six thousand to nine thousand metric tons per year. It is difficult to assess whether the total catch is greater or less than the roughly eight thousand metric tons that IMARPE, Dominique, and I had calculated in 1980. However, these figures do suggest that the fishermen continue to earn a livelihood, and that the catch remains well below any threshold of overexploitation. An echo-sounding study in the mid-1980s estimated a total biomass of ninety-one thousand metric tons in the open water of the lake (this technique does not work well in the reedbeds), an increase from the 1979 estimate of eighty-three thousand.

The one change was in the mix of species. The PELT reports confirmed what I had seen around Copacabana and what Cirilo had told me, that silverside were increasingly abundant and the carachi were less common. The studies suggested that carachi had begun to decline in the late 1980s. They did not indicate whether this change was due to changing physical and chemical conditions in the lake, to biological factors such as interactions among the species, or to the consequences of the activities of the fishermen. Nor did they mention that any of the native species had joined the umantu and become extinct. The catfish, the boga, and the ispi were scarce, but they were still found in numerous locations around the lake. The reports did not mention other rare *Orestias* species that the fishermen do not catch. However, it seems unlikely that these species would have become extinct, because they face less pressure from fishermen than the larger, more valuable species such as catfish, boga, and carachi.

The PELT reports made much of the pollution in the lake, though this problem seems to be localized to the area of ten square kilometers nearest to the point where untreated sewage from the city of Puno discharges into the Bahía de Puno. The pollution has led to dense growth of lakeweed in the formerly clear waters in this area. There has also been some decline in the portion of the reedbeds in the Bahía de Puno closest to the city, perhaps 1 or 2 percent of the total area. The rest of these beds seem to have maintained their densities, as have the other reeds at river deltas and other shore areas around the lake. René and the other biologists with whom I spoke reported that they continue to find birds in the reedbeds, including the one endemic species, the flightless short-winged grebe. It is understandable that they have not counted nests or made other estimates of the size of the bird populations, given the opposition of the local villagers to government intrusion in the reedbeds and the low budgets of the agencies that manage the Titicaca reserve.

It was not from PELT, though, that I heard of other paths that the lake might take. The biologist who headed the reserve and a local anthropologist friend, now a teacher at the university in Puno, mentioned a threat to which René had first alerted me a few days earlier. The national government had granted a Russian consortium the rights to drill exploratory wells for petroleum in the Lago Grande, close to the Capachica Peninsula. The consortium had hired guards to prevent villagers and others from entering the area where they were drilling, but rumors still circulated about severe pollution around the wells.

Several months after I left the altiplano, I received ten photographs taken by an employee of an international aid organization who had entered the concession on some pretext. I sent these photographs to Project Underground, a nongovernmental organization that supports indigenous groups whose lands are threatened by mining and oil firms. They agreed that the situation seemed threatening, though the photographs showed only localized pollution. By 1997 this threat had abated, at least temporarily. The Russian consortium had not followed up its exploratory drilling with an application for a permit for commercial extraction. However, the Peruvian government still lists these oil fields as available for future exploration and extraction.

While in Puno, I heard of a second threat, the Southern Peru Copper Corporation's desire for more water to produce and process ore on the arid Pacific side of the western cordillera. The corporation already had taken water from the nearby rivers and begun to tap a few lakes high up on the divide between the Pacific drainages and the altiplano. A number of rumors had circulated around Puno that the corporation was planning to dig a tunnel under the western cordillera that would divert water from the Río Huenque out of the altiplano and down the western slope to its smelter. The Río Huenque is one of the two major tributaries of the Río Ilave, the river that is second only to the Río Huancané in the volume of water that it brings to the lake. If the inflow into the lake were reduced, the lake itself would contract. Its level would drop, and it would lose area especially in the shallow basins of the Bahía de Puno and the Lago Pequeño. The consequences, though difficult to state precisely, could be severe. The reedbeds would shrink, since there would be smaller areas covered by water at the depths that totora requires. Because of this shift and other changes, the fish populations might be reduced, especially the carachi, ispi, and boga, the native species that require beds of totora and lakeweed for spawning. There is a significant risk that some of the rarer native species would become extinct. There might well be other negative consequences, such as lower agricultural yields if soil moisture declined.

This issue might prove to be a larger threat than the petroleum exploration, and it might also engender stronger opposition. Indigenous rights and environmental organizations have discussed a number of international water issues in South America. Several groups of Aymara activists have challenged transfers of water from the altiplano to the Pacific Coast in Chile. Moreover, the Southern Peru Copper Corporation is open to considerable public scrutiny, since its shares are traded on the New York Stock Exchange. Although much of the Río Huenque drainage is in remote grasslands high in the western cordillera, its large size means that it cannot be policed stringently. Unlike the Russian consortium, which was able to keep its operations out of sight, the Southern Peru Copper Corporation would not be able to conceal any dams and tunnels that it might build.

The staff of Project Underground gave me several names at a Peruvian nongovernmental organization that had sued the Southern Peru Copper Corporation over the air and water pollution it had caused near its smelters. They also mentioned several other organizations that address environmental and human rights issues in Latin America. These links, as well as my own ties to researchers and activists in southern Peru, have contributed to the formation of a network of individuals and organizations who discuss the transfer of water from the Río Huenque. Members of this network monitor and publicize the activities of the mining company and place water issues on the agendas of international agencies.

The growth of this opposition keeps me from falling into severe pessimism. I also draw some hope from the fact that other threats to the lake and to the villagers have abated—not just the petroleum exploration but an even greater peril from a path that many had spoken of, a path that was once metaphorical and soon became all too tangible: the Shining Path. From the United States I had followed this political force anxiously in the 1980s and early 1990s. Newspapers presented images of a country on the edge of chaos, as masked figures, members of the Shining Path, emerged in the central highlands and spread to other areas: Lima, cast into darkness as the Shining Path blew up power lines; highways, where passengers on buses, detained at unexpected blockades, were shot point blank; villages, the residents rounded up in small plazas to be forced to execute those who were deemed to be enemies of the people. The silence about such events in the letters that I received from Puno troubled rather than assured me. I assumed that the absence of any reference to the violent times indicated a fear that mail might be intercepted, and that reprisals might follow any reference deemed unfavorable by one side or the other.

It is difficult to characterize the Shining Path, the Sendero Luminoso, as it is known in Spanish. (A few militants proposed a name in Quechua, *ch'aska ñan*, which literally means "morning-star path." This phrase never caught on in village circles, around Lake Titicaca at least.) Though some people have found affinities between the Shining Path and Pol Pot's regime in Cambodia, there are no exact counterparts to it, and it is not immediately evident into which category of movement to place it. Some have called it a guerrilla movement, others a terrorist movement, but perhaps the most apt title is the phrase "extreme vanguardist party," which Deborah Poole and Gerardo Rénique use in their book *Peru: Time of Fear.* It was a party that sprang from one fraction of the highly divided Peruvian left of the late 1970s. It was vanguardist because a small cohort of adherents pressed for an immediate and violent revolution. It was extreme in many senses: extreme in its ideology of destroying the established order, extreme in the organization of its cells and the indoctrination of its members, and above all extreme in its use of violence as the only agent to purify a corrupt nation.

The reaction of the government was also extreme in its ideology and violence, in its disregard for democratic procedures and human rights. A brutal civil war ensued between the Shining Path and the unconstrained military counterinsurgency, brought to an end by the capture of key Shining Path leaders in 1992 and by the consolidation soon after of Alberto Fujimori's regime, characterized as "presidentialist" for its centralization and lack of democratic participation in another important book, Steve Stern's *Shining and Other Paths.* Along with other recent works, these books trace the complex history of the Shining Path to the economic stagnation in Peru in the 1980s, the failure of agrarian reform and other programs of the military government that had been in power from 1968 to 1980, the fragmentation of the left, and the widespread belief that Peru was a country whose backwardness was so extreme that it could be over-come only by violence. They examine as well the failure of what Stern calls "third paths," the participatory democratic alternatives to both the Shining Path and the military repression.

When I returned to Puno in 1995, I heard stories of the Shining Path. Many people told me of the internal refugees who had come to the city from the war-torn provinces of Melgar and Azángaro, to the north of the lake. One of Cirilo's daughters, who had worked as a schoolteacher in a small town in Melgar more than a hundred kilometers away, had fled when the Shining Path came near. She escaped unharmed, but colleagues of hers were executed. When working for the Ministry of Fisheries, René had driven to a smaller lake, Arapa, in Azángaro, for what he thought would be a meeting with a few village leaders. It turned into an ominous assembly with hundreds of villagers, their challenges to him containing menacing Shining Path slogans. It was only his fluent Quechua, he told me, that allowed him to tell a few jokes and defuse the tension enough that the crowd let his vehicle depart. Nonetheless, he received death threats after he returned to Puno, and his office abandoned all efforts to work at Arapa.

Studies of the Shining Path have traced in detail the unevenness of its penetration. It established control of certain regions of Peru, and it was unable even to enter others. This unevenness was particularly striking in the department of Puno. The Shining Path operated actively in some high-elevation grassland zones, such as Melgar and Azángaro, but made only minimal incursions in the lakeshore area. Many factors contributed to this difference. The more rugged topography of the grassland zones facilitated the movement of Shining Path units. The government could control the lakeshore area more easily because of the presence of larger towns and of military posts close to the border with Bolivia. The patterns of landholding also had an important influence. In previous decades, grassland zones had contained large, privately owned haciendas that raised livestock. The failure of agrarian reform programs in the 1970s to address issues of poverty and inequality in these provinces created po-litical tensions that the Shining Path exploited. By contrast, the lakeshore area was almost exclusively in the hands of villagers. Their established habits of keeping a watch on the borders of their lands may have contributed to the lack of Shining Path incursions in this region—and to the fact that they suffered less than villagers in many other parts of Peru during the civil war. As some observers have noted, the strengthening of village institutions of local control in several highland departments is one of the very few positive outcomes of the civil war.

The Shining Path, the paths of the lake and the fisheries, the paths of individuals like Cirilo, René, and Hilda: these are all specific and independent. Is it possible for me to unify them into a single path, much as a novelist might bring together the trajectories of different characters into a single coherent narrative line? Perhaps, since anthropologists are supposed to generalize from particular cases, it might be more appropriate for me to show that these many paths form an instance of some more general kind of path. Such a categorization might clarify the unfolding relations among people in the altiplano and between these people and their natural and cultural landscapes. It would show that the stories in this book could be of interest not only to satisfy a momentary curiosity about a remote and unique corner of the world, but also to offer insights that would bear on many people in many places.

Of the more general sorts of paths that social scientists discuss, two have come up many times as I have spoken with colleagues about the lakeshore villages. The first is the narrative of conquest. This path tells the story of indigenous peoples in their struggles for autonomy. It does not wind gently across its terrain, but shifts course sharply. It is punctuated by abrupt events of invasion and rebellion. This path, I might add, is one that has not been recognized as important until recently, because standard approaches to Latin American history have directed attention elsewhere. For many years it has been widely accepted that the history of Latin America, with the partial exception of Brazil, can be divided into three phases: the pre-Columbian times, when the native peoples lived in autonomous societies; the colonial period, when the region formed part of the areas ruled by the Christian monarchs of Spain and Portugal; and the republican period, after these former colonies became independent nations. This version of history contains sharp transitions. The decades between Columbus's landfall in 1492 in the Caribbean and such dates of

conquest as 1524 for the Aztecs and 1532 for the Incas mark the break between the first and the second phases. Even if one acknowledges that it
took additional time before the institutions of colonial rule began to operate fully, this break—the time of conquest—is still one of decades. The
shift from colony to republic occurred even more quickly, in not much
more than a decade in the first quarter of the nineteenth century.

In this view, then, conquest was confined to the gap between the first
and second periods. It marked the conversion of autonomous peoples
into subject castes. For many years, historians have viewed this conversion, for all its tragic nature, as brief, thorough, and irreversible. However, this understanding recently has changed greatly. Historians have
reexamined large-scale indigenous uprisings and rebellions and smaller
revolts, and have also described more localized, yet effective, forms of resistance in many everyday activities. Anthropologists, turning their attention to the pasts of the people with whom they conduct fieldwork,
have also found that the period of conquest did not sever all strands in
the history of native societies. Above all, indigenous peoples themselves
have claimed places in society, in politics, and in history that challenge
the view of the conquest as definitive. Even a few decades ago, it would
have been difficult to imagine major public recognition of Indians from
Latin America—that one of them would receive the Nobel Peace Prize,
as occurred in 1992 when this honor went to Rigoberta Menchú, a Maya
activist from Guatemala, or that one of them would appear in the inau-
guration of a new government, as occurred in 1993 in Bolivia, when the
newly elected vice president's wife attended the swearing in, dressed in
the indigenous round-topped hat and full skirts. Nor did many people
foresee the vast mobilization in 1992 in Ecuador, in which indigenous
peoples from every region of the country marched on the capital city of
Quito. Large delegations came from the Andean highlands and Amazonian lowlands, and representatives of the smaller groups on the Pacific
Coast joined in as well, all demanding recognition of their cultural and
political rights. The conquest, once seen as having been completed centuries ago, now appeared as unresolved, as ongoing; it has been not
merely challenged but even at times turned back.

Such a path of conquest, with its themes of invasion, subjugation, and the struggle for indigenous autonomy, could serve to conjoin many elements in the history of the lakeshore villages, of these people who have retained their languages and much more. They have kept their distinctive ways of understanding their world, as shown in the measurement of totora, the classification of winds, and the definition of work. They continue to control much of this world: it is examples such as the reedbeds and fishing grounds of Lake Titicaca that indigenous activists in the United States had in mind when they developed the slogan "Native Lands in Native Hands."

A recent book bears the provocative title *The Second Conquest of Latin America*. It discusses not the conquest of the sixteenth century that opened the colonial period, but another one that began in the nineteenth century after independence. At that time, Europe and North America did not generally turn to Latin America for colonies to rule directly, but rather for sources of raw materials to supply their growing industries. The editors, Steven Topik and Allan Wells, focus on coffee cultivation in highland Mexico and Guatemala, the production of henequen (a raw material for twine and rope) in Yucatan, and petroleum extraction on the Gulf Coast of Mexico—all areas where native peoples, who had maintained some autonomy until that time, were displaced from their lands.

Along such lines, it might be possible to speak of a third conquest, one that began in the late twentieth century and has continued into the twenty-first. Native peoples lose their lands through frontier colonization and mineral exploration in tropical forests, through the conversion of their fields and pastures to arid wastes by the diversion of water, through the building of roads and dams in remote canyons. The waters of Lake Titicaca might be another site of this third conquest. The reedbeds and fishing grounds offered cover to the rebel Urus who avoided Christianization for much of the seventeenth century, and they have eluded state control to the present. When Hilaria Quispe described the police who had confiscated the eggs she had gathered in the reedbeds near Huata, she alluded to a conquest path when she raised the image of invasion: "They take the eggs away from us. What are we going to feed our children with?" When she continued, "We are making sure we have our poles with us," she suggested another element of this path, the image of violent resistance.

Despite such instances, the notion that the theme of conquest could provide narrative unity to these diverse stories founders on the fact that the villagers tolerate and, on occasion, even embrace the presence of their purported conquerors, the state. The fishing villages avoided the navy and drove off CENFOR, but they accepted Eufracio, Hugo, and other IMARPE staff. IMARPE represented an ally against other state agencies that might tax them or impose certain restrictions—and as the fishermen from Huarisani mentioned in the training course for the catch survey, they hoped that IMARPE could support them in their conflicts with neighboring villages, as well. The census of fishermen and the catch surveys placed the villages in the archives of state agencies. This record, in turn, granted the villages a kind of permanence that could lead to concrete returns in the form of schools, clinics, and other programs, and to the more diffuse but equally important boon of recognition, of remaining unforgotten. Villagers raise flags to announce assemblies, even when they are planning to oppose government actions, not merely because the flags are a convenient and visible form of notification (the assembly dates have usually been arranged well in advance) or because their presence might deflect any interference from the police (they would be unlikely to intrude on such meetings). These flags display the villagers' understanding that their right to gather and to manage their affairs owes much to their position as Peruvians. Flying over village squares, the flags lend solemnity and legitimacy to the assemblies because they are identical to the ones that fly over the squares in Puno and Lima. It is such support that the villagers seek, as avidly as they seek autonomy. This notion of incorporation might even reach to so commonplace an event as Dora's question about whether the telephone works in Aymara. In asking this, she sought new ways of continuing her ties with her relatives. She did not propose that she and the aunt with whom she wished to speak withdraw into a separate, independent Indian world, but rather that they use the national communications network to continue the conversations they had begun, speaking face-to-face, in the village.

Since the path of conquest fits Lake Titicaca poorly, a second metaphorical, or analytical, path may be considered, that of development. It rests on the idea that nations undertake what one leading economist has called "journeys toward progress." Their historical movements lead them down a well-established path toward expansion and improvement. This notion is usually linked to economic well-being, a variable that has the advantage of being quantifiable. It is measured in monetary terms, most often the gross national product per capita, at times accompanied by other, secondary economic measures such as the equality of the distribution of income. As a measurable entity, this concept of development allows comparisons to be made between earlier and later phases of one country's history and between countries that are developed and ones that are termed underdeveloped, less developed, developing, or emerging. It permits debate over the conditions that facilitate improvement according to these measures. (I might add that the notion of development is linked to a view of the villagers as peasants, much as the notion of conquest emphasizes their position as Indians.)

Those who study the history of the idea of development find its roots in several trends in the eighteenth century—a general optimism about progress, a secularization of human history, the beginnings of the modern discipline of economics. They note that the notion of progress was used to justify the expansion of European and North American empires around the globe in the nineteenth century. The major unfolding of development has taken place since World War II. The idea of development provided a useful tool to organize discussions within the world of nations created by decolonization and the expansion of the United Nations, a stronger international presence than its timid predecessor, the League of Nations. At times the notion of development seems as if it has left the realm of theory and entered the world of common sense, as the most reasonable way to evaluate the success or failure of governments in meeting the needs of citizens. As persuasive as it is pervasive, it might be seen as the mortar that holds together the bricks that compose the edifices in which political discussion takes place—or as the oxygen breathed by the delegates who attend meetings in these buildings. Some new measure of development is proposed every time critics complain that the focus on economics and quantification excludes some fundamental dimension of human well-being. Quality-of-life measures have been constructed that include such indices as life expectancy, infant mortality, and literacy. When many environmentalists argued that economic growth was an underlying cause of major ecological problems such as global warming and the loss of biodiversity, the notion of sustainable development emerged. This resilience frustrates critics of development in general, who note that the concept of development closes off certain discussions even as it opens others. It tends to direct attention away from issues that are more difficult to measure, such as justice and human rights.

The concept of development exercises an astonishing power over the minds of people around the globe. It is worth pausing a moment to consider the case of Gapun, a small village in lowland Papua New Guinea, close to the coast, studied by the anthropologist Don Kulick. The inhabitants of Gapun maintain many elements of a centuries-old subsistence economy based on local resources. Their main food staple is the sago palm, and they obtain a good deal of meat by hunting in nearby forests. Despite the continuities of these traditions, the villagers had a tumultuous history in the twentieth century. They faced the advent of missionaries and Australian colonial rule in the 1920s and began to work as indentured laborers on copra plantations in the 1930s. Japanese and Australian armies passed through their lands during World War II. Cargo cults and the acceptance of Christianity in the late 1940s and early 1950s altered their religion. They began to cultivate rice for markets soon after, and entered coffee production in the 1960s. They have added other crops in recent years and sell carvings in the international trade in ethnic artifacts. However, they use money for customary ends, especially sponsoring the feasts that accompany funerals and the resolution of disputes. Accompanying these shifts has been a change in language. All the villagers know Tok Pisin, a pidgin vernacular used widely in Papua New Guinea. Most adults and adolescents know the local language, and the elderly often speak one or more other indigenous languages as well. The youngest children know only Tok Pisin.

Among these people, a key term in Tok Pisin is *kamap*, derived from the English "come up." Kulick shows its many meanings. The first is individual or human development: "Children are said to *kamap*, beginning as ego-centered creatures who *nogat save* (don't have knowledge) and developing into men and women, who, in rhetoric if not in fact, are concerned with each other and with the common good." The second has "connotations of economic development." Kulick notes that a village near Gapun whose inhabitants own many outboard motors and corrugated iron roofs has *kamap* in comparison to other villages in which these items are scarcer. He continues, "The village concept of *kamap* signifies a transformation towards the ways and existence of those whom the villagers call *ol kantri* ('countries,' i.e., the inhabitants of every other known country in the world except Papua New Guinea)."

Villagers describe how white men and women (*ol masta na misis*) live with many goods such as cars, canned food, and houses with bathrooms, and how they fight less among themselves. They discuss the relative effectiveness of different ways to *kamap* more rapidly and more thoroughly. Some argue that religion will bring a kind of magical transformation—a belief that Kulick sees as a reformulation of earlier cargo cults. Others favor hard work in agriculture or an expansion of the local schools.

Like the English word *development*, then, *kamap* refers to a broad range of phenomena. It allows the villagers to compare different periods in their history and to compare their nation with other nations. It can be used to justify different programs. In short, the villagers of Gapun use the path of development as a concept to organize their stories. If it serves so well in that setting, could it be adopted by the villagers around Lake Titicaca as well?

At first blush, the story of the fisheries would seem to be a classic case of economic development. The total catch has increased, slowly but steadily, as the result of the simplest of economic causes—improvements in infrastructure such as roads and technological innovation in the form of wooden boats, nylon gill nets, and some outboard motors. The gradual increase in income in Peru and in the altiplano has supported the expansion of the market for fish. The fishermen have made investments and earned higher incomes. One can even see an increase in the quality and price of fish. The proportion of fish that is dried has declined as the marketing systems have improved, allowing more fish to be sold fresh. (The *bolsas* that Dominique and I inadvertently helped spread around the lake are examples of a technology that has favored this switch.) This change is similar to the one that can be seen in the United States, Europe, and elsewhere, where consumers have shifted from canned to frozen to fresh vegetables.

In similar terms, the totora harvest has undergone development as well. In earlier decades it was harvested less intensively, principally as dry yellow totora, to be used in low-cost, labor-intensive craft production. Increasing quantities of fresh green totora are now harvested and used as cattle fodder. The integration of the lakeshore villages into a regional cattle-producing economy is a sign of economic expansion and rising incomes. The shift from roofs thatched with totora to ones covered with metal sheets is similar to the shift from craft to industrial items around the world.

This notion of development fits in with Dominique's account of TURFs. He was aware that the overexploitation of resources can be a negative side effect of economic development. It therefore becomes a priority in development policy to find a way to meld the biological aspects of resource use with the economic dimensions—the synthesis that gave rise to bioeconomic models. The unusual nature of TURFs lies in the fact that they represent a kind of sustainable resource use that emerges not from direct state intervention with quotas or closed seasons, nor from economic incentives such as landing taxes or auction of licenses, but rather through local control.

Has this language of development entered ordinary conversation in lakeshore villages, as it has in Papua New Guinea and many other parts of the world? There certainly are a number of instances in which the lakeshore villages talk of a steady improvement in material conditions that has come from the expansion of the fisheries and the totora harvest. Pedro Castillo remembers when, as a boy, he saw the first bicycle that anyone ever rode in his village of Piata—and now he owns a truck. Cirilo tends to focus more on the expansion of public services that are available in Socca, especially the schools, but he, too, speaks of improvement. Other villagers have mentioned changes in living conditions. They often mention that houses have wooden doors, rather than blankets or hide coverings.

Nonetheless, the villagers do not speak of development. They hear the word *desarrollo*, the Spanish term for this concept, in radio news programs and in speeches by political officials and candidates, but they do not use it when they speak Quechua. Nor have they adapted any Quechua term meaning "growth" or "unfolding" to use in its place, as speakers of indigenous languages in other parts of the world have done. (In Zimbabwe, for example, the Shona word *budiriro* refers to "emergence," "coming out," "growth," and "rising." Commonly offered examples are the emergence of the first leaves of crops in a planted field or the swelling of the breasts of an adolescent girl. It is now used to mean "development" in its extended economic and political sense as well.) This absence of any term for *development* in Quechua stems, in part, from the concrete recognition of the failures of local projects carried out in the name of *desarrollo*, such as the stream-based trout farms and the floating cages. It also reflects a general skepticism toward the government. Though villagers seek recognition from the government and welcome certain projects such as schools and clinics, they often doubt its blandishments.

Another factor has prevented the spread of words for *development* into the indigenous languages. Much as the diaries show a specific notion of work at some variance with economic measures, the villagers' accounts of their past show a view different from standard notions of development. Once again, the difference between villagers and economists lies in their reckoning of time. An economic view of work suggests that time is homogeneous, so that one can compare the returns for hours spent in different activities. An economic view of development similarly requires time to be homogeneous, so that the income in one year can be compared with previous years and with the growth projected into the future. Much as the diaries show that there are different kinds of time—a rhythm in each day of sleeping time and mealtime and work time—so too the villagers' accounts show that there are different kinds of years.

When Dominique and I asked fishermen about their decisions to buy boats, a number of them replied that they would make such a purchase in an *allin wata*, a good year. This phrase seems so ordinary, so lacking in any cultural specificity, that it failed at first to register in my mind. On reviewing my notes and other studies of time concepts in the Andes, I saw that this term contrasts with *yarqa wata*, a hunger year, when the crops produce poorly or fail altogether. Agriculture is indeed a risky enterprise

Flooded fields along the Río Ramis in a year of high water. Photograph by
Ben Orlove.

in the altiplano. El Niño–related events that occur a few times a decade
usually bring drought and poor harvests, and La Niña–related events
that are the opposite climatic extreme of El Niño ones can cause flooding. Even if the rains are sufficient, other natural events such as hail and
strong winds can damage the crops. Several factors must work together
for a year to be good, so that there might be a surplus that could be spent
to purchase an item such as a boat. The villagers monitor the natural
world closely for the signs—the appearance of the Pleiades in the night
sky, the patterns of birds' nests, the places where foxes are heard calling—that indicate what kind of year lies ahead. Their involvement in
many rituals is also directed toward assuring the cooperation of supernatural entities.

The villagers' notions of time are not limited to an endless sequence
of good, ordinary, and poor years. Recent studies have shown the complexity of their views of their own past. One key unit of time is the

notion of generations. Villagers speak of double-generations. "In time of our grandparents" is a common phrase. They mention their grand-parents' grandparents, the *tatarabuelos,* or great-great-grandparents, far more frequently than the *bisabuelos* or great-grandparents. These double-generations are important because of the central role of eyewitnesses in describing events. To hear about past events from a grandparent is to re-ceive direct testimony from someone who had seen them—a much more reliable source than hearsay. The great drought of the 1930s and 1940s re-mains vivid in local understanding because of such evidence. In turn, the grandparents' accounts of what they had heard from their own grand-parents provide knowledge of an earlier time—for example, when umantu were abundant in the lake. This notion of generations comes a bit closer to the idea of development, because villagers can compare current conditions to past ones. They note the numerous improvements in mate-rial life, such as the advent of radios, portable record players, and cassette recorders. Rather than discussing the economic factors alone, the vil-lagers often speak of the end of the *abusos,* injustices, that prevented them from building schoolhouses or opening markets in rural areas, and that led them to be subject to the arbitrary whim of police and judges. How-ever, the changes are not all positive. Villagers note also that the fields do not produce crops as abundantly as they once did, that thieves are more numerous and more brazen than they once were, and that people do not live as long as they used to. They often interpose such comments of de-cline in their discussions of improvement.

In addition, the generations do not extend as far back in the past as the homogeneous temporal perspective of development would sug-gest. In the villagers' accounts, the generations before their great-great-grandparents merge into a more mythical time, a sequence of epochs separated by transformations or cataclysms. These are known not from eyewitness accounts, but from often-told legends and from the landscape itself. Scattered throughout the altiplano lie ancient stone towers and other ruins, such as the sunken plazas on the summit of Isla Soto, that are evidence of the first journey of a human at the time when the race of giants was conquered and sent beneath the earth. Mountains, hills, lakes: they too have distinctive forms that record earlier epochs. The summits of the cordilleras and the lower peaks closer to the lake were formed at the time of creation, in the remote past. The winds that these mountains send across the altiplano testify to their continued vigor. The small pond that Dante showed me, high up on the slopes of Ccapia, contains treasures from the time of the Incas, or even earlier. Lake Titicaca itself bears witness to the flood that destroyed the beings of a previous epoch.

In this inevitably, and perhaps excessively, brief summary of the complex subject of temporal consciousness, I have suggested that different units of time—years, generations, epochs—each correspond to different ways of knowing—direct observation, reports of eyewitnesses, a recounting of legends whose veracity is affirmed by visible signs in the landscape. However, I do not want to propose that the villagers have a tightly organized system for reckoning time. It is sufficient to say that these units provide a sense of time very different from the linear, homogeneous time that underlies the concept of development. The notion of epochs challenges development by leaving open the possibility that another cataclysm might bring change in the future.

A noted historian has discussed the recurrence of utopian thinking in Andean Peru. Such thinking may have contributed to the appeal in the altiplano of Protestant missionaries, who proposed an overturn of religious and secular hierarchies and an imminent return of Christ to earth. The sequence of generations and of different kinds of years undercuts development in a different way, by emphasizing cyclical rather than linear time and by pointing to continuities rather than changes within epochs. For the villagers in Gapun, metal roofs and outboard motors are a sign that they have *kamap*. These same objects entered the altiplano around the same time that they came to Papua New Guinea. Lakeshore villagers comment on them and view them as an indication of greater comfort, but they do not take them as unambiguous signs of progress, as elements in a single process of development. People who accept the notion of development believe that in coming years they will have more material goods. In contrast, the villagers hope that they will have enough.

In sum, the economic concept of development, like the narrative of conquest, fails to represent the history of the villagers adequately. Unlike these metaphorical paths, the actual paths, the ones that are literally on the ground, convey this story effectively. The villagers make these paths in tangible ways. At community assemblies, they discuss how repairing or widening a path will make it easier to bring fish and crops and animals to market, how the schoolteachers may be absent less often if their trip back after a weekend away is shortened. They agree to form work parties to carry out the necessary labor—the *trabajo en el camino* that the diaries mention. They show up on time, men with picks and shovels, women with pots and carrying cloths filled with food for the large midday meal. At the assemblies, the villagers also voice their concerns about widening paths. Thieves can enter quickly, steal an animal or a bicycle, and be gone before they are noticed. It is no coincidence that the only villages without dogs are the ones located on the islands in the lake, since no thief would risk traveling by boat. The police travel more readily by car as well, making it easier for them to surprise villagers when they arrive and ask questions about fishing licenses, goods smuggled in from Bolivia, or other uncomfortable topics. Some villages keep watch over their roads as they keep watch over their fields, pastures, reedbeds, and fishing grounds. Government officials who drive unannounced down village paths can be confronted by a hostile crowd, as Eufracio and Hugo learned when they traveled in the IMARPE vehicle to Cohasía. A few villages that are most concerned with excluding outsiders, such as Cachipucara, have organized patrols to control access to their village lands. The first signs of an outsider's approach—dogs running out to bark at a car, a plume of dust on a dry day—might be welcomed by people who await a truck to take them to a weekly market, or who have planned to see a public-health nurse who is scheduled to come to the village. However, these same signs awaken suspicion if no vehicle is expected.

The paths also play an ambivalent role in the realm of memory. They facilitate the process of record keeping. Had it not been for the roads that placed nearly all the lakeshore villages within a day's drive of Puno, it would have been harder for IMARPE staff to travel out to them, and thus to carry out the forms of registration and recording that mattered so much to the fishermen, such as enumeration in the census and their participation in the catch surveys. The paths can bring visitors who can record and remember villages, protecting them against the risk of oblivion. Villagers serve enormous meals to the guests who arrive from outside, not so much from a habitual generosity or as a calculated bribe to seek some immediate return, but in the hope that the abundant food will leave a positive and enduring recollection. However, paths are also places of forgetting. Visitors may depart and not recall the place where they were received warmly, consigning it to the fate of becoming a *pueblo olvidado*, a forgotten town. As numerous songs attest, lovers travel away and then abandon their promises of constancy. When a son or daughter is about to leave the village, parents often fear that they will never see him or her again. The parents' farewells, filled with wails and laments, often take place at the edge of a path that links the village with the wider world.

The path that represents the villages, then, is not a metaphorical path of conquest or of development, but a real path itself. Needed and feared, these paths can allow a measure of prosperity or bring sudden losses. They can create a record of the villages or contribute to their gradual erasure. They evoke the opposed forces in the villagers' lives. For all the tenacity with which villagers hold on to their lands and their self-governance, for all the resilience with which they face new circumstances, they remain vulnerable to powerful forces beyond their control. For all the strength of their links to their past, they recognize the threat of oblivion. It was this ambivalence that struck me with sudden force when I left the altiplano and was beseeched by the villagers not to forget.

And now it is not I who is about to depart, but you, the reader: you are about to depart from the pages of this book. Your stay in the altiplano is coming to an end. You will stop hearing the voices of its inhabitants, who have traveled to you, even if indirectly, through words printed on a page. These voices, these images that you have seen, may remain as memories, if you can respond to the call, even at this remove, not to forget.

How can this not forgetting take place in the lives of readers of books like this one? It might seem that there is hardly any place for these memories at all in our present world, a world that seems to be speeding up in its course toward the future, a world that is increasingly oriented toward novelty. But much as there are many forms of not forgetting—the song to the departing child or lover, the request to the official or traveler who is about to leave—so too different readers may recall these memories at different times. Even in the United States or Europe, you may find yourself in the presence of someone who grew up in a Quechua-speaking village, even if not directly from the shores of Lake Titicaca: a group of poncho-wearing musicians at a park or a subway stop, playing flutes, panpipes, drums, and odd stringed instruments; merchants with braids, the men as well as the women, in stalls at a crafts fair. For you, these memories may lead you to recognize that these musicians and vendors have not arrived from a timeless realm of evocative melodies and distinctive weavings. They have traveled from villages on journeys not unlike the trips of the fishermen to the new fishing grounds—a longer distance by airplane to the United States or Europe than by boat to new areas in the lake, certainly, but still an exploration of new grounds. Your thoughts may linger on the journeys that have been taken by other new immigrants. Without ponchos or braids, with only their labor to sell, rather than their music or crafts, they arrive nonetheless, they are glimpsed through the door of a restaurant kitchen, they appear in a photograph that accompanies a newspaper article about garment factories; they come not from the shores of Lake Titicaca, perhaps, but from some other village world whose richness and fragility you may understand from your memories of the altiplano.

Some readers, on seeing such immigrants, may envision images of planetary environmental crisis: the warning of the rapid loss of biodiversity, the concern for endangered species. One of the Titicaca fish has already joined the dodo and the passenger pigeon in extinction. Stories on television, in newspapers and magazines, often juxtapose a person and an animal, though with differing messages. Is the tall African man standing next to the elephant to be understood as the local tour guide who will protect it or the poacher who will destroy it? Does the barefoot, brown-skinned woman in a nondescript blouse and skirt, who gazes at a tapir at the edge of a clearing, wish to see the forest remain standing, this great source of herbs for healing, or does she want to clear a large tract to grow crops? Will the fur-clad hunter on the ice floe, close to the seal, be the one to kill it or to prevent an oil company from drilling? For you, confronted with these images, the memories of the altiplano may remind you of the length and depth of commitments to local places. They may demonstrate to you the ability of people to live in such places, continuing to speak the language of their grandparents and great-great-grandparents, the language that has come to them from prior epochs; admitting some new words—*boat, net*—and not others—*fisherman, development*—and keeping old words for which there is no substitute: *ch'eqa thaya* for left-wind, *pichu* for chestful, *yarqa wata* for hunger year.

There may be other moments when you will realize that you have not forgotten the lakeshore villagers. I cannot fully anticipate what these occasions might be. We have all taken a path into a new century, a new millennium. We have left behind a formidable century, a century of great hope and great horror, with the depressions and world wars of its first half, the heralded ends of colonialism and communism in its second half, which have not always brought the hoped-for freedom and prosperity. We live in an era when remote corners of the world spring suddenly to our attention: Kosovo, Chechnya, East Timor as I write, though others will replace them in the news. Let us not forget that it has been a formidable century as well even in the distant altiplano, less prone to appear on television screens. Let us not forget the people who have held on firmly to their mountain world throughout the twentieth century and who hold on to it still as they enter the next, drawing a living from the vast lake that lies at its center.

Notes

PREFACE

xi   **Water: the most commonplace of liquids**   I would like to thank David
     Robertson, and indeed the entire Nature and Culture Program at the Uni-
     versity of California at Davis, for their assistance in conceiving and devel-
     oping this chapter and for their encouragement in thinking about the issues
     of place that pervade this book.

xx   **One old man**   Henry David Thoreau, *Walden and Civil Disobedience* (New
     York: The Penguin American Library, 1983 [1854]), 351–52.

xxiv **Its breezes**   Garrison Keillor, *Lake Wobegon Days* (New York: Penguin,
     1995), 2.

xxiv **Prudence, the New England missionary**   Ibid., 28.

xxiv **The lake's fish**   Ibid., 75, 149, 150, 241.

xxiv **This second set of books**   To be sure, some books about lakes do not fit
     neatly into either of these categories. Marilynne Robinson's evocative *House-
     keeping* might be placed in the first category, since the protagonist, Ruth, is
     transformed by the years of her childhood that she spends at a lake in

Idaho, and since the book has a clear narrative that unfolds in time. As in *Hotel du Lac,* a person arrives at a lake in some difficulty, spends time there, and leaves after some deep realizations linked to a boat trip on the lake. Indeed, it might be said that the initial closeness of Ruth to her sister, Lucille, and their later separation can be seen as much in their changing relations to the lake that they visited so often as young orphans, living with relatives, as in their changing ties to their eccentric aunt, Sylvie. Yet this book fits into the second category as well, since the lake—in which the girls' grandfather died in an accident and their mother committed suicide—evokes memory and grief, the weight of history, and the immediacy of the present.

J. M. Coetzee's *Waiting for the Barbarians* is similarly difficult to pigeonhole. The story is told by an official who is posted to a settlement at the edge of civilization, and who lives through a war. A lake separates the areas under government control from the wilder regions, inhabited by nomads, and the official's journeys along the shores of the lake are critical to his changing understandings of these nomads. Like other books in the second category, this one consists of partially linked personal narratives. The lake appears in a different guise in every chapter. In one, the official, confined to a prison, sees a plume of smoke from burning reeds on the lakeshore. His deepening understanding of the profound incompatibilities of the different groups in the region parallels his discovery of different aspects of the lake. This book, although closer to the second category, still has elements of the clear narrative, tight structure, and well-defined transformation of the books in the first. In other words, the two categories that I propose are not firm and fixed.

xxvi **Nor do these books contain myths**   A collection of Andean myths and folktales that includes a number of stories about lakes is Efraín Morote Best, *Aldeas sumergidas: Cultura popular y sociedad en los Andes* (Cuzco: Centro de Estudios Rurales Andinos Bartolomé de las Casas, 1988).

xxvii **Much as the capacities**   Edward Scott Casey, *The Fate of Place: A Philosophical History* (Berkeley and London: University of California Press, 1997), offers a thoughtful examination of the phenomenology of place and movement.

CHAPTER I. NOT FORGETTING

2 **I could reply easily to these questions**   In transcribing Quechua words and phrases, I have improvised an orthography to represent the sounds of that language. I chose the particular system that I use because it seems to me to be more comprehensible than any alternative to readers whose na-

tive language is English. A linguist might render the second Quechua word in the paragraph as *qunqawaychu,* to represent faithfully the understanding that Quechua has only three distinct vowel sounds, though some purists prefer *qunqawayču,* on the grounds that each sound (or, to be precise, each phoneme) should be indicated by a single symbol. In his letters to me, Cirilo writes this word as *cconccahuaychu,* using a double *cc* for the sound that I indicate with a *q,* a kind of *k* sound pronounced at the back of the throat, and borrowing the *hu* from Spanish to indicate the *w* sound. I recognize that many people who speak Quechua have strong feelings about orthography, as they do about many issues of representing Andean life and culture. I apologize to those whom I may offend by my somewhat Anglicized rendering. I hope that the comprehensibility of my system will help in some small measure to convey the richness of the Quechua language to those who have no knowledge of it, and I trust that those who are familiar with it will recognize the words that I have transcribed.

4   **I was surer**   A number of anthropologists have written on the theme of exchange in Andean societies. They suggest that an ongoing series of exchanges can serve to maintain relationships and to keep them current in the memory of the participants. See particularly Olivia Harris, "Labour and Produce in an Ethnic Economy, Northern Potosí, Bolivia," in *Ecology and Exchange in the Andes,* ed. David Lehmann (Cambridge: Cambridge University Press, 1982), 70–96; Sarah Lund Skar, "Appropriating Pawns: Andean Dominance and the Manipulation of Things," *Journal of the Royal Anthropological Institute* 1 (4): 787–803 (1995); Thomas Alan Abercrombie, *Pathways of Memory and Power: Ethnography and History among an Andean People* (Madison: University of Wisconsin Press, 1998); Mary J. Weismantel, *Cholas and Pishtacos: Race, Sex, and Popular Culture in Andean South America* (Chicago and London: University of Chicago Press, 2001).

5   **In one song**   "Escapulario de mi pecho," on the album *Los Preferidos,* performed by the Conjunto Velille de Chumbivilcas, IEMPSA (Industrias Eléctricas y Musicales Peruanas, Sociedad Anónima) no. ELD-2075.

6   **After a couple of hours**   "Maldito amor," on the album *Hermosa Tinta,* performed by the Trio Los Amaru de Tinta, El Virrey Industrias Musicales no. P-6324262.

6   **But the link**   "Lamento," performed by the Conjunto Velille de Chumbivilcas on the album *Cada Vez Mejor,* IEMPSA no. ELD-2188.

7   **The switch from Spanish to Quechua**   Elsewhere I have discussed this switch from Spanish to Quechua in another common genre, jokes: "Surfacings: Thoughts on Memory and the Ethnographer's Self," in *Jews and Other Differences: The New Jewish Cultural Studies,* ed. Jonathan Boyarin and Daniel Boyarin (Minneapolis: University of Minnesota Press, 1997), 1–29.

8   **They are called**   These themes are quite common. For *ingrato,* "Amor ingrato," on the album *Arriba el Folklore,* performed by Los Chankas de Apurimac, IEMPSA no. ELD-2194; for *pretencioso,* "Pretenciosa," lyrics printed in *Cantares serranos* (Lima: Editorial Mercurio, n.d.), 30. This thin collection, which I purchased in a marketplace in the early 1980s, does not have a publication date.

9   **At its end**   Both the Quechua and the Spanish appear in the Spanish edition of the novel (Buenos Aires: Editorial Losada, 1958). The Quechua orthography is Arguedas's. I have taken the English translation from an English-language edition of the novel, *Deep Rivers,* trans. Frances Horning Barraclough (Austin: University of Texas Press, 1978).

12   **Perhaps, I thought**   In her study of migration from a district on the shores of Lake Titicaca to a frontier settlement area in the Amazon, Jane Collins documents the villagers' concern that the migrants will forget their ties to their communities (*Unseasonal Migrations: The Effects of Rural Labor Scarcity in Peru* [Princeton: Princeton University Press, 1988], 185). Studies from other parts of the world have found similar concerns that migrants will forget their families in their home villages; James Ferguson's study of Zambia offers particularly striking instances of this phenomenon (*Expectations of Modernity: Myths and Meanings of Urban Life on the Zambian Copperbelt* [Berkeley: University of California Press, 1999]).

13   **When I entered**   The four books are Walter Sáenz Lizarzaburu, *Racarrumi, breve historia de un pueblo olvidado* (Lima: n.p., 1975); Augusto Chávez-Costa, *El Perú, un pueblo olvidado y sin voz* (Lima: Programa Editorial, 1978); Juan Illahuamán Chipana, *Pueblos olvidados de Andahuaylas* (Lima: n.p., 1978); Pedro Hernán Portilla Salas, *Apurímac, el perfil de un pueblo olvidado del Perú* (Lima: Editorial Colmena, 1985). The quotations are from Illahuamán Chipana, who speaks specifically about the people from the villages and towns of Andahuaylas who live in Lima. The reference to "sons and daughters" *(hijos)* is on p. 81. He mentions that the tie to the homeland is based on memory (*cada corazón . . . nunca olvida el terruño que le vió nacer;* every heart will never forget the homeland of its birth), 59, 61. The villagers return for patron saint festivals not to enjoy the familiar foods or to hear the traditional music but "to celebrate the village saint with devotion" *(para festejar con devoción a la patrona del Pueblo),* 70. They send money for telegraph lines, schools, and health posts as a kind of help *(ayuda)* because their fellow villagers are in need *(necesidad).*

13   **In this simple**   In her innovative works, Brackette Williams shows that national cultures often consist of debates over the relative position of different segments within the history of the nation as a whole. In this process of remembering and forgetting, entire segments of the population, usually

defined by race and ethnicity, can shift their position in the nation as a whole. Williams's writings that have most influenced me are "A Class Act: Anthropology and the Race to Nation across Ethnic Terrain," *Annual Review of Anthropology* 18 (1989): 401–44, and *Stains on My Name, War in My Veins: Guyana and the Politics of Cultural Struggle* (Durham, N.C.: Duke University Press, 1991). She does not, however, contemplate this possibility of utter oblivion and disappearance from the nation altogether.

In the case of the altiplano, this theme of forgetting, concretized in the image of the *pueblo olvidado,* contains an amalgam of regional, class, racial, and ethnic identities. Much as people of a variety of backgrounds held *despedidas* for me, so too Spanish-speaking townspeople and Indian villagers asked me, or an official, not to forget them. I have focused more extensively on the rural indigenous side. It does bear noting, though, that even *despedidas* from wealthy families in the departmental capital of Puno leaned toward a regional and in some sense indigenous side: the food that was served often consisted of regional specialties with local ingredients, such as the *ch'ayru* (stew with freeze-dried potatoes), and regional music such as *huaynos.* This stands in marked contrast to the emphasis that these families in Puno place on national or cosmopolitan culture at other events. Wedding receptions, for example, open with champagne and waltzes, which are followed by more contemporary mixed drinks and rock-influenced dances.

CHAPTER 2. MOUNTAINS

41　**The most recent**　The geological history of the lakes is discussed in A. Lavenu, "Formation and Geological Evolution," in *Lake Titicaca: A Synthesis of Limnological Knowledge,* ed. Claude Dejoux and André Iltis (Dordrecht, Holland: Kluwer Academic Publishers, 1992), 3–15; and Geoffrey O. Seltzer, "Recent Glacial History and Paleoclimate of the Peruvian-Bolivian Andes," *Quaternary Science Reviews* 9 (2–3): 137–52 (1990). A review of lake levels in the late Quaternary can be found in Paul A. Baker et al., "The History of South American Tropical Precipitation for the Past 25,000 Years," *Science* 291 (5504): 640–44 (2001).

41　**The age that is required**　The concept of ancient lakes is discussed in several articles. Of particular importance are A. Gorthner, "What Is an Ancient Lake?" *Advances in Limnology* 44 (5): 285–317 (1994); Koon Martens, "Speciation in Ancient Lakes," *Trends in Ecology and Evolution* 12 (5): 177–82 (1997);.H. Kawanabe, G. W. Coulter, and A. C. Roosevelt, *Ancient Lakes: Their Cultural and Biological Diversity* (Ghent: Kenobi Productions, 1999).

42   **They consist of small hunter-gatherer settlements**   For a discussion of these early settlements, see Alan Kolata, *The Tiwanaku: Portrait of an Andean Civilization* (Cambridge and Oxford: Blackwell, 1993), and Clark S. Erickson, "The Lake Titicaca Basin: A Pre-Columbian Built Landscape," in *Imperfect Balance: Landscape Transformations in the Pre-Columbian Americas,* ed. David L. Lentz (New York: Columbia University Press, 2000), 311–56.

CHAPTER 3. NAMES

45   **There was very little traffic**   Five steamships carried cargo to a few ports, and some larger balsas occasionally carried villagers across bays and straits. The history of the steamers is covered in Brian Fawcett, *Railways of the Andes* (London: George Allen and Unwin, 1963).

47   **They often use resources**   Any simple generalization within the complex field of environmental history is subject to exception. Governments and private firms have regulated resources successfully on many occasions. Nonetheless, much evidence points toward the value of systems of comanagement of resources, in which local populations have a strong voice, and toward the shortsightedness of corporations. For a fuller discussion of these points, see Benjamin Orlove and Stephen Brush, "Anthropology and the Conservation of Biodiversity," *Annual Review of Anthropology* 25 (1996): 329–52.

47   **Before I begin telling the story**   I first presented this discussion of names in 1991 to the Agrarian Studies seminar at Yale University. I would like to thank Jim Scott for inviting me, Angie Haugerud for presenting my paper, and the numerous participants for their thoughtful comments on this material.

48   **Were we to adopt it**   The most sustained comparative effort to examine the importance of gender in fishing economies and societies is Jane Nadel-Klein and Dona Lee Davis, eds., *To Work and to Weep: Women in Fishing Economies,* Memorial University of Newfoundland Institute of Social and Economic Research Social and Economic Papers no. 18 (St. John's, Newfoundland, 1988). The volume examines the gender division of labor in work and subsistence and also considers gender in relation to social status, expressive culture, and development projects. The various authors use a number of terms for "persons-who-fish," both male and female, and do not strive to reach consensus on a single term. Charlene Allison's contribution to this volume is "Women Fishermen in the Pacific Northwest" (pp. 230–60), a study of a group of women who work on, and sometimes own, fishing boats; these women call themselves "fishermen." This complex is-

sue of terminology also surfaces in a study of a Portuguese fishing village, Sally Cooper Cole's *Women of the Praia: Work and Lives in a Portuguese Coastal Community* (Princeton: Princeton University Press, 1991). To refer to men and women who fish, Cole sometimes uses *fisherman* and *fisherwoman*, sometimes the Portuguese terms *pescador* and *pescadeira*. When referring to both, she uses "fisherwomen and men" (p. 5) or "fishermen and women" (pp. 55, 89). She uses the word *pescadores* as it is used in standard Portuguese, at times to refer to both men and women (pp. 44, 53), at times to men only (p. 49).

48   **I sometimes went on**   There is an extensive, rich literature on issues of gender in the Andes. Some of the early works that argue for the existence of a distinctively Andean form of gender complementarity in social, economic, and ritual domains are Billie Jean Isbell, "La otra mitad esencial: Un estudio de complementaridad sexual en los Andes," *Estudios Andinos* 5 (1): 37–56 (1976); Bernd Lambert, "Bilaterality in the Andes," in *Andean Kinship and Marriage,* American Anthropological Association Special Publication no. 7, ed. Ralph Bolton and Enrique Mayer (Washington, D.C., 1977), 1–27; Olivia Harris, "Complementarity and Conflict: An Andean View of Women and Men," in *Sex and Age as Principles of Social Differentiation,* ed. J. S. La Fontaine (London: Academic Press, 1978), 21–40; and Harris, "The Power of Signs: Gender, Culture, and the Wild in the Bolivian Andes," in *Nature, Culture, and Gender,* ed. Carol P. MacCormack and Marilyn Strathern (Cambridge: Cambridge University Press, 1980), 70–94. This view, with an added postcolonial emphasis, also appears in Irene Silverblatt, *Moon, Sun, and Witches: Gender Ideologies and Class in Inca and Colonial Peru* (Princeton: Princeton University Press, 1987).

The emphasis on complementarity was challenged by studies of the economic and political obstacles that highland women face, including Susan Bourque and Kay Warren, *Women of the Andes: Patriarchy and Social Change in Two Peruvian Towns* (Ann Arbor: University of Michigan Press, 1981); Benjamin Orlove, "A Stranger in Her Father's House: Juanita's Suicide," in *Lucha: Latin American Women Coping with Adversity,* ed. Connie Weil (Minneapolis: University of Minnesota Latin American Studies Program, 1988), 161–201; and Florence E. Babb, *Between Field and Cooking Pot: The Political Economy of Marketwomen in Peru* (Austin: University of Texas Press, 1989).

The intertwining of gender with race and class distinctions in the highlands is a central theme in more recent works, such as Mary J. Weismantel, *Food, Gender, and Poverty in the Ecuadorian Andes* (Philadelphia: University of Pennsylvania Press, 1988); Marisol de la Cadena, "'Las mujeres son mas indias': Etnicidad y género en una comunidad del Cusco," *Revista Andina* 9 (1): 7–29 (1991); Lesley Gill, *Precarious Dependencies: Gender, Class, and Do-*

mestic Service in Bolivia (New York: Columbia University Press, 1994); and Silvia Rivera Cusicanqui, ed., *Ser mujer indígena, chola o birlocha en la Bolivia postcolonial de los años 90* (La Paz: Ministerio de Desarrollo Humano, Secretaría Nacional de Asuntos Etnicos, de Género y Generacionales, Subsecretaría de Asuntos de Género, 1996).

Representational and performative dimensions in gender, once again in a context of race and class, are treated in Marisol de la Cadena, "The Political Tensions of Representations and Misrepresentations: Intellectuals and Mestizas in Cuzco (1919–1990)," *Journal of Latin American Anthropology* 2 (1): 112–47 (1996); Deborah Poole, *Vision, Race, and Modernity: A Visual Economy of the Andean Image World* (Princeton: Princeton University Press, 1997); and Mary J. Weismantel, *Cholas and Pishtacos: Race, Sex, and Popular Culture in Andean South America* (Chicago and London: University of Chicago Press, 2001).

48   **On a few occasions**   With audiences willing to pursue the matter further, I suggested that relations of gender, work, income, and power were still more complicated. Though women made up the majority of the fish vendors in markets, there were some men as well, who specialized in the sale of the most expensive fish species. This point also led the discussion to shift from specific details of the case to a consideration of a more general issue, in this instance the relation of male domination to capitalism or the market economy. This conversation, however, did not tend to prove very satisfactory, since there were many consequences of capitalism for the Lake Titicaca region besides the differences between male and female fish vendors, and many other cases that would serve to examine these broad comparative and historical issues.

55   **a "slimy green-faced alien"**   Carol Titelman, ed., *The Art of Star Wars* (New York: Ballantine Books, 1979), 70.

55   **Greedo uses the agentive suffix -*q***   Since a direct transliteration of the alien's words, *"Jaba waninchikuq hamushani t'aytani wañu usqhaq,"* does not make sense, I have rearranged the second word and altered two phonemes to obtain intelligible dialogue. I do not know whether to attribute the confusion in the lines as spoken to an incorrect original script, to errors in my transcription, or to the inadequate Quechua training or ability of the actor who delivered the lines.

55   **The suffix -*q***   I greatly appreciate the generosity of linguistic anthropologist Nancy Hornberger, who has reviewed this material carefully. She points out that there are three closely related, though conceptually distinct, uses of the suffix -*q*. In the fragment of dialogue from *Star Wars*, for example, the first use is as a nominalizer that forms a subordinate clause following a verb of motion and is usually translated in English with the infini-

tive form "to ___"; the second is an agentive nominalizer that marks an action and is usually translated in English with -er. (The third form is a nominalizer that forms a complement to a sensory verb, indicating an action simultaneous to that of a main verb, e.g., *qanta qhorqoqta uyarirqansi*, "She says she heard you snoring," which English translates most often with the gerund form, ending in -*ing*.) Further details about these agentives may be found in Quechua grammars such as Antonio Cusihuamán, *Gramática quechua, Cuzco-Collao* (Lima: Ministerio de Educación, 1976); and Rodolfo Cerrón Palomino, *Lingüística quechua* (Cuzco: Centro de Estudios Rurales Andinos "Bartolomé de Las Casas," 1987).

57   **The key difference**   The use of -*man* in English is inconsistent. Terms such as *fisherman* and *washerwoman* use both -*er* and -*(wo)man*, while *hunter* and *baker* use just -*er*.

57   **The villagers have adopted**   Some propose *amauta* or *yachachiq* for "teacher," but these are rather self-conscious efforts to extirpate Spanish loan-words and are restricted to small, though important, *indigenista* circles.

58   **The adherents of each**   I will not examine these debates closely here, because interested readers can turn to several excellent reviews. In my writings on the Andes over the last two decades, I have shifted from a firmly held, though perhaps not very tightly argued, neo-Marxist position favoring class over ethnicity to a muddier synthesis of the two. My strongest statements of the "class" position date back to the 1970s ("Urban and Rural Artisans in Southern Peru," *International Journal of Comparative Sociology* 15 (3–4): 193–211 [1974]; *Alpacas, Sheep, and Men: The Wool Export Economy and Regional Society in Southern Peru* [New York: Academic Press, 1977]). I would like to believe that more recent pieces show my efforts at synthesis ("The Dead Policemen Speak: Mestizo Accounts of the Killings at Molloccahua, 1931," in *Unruly Order: Violence, Power, and Identity in the Southern High Provinces of Peru*, ed. Deborah A. Poole [Boulder, Colo.: Westview Press, 1994], 63–95; Benjamin Orlove and Ella Schmidt, "Swallowing Their Pride: Indigenous and Industrial Beer in Peru and Bolivia," *Theory and Society* 24 (2): 271–98 [1995]; "Down to Earth: Race and Substance in the Andes," *Bulletin of Latin American Research* 17 (2): 207–22 [1998]).

My trajectory is, at any rate, not unique. To be sure, some books have taken clear positions on the ethnicity side, such as Catherine Allen, *The Hold Life Has: Coca and Cultural Identity in an Andean Community* (Washington, D.C.: Smithsonian Institution Press, 1988), or the class side, such as Gavin Smith, *Livelihood and Resistance: Peasants and the Politics of Land in Peru* (Berkeley: University of California Press, 1989), and Carmen Diana Deere, *Household and Class Relations: Peasants and Landlords in Northern Peru*

(Berkeley: University of California Press, 1990). However, the two positions are not as sharply defined as they once were. An interest in issues of politics and ideology has led some of the more firm "class" theorists to consider culture, and a concern with issues of domination has directed "ethnicity" theorists toward power and the state. Works that link class and ethnicity in the context of resistance to colonial and postcolonial rule include Silvia Rivera Cusicanqui, *Oprimidos pero no vencidos: Luchas del campesinado aymara y qhechwa de Bolivia, 1900–1980* (La Paz: HISBOL, 1984); Alberto Flores Galindo, *Buscando un inca: Identidad y utopia en los Andes* (Lima: Instituto de Apoyo Agrario, 1987); and Steve J. Stern, ed., *Resistance, Rebellion, and Consciousness in the Andean Peasant World, Eighteenth to Twentieth Centuries* (Madison: University of Wisconsin Press, 1987).

The general reawakening of interest in nationalism in the 1980s and 1990s, signaled in books such as Florencia E. Mallon, *Peasant and Nation: The Making of Postcolonial Mexico and Peru* (Berkeley: University of California Press, 1995), has converged with a concern about race, leading to a considerable reconfiguration of the "ethnicity" position, as shown in such works as Andrés Guerrero, *La semántica de la dominación: El concertaje de indios* (Quito: Ediciones Libri Mundi, 1991); Thomas Abercrombie, "To Be Indian, to Be Bolivian: 'Ethnic' and 'National' Discourses of Identity," in *Nation-States and Indians in Latin America,* ed. Greg Urban and Joel Sherzer (Austin: University of Texas Press, 1991), 95–130; Stephen Eisenman and Mary J. Weismantel, "Race in the Andes: Global Movements and Popular Ontologies," *Bulletin of Latin American Research* 17 (2): 121–42; Marisol de la Cadena, *Indigenous Mestizos: The Politics of Race and Culture in Cuzco, 1919–1991* (Durham: Duke University Press, 2000); and Zoila Mendoza, *Shaping Society through Dance: Mestizo Ritual Performance in the Peruvian Andes* (Chicago: University of Chicago Press, 2000). An attention to the performative, rather than the ascriptive, dimension of racial categories, evident to some extent in all these works, is particularly clear in the last two.

As the range of positions has expanded from a simple dichotomy of analyses based on ethnicity or class, there has also been a loosening of the connections between the choice of labels and the choice of models—or, in less formally analytic terms, between the choice of names and the choice of stories. Through the early 1980s or so, to use the term *peasant* was to adopt class models, and to use the word *Indian* and its politer variants was to adopt models of ethnic relations. With growing analytical flexibility, these terms lost some of their dogmatic quality. Despite this expansion within Andean studies, I continue some of my earlier reluctance to use the term *Indian,* though this concern is derived not so much from a Marxist suspicion of ethnicity as false consciousness as from an aversion to the picturesque: The more I gave talks on my research around Lake Titicaca, the less I tended to show slides. The distinctively dressed and dark-skinned villagers in the foreground, the spectacular mountain scenery in the background, and the thatched adobe houses in the middle distance mesmerized a sizable fraction of my listeners, whose attention was diverted from the economic and political matters that I wished to discuss to a conceptualization of the villagers as exotic Indians. It took little more than a few poncho-clad villagers and a llama or two for my listeners to begin to dream that they were looking at a people whose ancient customs had been relatively uncontaminated by the modern world.

60   **The word** *village* **can refer**   For some readers, *village* may suggest a cluster of houses. Though there are such nucleated villages around Lake Titicaca, I note that the houses in many portions of the lakeshore are dispersed among the fields, rather than being concentrated in a single village center.

60   **Whereas** *Indian* **implies a cultural difference**   There is a lengthy literature on Andean Indians in cities. Billie Jean Isbell's major 1978 monograph on a rural highland community discusses migrants to a capital city (*To Defend Ourselves: Ecology and Ritual in an Andean Village* [Austin: University of Texas Press, 1978]), as does Lesley Gill's *Precarious Dependencies,* mentioned previously. Other works on this topic include Xavier Albó, *Khitïpxtansa? quienes somos?: Identidad localista, étnica y clasista en los aymaras de hoy* (La Paz: CIPCA, 1979); Xavier Albó, Thomas Greaves, and Godofredo Sandoval, *Chukiyawu: La cara aymara de La Paz* (La Paz: CIPCA, 1987); José Matos Mar, *Las barriadas de Lima, 1957* (Lima: Instituto de Estudios Peruanos, 1977), and *Desborde popular y crisis del estado: El nuevo rostro del Perú en la década de 1980* (Lima: Instituto de Estudios Peruanos, 1984); Frank Salomon, "Killing the Yumbo: A Ritual Drama of Northern Quito," in *Cultural Transformations and Ethnicity in Modern Ecuador* (Urbana: University of Illinois Press, 1981), 162–208; Xavier Albó and Matás Preiswerk, "El Gran poder: Fiesta del aimara urbano," *América Indígena* 51 (2–3): 293–352 (1991); Hans Buechler and Judith-Maria Buechler, *The World of Sofía Velasquez: The Autobiography of a Bolivian Market Vendor* (New York: Columbia University Press, 1996); Gregorio Condori Mamani, *Andean Lives: Gregorio Condori Mamani and Asunta Quispe Huamán,* ed. Ricardo Valderrama Fernández and Carmen Escalante Gutiérrez, trans. from the Quechua with annotations and revised glossary by Paul H. Gelles and Gabriela Martínez Escobar (Austin: University of Texas Press, 1996).

62   **"we who eat** *máchica***"**   Weismantel, *Food, Gender, and Poverty,* 161.

62   **One of my most significant encounters**   The notion of a contact zone is first presented explicitly in Mary Louise Pratt, *Imperial Eyes: Travel Writing and Transculturation* (London: Routledge, 1992).

62   **I made two trips, each a few weeks long**   I would like to thank two Bolivian anthropologists whom I visited a number of times in La Paz and the surrounding countryside, Silvia Rivera Cusicanqui and Xavier Albó. I would also like to acknowledge the members of the anthropological community in Bolivia with whom I spent time in La Paz and traveled to the countryside: Phil Blair, Deborah Caro, Valerie Estes, Ricardo and Karen Godoy, Inge Harman, Martha Lamborn, Jean Meadowcroft, Winston Moore, Tristan Platt, Roger Rasnake, and Mike and Susan Reed. I particularly would like to thank Phil Blair for his generous hospitality.

64   **Dora was certainly accustomed**   Several books document the history of Bolivian radio: Xavier Albó, *Idiomas, escuelas, y radios en Bolivia* (Sucre: ACLO-UNITAS, 1981); Raúl de la Quintana Condarco and Ramiro Duchén Condarco, *Radio Illimani: Los primeros años de su historia (1933–1937)* (La Paz: CIMA, 1986); Ronald Grebe López, *Radio y educación en Bolivia* (La Paz: Centro de Estudios Sociales, 1989); Alfonso Gumucio Dragon and Lupe Cajías, eds., *Las radios mineras de Bolivia* (La Paz: CIMCA-UNESCO, 1989); Raúl de la Quintana Condarco, *Aproximación a un catálogo bio-bibliográfico de la radiodifusión boliviana* (La Paz: CIMA, 1999).

65   **Dora's question about the telephone**   A similar story has been told about Swedish-speakers in Wisconsin in 1881 who did not believe that the telephone would work in their native language. One such doubter was quoted as saying, "By yimminy, she talks Swedish!" Angus Hibbard, *Hello Goodbye, My Story of Telephone Pioneering* (Chicago: A. C. McClurg, 1941), cited in Claude Fisher, *America Calling: A Social History of the Telephone to 1940* (Berkeley: University of California Press, 1992), 141.

CHAPTER 4. WORK

74   **My contacts with the main office**   I would like particularly to thank Don Chapman. Wayne Wurtsbaugh and Tim Kittel were also helpful in the early stages of contacting IMARPE and designing the research with the fishermen.

82   **We knew that migration was common**   An early monograph on this subject had broad influence: Héctor Martínez, *Las migraciones altiplánicas y la colonización del Tambopata* (Lima: Ministerio de Trabajo y Asuntos Indígenas, Plan Nacional de Integración de la Población Aborigen, 1961). A more detailed study of migration from the lakeshore district of Moho to an agricultural colonization zone in the upper reaches of the Amazon basin is Jane L. Collins, *Unseasonal Migrations: The Effects of Rural Labor Scarcity in Peru* (Princeton: Princeton University Press, 1988). A study of the migra-

tion of musicians from the adjacent district of Conima to Lima is Thomas Turino, *Moving Away from Silence: Music of the Peruvian Altiplano and the Experience of Urban Migration* (Chicago: University of Chicago Press, 1993). The theme of the last two studies—that migrants from specific villages move to another region in which they share a new occupation—is also demonstrated in Jorge Recharte, *Qori Llank'ay: Gold Mining Technology in a Community Mine, Northern Region of Puno (Perú),* Production, Storage, and Exchange in a Terraced Environment on the Eastern Andean Escarpment Project, monograph no. 2 (Chapel Hill: University of North Carolina, Department of Anthropology, 1993).

88   **"It's been too long a week"**   I am grateful to a number of people who assisted me with the data analysis, especially Linda Thorpe, Peter Hunter, and Rod Thompson of the Division of Environmental Studies at the University of California at Davis.

90   **This view developed in the 1950s and 1960s**   A useful review of this history can be found in Geoffrey Waugh, *Fisheries Management: Theoretical Developments and Contemporary Applications* (Boulder, Colo.: Westview, 1984). The classic statement of this position is Garrett Hardin, "The Tragedy of the Commons," *Science* 162 (December 13, 1968): 243–48.

91   **This local control would convert**   This approach of common-property management has been used by anthropologists since the 1980s in such works as Fikret Berkes, "Common Property Resource Problems and the Creation of Limited Property Rights," *Human Ecology* 13 (2): 187–208 (1985), and the important collection of Bonnie J. McCay and James M. Acheson, eds., *The Question of the Commons: The Culture and Ecology of Communal Resources* (Tucson: University of Arizona Press, 1987). A highly influential work that discusses this approach is Elinor Ostrom, *Governing the Commons: The Evolution of Institutions for Collective Action* (Cambridge: Cambridge University Press, 1990); this book also contains a thoughtful review of the intellectual antecedents of the debates on the topic. Recent reviews of work that derive from the common-property-management approach include Bonnie J. McCay and Svein Jentoft, "Market or Community Failure? Critical Perspectives on Common Property Research," *Human Organization* 57 (1): 21–29 (1998), and Arun Agarwal and Clark Gibson, "Enchantment and Disenchantment: The Role of Community in Natural Resource Conservation," *World Development* 27 (4): 629–49 (1999).

93   **We found that the fishermen were catching**   For each of these types of trips, Dominique and I had to make two sorts of calculations. We calculated the amount of time that a particular net had been in the water, though in the case of check trips, we had to refer back to the first trip, when the net originally had been placed. We also measured the amount of time that each

fisherman was working. We knew that we would include all the time that a fisherman spent on the water, whether he was actively rowing or handling the nets, or simply sitting in his boat. After a little discussion, we decided to count the time that a fisherman spent walking between his house and the shore, since this travel was an essential part of fishing. It took a longer conversation to decide not to include the time that a fisherman spent asleep out on the water. He would have slept anyway, we reasoned. Before we made a final decision to implement these calculations, we reviewed them with Cirilo. He burst into laughter when we told him that we had even considered counting as work the time that a fisherman spent sleeping. Of the many strange notions that gringos like us had suggested to him, that one struck him as the most absurd.

95   **He was well aware**   In our understanding of village social and political life, Dominique and I both benefited from the assistance of an anthropologist from Puno, Mario Núñez, whose help we gratefully acknowledge.

95   **As Dominique argued**   The title of his 1987 dissertation at the University of British Columbia is "Territorial Use-Rights in Fishing (TURFs) and the Management of Small-Scale Fisheries: The Case of Lake Titicaca (Peru)."

96   **Still, I felt that something was missing**   A similar effort to expand the discussion of common-property institutions can be found in McCay and Jentoft, "Market or Community Failure?"

96   **The villagers' control of their fishing grounds**   This effort to assure local control of distinct territories with different production possibilities brings to mind the theme, once widely discussed in Andean studies, of verticality, the tendency of Andean societies to maintain direct control of a maximum number of ecological zones at different elevations. The first major statement of this theme was made by John V. Murra in "El 'control vertical' de un máximo de pesos ecológicos en la economía de las sociedades andinas," in *Visita de la provincia de León de Huánuco en 1562,* vol. 1, *Visita de los yacha y mitmaqkuna cuzqueños encomendados en Juan Sánchez Falcón,* ed. John V. Murra (Huánuco: Facultad de Letras y Educación, Universidad Nacional Hermilio Valdizán, 1972), 427–76. For other discussions of verticality, see Enrique Mayer, "Un carnero por un saco de papas: Aspectos del trueque en la zona de Chaupiwaranga, Pasco," *Revista del Museo Nacional del Perú* 37 (1): 184–96 (1971); Stephen B. Brush, "Man's Use of an Andean Ecosystem," *Human Ecology* 4 (2): 147–66 (1976); and Benjamin Orlove, "Integration through Production: The Use of Zonation in Espinar," *American Ethnologist* 4 (1): 84–101 (1977).

98   **What kept the rest of the villagers**   At one point when I was writing this chapter, when I was most fascinated with the commitment of the fishermen to agriculture, I contemplated using as a title for the book *Fishing for Com-*

plements, since the fish provide a supplement to the diet and income of the households, rather than forming their core.

98 **The profitability issue lingered in my mind** My understanding of the villagers' ideas about economic matters owes a great deal to conversations with colleagues. I first presented this chapter at the economic sociology colloquium at the University of California at Davis, and it benefited particularly from comments by Fred Block, Miriam Wells, and Nancy Folbre. Peggy Barlett's comments on the material in this chapter were also very helpful to me.

98 **We certainly had detailed information** One could question the value we placed on the fish that the fishermen and their families consumed at home or distributed to immediate kin and neighbors, roughly one-sixth of the catch. They might have eaten fish that were worth less because they were smaller, or were damaged during removal from the nets. Moreover, they might make very different economic decisions about the food they purchased and the food they produced themselves. In our decision to use local prices to estimate the value of fish, we drew on the discussion in an important article on this subject, Michael Chibnik, "The Value of Subsistence Production," *Journal of Anthropological Research* 34 (4): 561–76 (1978). A more recent discussion, also influenced by this article, shows the difficulty of bringing subsistence and market goods into a single accounting framework: Wiktor L. Adamowicz, et al., "In Search of Forest Resource Values of Indigenous Peoples: Are Nonmarket Valuation Techniques Applicable?" *Society and Natural Resources* 11 (1): 51–66 (1998).

98 **But what about the labor input?** I would like to thank my friend and colleague Steve Brush for his willingness to discuss these questions of labor input at length, and for the insights that he gave me in these matters.

100 **We found that it was slightly more common** We were interested to note that this crew size varied relatively little from one type of trip to another. The mean crew size for overnight trips was 1.36, for double trips 1.53, and for check trips 1.46. The mean for trips with *wayunaqanas* (large trawl nets) and other traditional gear was 1.85, pulling the overall average mean crew size up to 1.56.

100 **The fishermen had a standard way of phrasing** In Quechua this phrase is indicated by a suffix, *-ysi-,* which can be attached to a verb stem. Especially when used with words of motion, it carries a sense of accompanying rather than assisting.

101 **Quechua-speakers distinguish** An important early article on Andean categories of work is Jesús Contreras, "La valoración del trabajo en una comunidad campesina de la sierra peruana," *Boletín Americanista* 30 (1): 41–

72 (1980). Contreras also notes that Quechua-speakers often include a third term, *trabajay,* to work for an employer for wages.

102   **"My wife herds the sheep"**   September 17, 1980. I will give citations for the date and author of these quotations. A set of typescripts of these diaries may be consulted in the archives of the Ministerio de Asuntos Campesinos y Agricultura in La Paz. Since they are unpaginated, I do not refer to the quotations by page number.

102   **"On Tuesday, the whole family woke up very early"**   Tomás Hoyo, April 17, 1979.

103   **These Andean diary-keepers**   I am grateful to Frank Salomon for his suggestion that the repetitive nature of these entries, rather than reflecting an unfamiliarity of the diary-keepers with diary-keeping, might indicate their long experience with other forms of regular written accounting of economic activity. He mentioned both the *libros de actas,* the village record books that provide detailed information on the allocation of labor and foodstuffs to community projects, and the famous *khipu,* or knotted cords, used in Inca times to keep track of goods and labor. See Frank Salomon, "Los *quipus* y libros de la Tupicocha de hoy," in *Arqueología, antropología, e historia de los Andes: Homenaje a María Rostworoski,* ed. Rafael Varón Gabai and Javier Flores Espinoza (Lima: Instituto de Estudios Peruanos, 1997), 241–58; Gary Urton and Jeffrey Quilter, eds., *Inscription and Narrativity in Andean Knot-Records* (Washington, D.C.: Dumbarton Oaks, 2000); Frank Salomon, "How an Andean 'Writing without Words' Works," *Current Anthropology* 42 (1): 3–29 (2001).

103   **"we would write a book"**   Pedro Maquera, undated four-page introductory statement.

103   **"to write each day"**   Ramón Mamani, April 18, 1979.

104   **Why did the fishermen record**   For a detailed discussion of the check survey mentioned in this paragraph, see Levieil, "Territorial Use-Rights in Fishing."

104   **I found the box containing the diaries**   I would like to thank Shelly Diaz for her assistance in analyzing the entries in the diaries. My understanding of the diaries has deepened through conversations with Enrique Mayer and Frank Salomon.

105   **"On Wednesday morning we woke up"**   Pedro Maquera, June 27, 1979.

105   **"On Monday we went to Bacoma to harvest maize"**   Tomás Hoyo, January 7, 1980.

107   **On only one occasion was a lawyer described as "working"**   This instance shows that work is not as tightly linked to money as in the United States; not only is much work outside the wage and market economy, but some paid activities do not count as work. In general, the activities that are

not listed as work overlap with contemporary Western definitions: sleep, rest, festivities, and visits never appear as work. The diary-keepers do not discuss travel time in detail or consider it as a kind of work, unlike westerners, who often separate out commuting as another type of activity and discuss the amount of time that it takes. Eating is omitted as well: unlike American office workers, who might "have a working breakfast" if they met someone for an early-morning meal and discussed business matters, or who could "work through lunch" while eating at their desks, the villagers do not work while they eat. For a rich account of cultural understandings of work in America that has influenced this chapter, see Studs Terkel, *Working: People Talk about What They Do All Day and How They Feel about What They Do* (New York: Pantheon Books, 1974).

108   **Of the seven diary-keepers**   This sample of seven male villagers is not large enough to be statistically significant. However, I note that the diary-keepers are more likely than most villagers to have kept track of monetary income and expenditures, since they are men, since they are more educated, and since their positions as village officials led them to discuss budgets.

108   **"My wife has taken care of the animals"**   Pedro Maquera, August 15, 1979.

109   **"Today Wednesday, my wife winnowed two donkey-loads of barley"** Julio Constantino Maquera, August 6, 1980.

109   **"Today we get up very early"**   Justo Yanarico, January 20, 1980.

110   **"We get up at 6 A.M."**   Julio Constantino Maquera, May 18, 1979.

110   **Though he mentions the specific time on five occasions**   As this entry shows, he is distinctive in other ways as well. The most observant Protestant in the set, he mentions prayers more often than the others, and he is the only one to have detailed the ingredients that his wife used to prepare meals. This variation in the diaries suggests the relative independence that the diary-keepers had in selecting what topics and details to mention. Furthermore, the fact that the authors retained these distinctive characteristics throughout the period of diary-keeping supports the notion that the project staff did not edit the diaries or suggest revisions to the diary-keepers.

111   **When Justo Yanarico became ill**   He describes these events in the entries for June 17–20, 1980.

111   **The diary-keepers had a particular way of describing**   This sequence of activities suggests the close attachment to the village as a place. The diary-keepers described the daily movements of all the family members and animals from the house and corrals out to field and pasture and then back again. These movements were so expected that the diary-keepers often specifically reported that they were staying at home if they remained at their house to make craft items.

111   **Rather than tallying hours**   The diary-keepers noted variation in the time they spent at work by describing the time when they awakened. Justo Yanarico usually wrote that he had awakened *temprano*, early, but he occasionally used the phrase *bien temprano*, very early. He would get up earlier than unusual when he had several tasks to carry out on one day, or when he had a task that might last a long time. For example, he indicated that he woke up *bien temprano* one morning when he was walking in the hills above his village to cut grasses to bring back as fodder. He was uncertain how much time he would need to gather a full donkey-load, so he set off early in order to be able to return home before dark.

112   **Since they did not tally their working hours**   An article on the analysis of time allocation that has influenced my thought is E. P. Thompson, "Time, Work-Discipline, and Industrial Capitalism," *Past and Present* 38: 56–97 (December 1967).

112   **"On Monday and Tuesday I went all day"**   Justo Yanarico, February 23 and 24, 1981.

113   **"Today Tuesday I also went to the river to fish"**   Justo Yanarico, April 15, 1981.

113   **This steadiness is also shown**   This discussion refers to the trips in which fishermen hung gill nets. Many factors enter into the calculations of the returns to trips. The returns can differ depending on whether they are calculated in relation to the individual trip, to economic time (time when the fisherman is actually working), or to ecological time (time when the nets are in the water). The fishermen have more free time in some months, but the returns to fishing may vary. For example, the returns are higher to overnight trips from May through August, but the length of the trips is greater, suggesting that the fishermen travel farther to reach better fishing grounds. The catch per hour for the check trips is higher in the busy months, though the trips are shorter, suggesting that the fishermen could fish more if they were not also occupied with farming.

114   **These concepts of work contrast**   To be sure, economists can model the notion of nonhomogeneous time, which could be used to explain why workers receive additional compensation when they work on holidays. Still, the diaries show a notion of time that is strikingly at variance with the views of conventional economists.

CHAPTER 5. FISH

118   **The other twenty-two are found**   *Orestias luteus* occurs in two lakes that drain into Lake Titicaca, Lago Arapa and Lago Umayo, and *O. puni* is found in Lago Umayo; *O. pentlandii* is more widely distributed in these

lakes and associated rivers, and in rivers in the department of Cuzco, to the north of the altiplano, as well.

119   **It opens with the arrival of hunter-gatherers**   A number of sources describe this period. Useful information can be found in the following works, all of which concentrate on later periods: Catherine J. Julien, *Hatunqolla: A View of Inca Rule from the Lake Titicaca Region* (Berkeley: University of California Press, 1993); Clark L. Erickson, *Investigación arqueológica del sistema agrícola de los camellones en la Cuenca del Lago Titicaca del Perú* (La Paz: Piwa, 1996), and "The Lake Titicaca Basin: A Precolumbian Built Landscape," in *Imperfect Balance: Landscape Transformations in the Precolumbian Americas,* ed. David Lantz (New York: Columbia University Press, 2000), 311–56; and Nathan Wachtel, *Le retour des ancêtres: Les Indiens Urus de Bolivie, XXe–XVIe siècle: Essai d'histoire régressive* (Paris: Gallimard, 1990).

121   **Rather than paying tribute to the Incas**   A discussion of this period can be found in Nathan Wachtel, "Men of the Water: The Uru Problem (Sixteenth and Seventeenth Centuries)," in *Anthropological History of Andean Polities,* ed. John V. Murra, Nathan Wachtel, and Jacques Revel (Cambridge: Cambridge University Press, 1986), 263–310.

121   **This map includes a few details**   Sources on the mining economy at large include Carlos Sempat Assadourian, *Minería y espacio económico en los Andes, siglos XVI–XX* (Lima: Instituto de Estudios Peruanos, 1980); Enrique Tandeter and Nathan Wachtel, *Precios y producción agraria: Potosí y Charcas en el siglo XVIII* (Buenos Aires: Centro de Estudios de Estado y Sociedad, 1983); and Peter Bakewell, *Miners of the Red Mountain: Indian Labor in Potosí, 1545–1650* (Albuquerque: University of New Mexico Press, 1984). For details on trade to Potosí, see Robson Tyrer, *Historia demográfica y económica de la Audiencia de Quito: Población indígena e industria textil, 1600–1800* (Quito: Banco Central del Ecuador, 1988); and Brooke Larson, *Colonialism and Agrarian Transformation in Bolivia: Cochabamba, 1550–1900* (Princeton, N.J.: Princeton University Press, 1988).

121   **The hypothetical museum curator**   The key work for this section is Wachtel, *Le retour des ancêtres.*

122   **In 1780, Tupac Amaru, a minor Indian noble**   The key work on this movement in the altiplano is Augusto Ramos Zambrano, *Puno en la rebelión de Tupac Amaru* (Puno: Universidad Nacional Técnica del Altiplano, 1982).

124   **This sequence may be repeated several times**   At present, the use of these huge nets differs somewhat from the way they were used in the past. Contemporary fishermen often use sails, rather than paddles, to bring their boats into the water. The number of helpers is often smaller as well. Nonetheless, the coordination of partners, the repetition of the trawls, and the division of the catch remain unchanged.

125 **Fishermen from two neighboring villages rowed out** This scene is recorded in Guillermo Billinghurst, *Reconocimiento militar del río Desaguadero
y de la Altiplanicie andina* (Lima: Imprenta de "La Patria," 1880). I would like
to thank Christina Huenefeldt for providing me with this reference.

125 **The steps in its use** Fishermen have now replaced the cotton or wool
thread of earlier decades with synthetic fiber, which weighs less and dries
more quickly.

126 **Here, the quote is from David Forbes** David Forbes, *On the Aymara Indians of Bolivia and Peru* (London: Taylor and Francis, 1870).

127 **The last and most lovely of the old types** These basket traps are discussed in detail in Edgar Farfán's unpublished report, "Aparejo y método
para la estracción del 'ispi' (Orestias sp. [Tchernavin 1994]) en el Lago Titicaca" (Puno: Instituto del Mar del Perú, 1974).

132 **At first the villagers were excited** In part as a favor to the congressional
delegation from Puno, the government of President Bustamante y Rivero
(1945–48) granted title of these newly exposed lands to lakeshore communities in 1946, at a time when the level of the lake was beginning to rise
again. In general, the villagers were pleased to gain official recognition of
their claims to these lands. However, they believed that the lands had been
theirs all along.

132 **Many other sources confirm the existence of the drought** The lake level
is reported in M. A. Roche et al., "Climatology and Hydrology of the Lake
Titicaca Basin," in *Lake Titicaca: A Synthesis of Limnological Knowledge,* ed.
André Iltis and Claude Dejoux (Dordrecht: Kluwer, 1992), 63–83. For the
ice-core records, see L. G. Thompson et al., "El Niño Southern Oscillation
Events Recorded in the Stratigraphy of the Tropical Quelccaya Ice Cap,
Peru," *Science* 226 (4670): 50–53 (1984); L. G. Thompson et al., "A 1,500-Year
Record of Tropical Precipitation in Ice Cores from the Quelccaya Ice Cap,
Peru," *Science* 229 (4717): 971–73 (1992); L. G. Thompson et al., "Ice-Core
Paleoclimate Records in Tropical South America since the Last Glacial
Maximum," *Journal of Quaternary Science* 15 (4): 377–94 (2000).

133 **These wages, which had formed one element of the village economy**
Works that trace the economy of the altiplano through the depression in-
clude Gordon Appleby, "The Development of a Central-Place Marketing
System in the Department of Puno, Peru" (Ph.D. dissertation, Department
of Anthropology, Stanford University, 1976); Gordon Appleby, "The Role
of Urban Food Needs in Regional Development, Puno, Peru," in *Regional
Analysis,* vol. 1, *Economic Systems,* ed. C. A. Smith (New York: Academic
Press, 1976), 147–78; and Nils Jacobsen, *Mirages of Transition: The Peruvian
Altiplano, 1780–1930* (Berkeley: University of California Press, 1993).

133 **In 1935, the Peruvian and Bolivian governments agreed** A valuable
source on the introduction of trout to Lake Titicaca is Ramon Laba, "A

Story of Development: Lake Titicaca 1935–1977" (Master's thesis, Department of Political Science, University of Wisconsin, 1978). This particular point is mentioned on p. 6.

134 **Of James's five recommended species** The five species that James recommended were whitefish *(Coregonus clupeaformis),* lake trout *(Salvelinus namaycush),* brook trout *(Salvelinus fontinalis),* brown trout *(Salmo trutta),* and rainbow trout *(Oncorhynchus mykiss,* the fish formerly known as *Salmo gairdineri).* The first three failed completely, since no specimens were found in the years after they were released. Nor did the brown trout colonize the lake, though small populations developed for a while in the Río Ilave, the only sizable river that enters Lake Titicaca from the Cordillera Occidental.

134 **One could even say** Useful sources on extinctions of lake fish species include Tijs Goldschmidt, *Darwin's Dreampond: Drama in Lake Victoria* (Cambridge: MIT Press, 1996); Christopher Lever, *Naturalized Fishes of the World* (San Diego: Academic Press, 1996); Melanie L. J. Stiassny, "An Overview of Freshwater Diversity with Some Lessons from African Fishes," *Fisheries* 21 (9): 7–13 (1996); and Ian J. Harrison and Melanie L. J. Stiassny, "The Quiet Crisis: A Preliminary Listing of the Freshwater Fishes of the World That Are Extinct or 'Missing in Action,'" (New York: American Museum of Natural History, 1996, manuscript).

134 **Granted this danger, it is remarkable** The source for the most recent documented capture of an umantu is H. C. Gibson, "The Percy Sladen Expedition to Lake Titicaca, 1937," *Geographical Journal* 88 (3): 533–42 (1939).

135 **The umantu was the largest of the** *Orestias* Two sources give useful information on the evolution, physiology, and ecology of the native fish of Lake Titicaca: Lynne R. Parenti, "A Taxonomic Revision of the Andean Killifish Genus *Orestias (Cyprinodontiformes, Cyprinodontidae),"* *Bulletin of the American Museum of Natural History* 178 (2): 334–557 (1984), and L. Lauzanne, "Native Species: The Orestias," in *Lake Titicaca,* ed. Iltis and Dejoux, pp. 405–19.

135 **Current estimates suggest that it began to evolve** These dates draw on the discussion in A. Parker and I. Kornfield, "Molecular Perspective on Evolution and Zoogeography of Cyprinodontid Killifishes *(Teleostei, Atherinomorpha),"* *Copeia* 95 (1): 8–21 (1995).

135 **The scientific travelers, from S. W. Garman in the 1870s through Gibson in the 1930s** Sources include Alexander Agassiz and S. W. Garman, *The Exploration of Lake Titicaca* (Cambridge: Harvard University, Bulletin of the Museum of Comparative Zoology, 1876); Maurice Neveu-Lemaire, *Les lacs des hauts plateaux de l'Amérique du Sud* (Paris: Imprimerie Nationale, 1906); and Gibson, "The Percy Sladen Expedition."

135 **There might well have been another kind of extinction** This use of the word *extinction* raises the question of the analogies, or relations, between

biological and cultural evolution. This topic is being explored in anthropology and ecology, as shown by such works as Robert Boyd and Peter J. Richerson, *Culture and the Evolutionary Process* (Chicago: University of Chicago Press, 1985); William H. Durham, *Coevolution: Genes, Culture, and Human Diversity* (Stanford: Stanford University Press, 1991); and Luigi Luca Cavalli-Sforza, *Genes, Peoples, and Languages* (New York: North Point Press, 2000). For some readers, the notion of "cultural extinction" is a firm analytical construct; for others, it serves as a more casual metaphor.

136 **Historians of fisheries have documented** Sources include Geoffrey Waugh, *Fisheries Management: Theoretical Developments and Contemporary Applications* (Boulder, Colo.: Westview, 1984), and J. R. McGoodwin, *Crises in the World's Fisheries: People, Problems, and Policies* (Stanford: Stanford University Press, 1990).

137 **It would have been unrealistic to expect** Alfred W. Crosby, *Ecological Imperialism: The Biological Expansion of Europe, 900–1900* (Cambridge: Cambridge University Press, 1986), traces the early history of fish introductions. A work that shows the great popularity of such introductions in the first half of the twentieth century is Christopher Lever, *Naturalized Fishes of the World* (San Diego: Academic Press, 1996).

137 **Even by the standards of the time** This story is detailed in Laba, "A Story of Development."

137 **His report, eighteen pages long** M. C. James, "Informe sobre la vigilancia para el desarrollo de pesquerías en el Lago Titicaca" (La Paz: Archives of the Ministerio de Asuntos Campesinos y Agricultura, 1936, typescript).

138 **Completely unaware of village control of fishing grounds** The quotations in this paragraph are found in James, "Informe sobre la vigilancia," p. 17.

138 **He lost one set of whitefish eggs** This detail is reported in Laba, "A Story of Development," pp. 8–9.

143 **Dominique and I believed that the answer** As this book was moving into production, Dominique e-mailed me with another possible explanation, which has to do with technology. The boatwrights were unfamiliar with clinker-building, in which each plank overlaps with the one below it. In the absence of this technique, it would be necessary to ensure, Dominique wrote, "that . . . the shape of each plank is adapted precisely to its position along the side of the boat (you cannot keep planks as simple rectangles and you need also to plane the upper and lower edges to give them a certain angle to fit with the upper or lower planks). . . . Not knowing or not knowing how to use a plane was also a major handicap." This note on technology may help explain the upper limit on the size of boats, though

I remain persuaded that the satisfaction of the fishermen with their small boats also accounts in part for the lack of change.

148   **The fishermen checked their nets**   In the first years of the cannery's operation, fishermen brought trout directly to the cannery. The year when this and the three canneries that subsequently opened began sending representatives out to meet the fishermen is given as 1964 in G. Everett, *The Rainbow Trout of Lake Titicaca and the Fisheries of Lake Titicaca* (Puno: Report to the government of Peru, 1971), 20. Everett later published some results from this report in an article, "The Rainbow Trout *Salmo gairdineri* (Rich.) Fishery of Lake Titicaca," *Journal of Fisheries Biology* 5 (5): 429–40 (1973).

151   **It is a striking fish nonetheless**   The English word *silverside* refers to a number of species that have this distinctive mark. The Spanish term *pejerrey*, or kingfish, has been adopted into Quechua and Aymara. The fish's scientific name is *Basilichthys bonaerensis*.

153   **As biological reports on the silverside began to appear**   The first report was W. A. Wurtsbaugh, *Biología y pesquería del pejerrey* (Basilichthys bonaerensis) *en el Lago Titicaca* (Puno: Instituto del Mar del Perú, 1974). Other reports include G. Hanek et al., *La pesquería en el Lago Titicaca (Perú), presente y futuro* (Rome: United Nations Food and Agriculture Organization, 1982); and P. Vaux et al., "Ecology of the Pelagic Fishes of Lake Titicaca, Peru–Bolivia," *Biotropica* 20 (3): 220–29 (1988). This research on the silverside indicates that it may have been responsible for introducing protozoa into the lake that parasitize the *Orestias* species, as shown in W. Wurtsbaugh and R. Alfaro, "Mass Mortality of Fishes in Lake Titicaca (Peru–Bolivia) Associated with the Protozoan Parasite *Ichthyophthirius multifiliis*," *Transactions of the American Fisheries Society* 117 (2): 213–17 (1988).

153   **In their native habitat, females spawn**   The normal temperature range for spawning in the silverside's native habitat is 15 to 21 degrees Celsius; the fairly narrow optimum is 17 to 18 degrees. Though surface temperatures as high as 17 degrees have been observed in the main lake, and the shallower Lago Pequeño has warmed to as high as 18.5 degrees, such temperatures are unusual. The surface temperatures in the warmest month of the year average only 14.4 degrees.

156   **During the week in 1981 that I went down to the navy base**   I would like to thank the personnel of the Peruvian navy for their assistance, especially Amanda Castillo, for her help in locating the records in the archive at the base.

157   **The navy officials registered boats and fishermen**   My thoughts on this topic have been influenced by a book on the perspective of state agencies, James Scott, *Seeing Like a State: How Certain Schemes to Improve the Human Condition Have Failed* (New Haven: Yale University Press, 1998).

157   **By 1981, when the registration had tapered off**   For many reasons, the balsas were never registered. The strong similarities among these small craft made them difficult to distinguish from one another. The government's practice of painting the name on the boat would have been difficult to apply to them, since they were essentially large bundles of reeds bound together with twine. Moreover, the balsas usually lasted for only six months or so before they became so waterlogged that they needed to be replaced, so a fisherman would have needed to register two of them each year.

160   **The fishermen who lived in the villages closest to the provincial capitals**   The precise figures are as follows: 316 licenses were issued to fishermen in the three capitals, out of a total of 543 who lived in the corresponding districts; 724 licenses were issued to the fishermen who lived in other districts, out of a total of 2,583.

162   **As imported fish**   I have explored this Latin American fascination with imports in a volume I edited: *The Allure of the Foreign: Imported Goods in Postcolonial Latin America* (Ann Arbor: University of Michigan Press, 1997).

162   **The first of the aquaculture projects**   I would like to acknowledge the assistance I received in gathering information on these development projects from the personnel of the Puno regional office of the Ministry of Fisheries, especially Jorge Sánchez.

163   **As the trout farms began to run into difficulties**   Sources for the cage culture projects include Benjamin Orlove and Dominique Levieil, "Some Doubts about Trout: Fisheries Development Projects in Lake Titicaca," in *State, Capital, and Rural Society: Anthropological Perspectives on Political Economy in Mexico and the Andes,* ed. Benjamin Orlove, Michael W. Foley, and Thomas F. Love (Boulder, Colo.: Westview, 1989), 211–46; H. Treviño, J. Torres Calderón, and M. Roncal Gutiérrez, "The Fishery Potential," in *Lake Titicaca,* ed. Iltis and Dejoux, pp. 539–50; Ministerio de Pesquería y Agencia Española de Cooperación Internacional, *Ordenamiento Pesquero del Recurso Trucha en la Región Sur* (Puno: Dirección Regional de Pesquería, 1999).

168   **In the meantime, at least, few shifts have occurred in the fisheries**   The sources for information on the fisheries in the 1990s discussed in this section include a set of reports prepared by a development project in the altiplano run jointly by the Peruvian and Bolivian governments: Repúblicas de Perú y Bolivia, *Diagnóstico y estudio de desarrollo pesquero* (Puno: Plan Director Global Binacional de Proteccion-Prevención de Inundaciones y Aprovechamiento de los Recursos del Lago Titicaca, Río Desaguadero, Lago Poopó, y Lago Salar de Coipasa, 1993). Other sources are Instituto Nacional de Desarrollo, *Diagnóstico Pesquero del Area Circunlacustre del Lago*

Titicaca (Puno: Proyecto Especial Binacional Lago Titicaca, 1993), and Ministerio de Pesquería y Agencia Española de Cooperación Internacional, *Ordenamiento Pesquero del Recurso Trucha en la Región Sur* (Puno: Dirección Regional de Pesquería, 1999).

CHAPTER 6. REEDS

174 **Like other wetlands** Sources on aquatic plants include A. Raynal-Roques, "The Higher Plants," in *Lake Titicaca: A Synthesis of Limnological Knowledge,* ed. André Iltis and Claude Dejoux (Dordrecht: Kluwer, 1992), 223–31; and Isaac Ticona Zuñíga, "Determinación del cariotipo de la totora en el Lago Titicaca" (Master's thesis in agronomy, Universidad Nacional Técnica del Altiplano, Puno, 1980).

174 **Reproducing chiefly by sprouting** Raynal-Roques indicates that plants in shallow waters usually flower after two to three years; they require four or five years in deeper waters, and some of them never flower at all. The flower spikes, a dull brown, are seven to eight centimeters across and hence quite small in proportion to the stem.

178 **In years of very low lake levels** Government officials oppose such burning. See, for example, the article in the August 8, 1998, issue of *El Comercio,* a leading national newspaper, "Por falsa creencia queman totorales de la Reserva Nacional del Titicaca."

182 **Through the late 1930s** If the villagers had used totora as cattle feed earlier in the century, it is unlikely that Weston LaBarre, an anthropologist who traveled extensively through the altiplano in 1938 and 1939, would have failed to mention it in his detailed account of local culture, *The Aymara Indians of the Lake Titicaca Plateau, Bolivia* (Washington, D.C.: American Anthropological Association, 1948). In his descriptions of livestock raising (pp. 70–76, 152), LaBarre lists a number of wild and cultivated plants provided to different species of domesticated animals and takes care to describe two types of lakeweed that served as fodder for cattle near the lake. Since he mentions that donkeys and mules were fed green totora stalks, it is unlikely that he would not have reported the same practice for cattle. There is also no mention of the use of totora as cattle feed in another, somewhat less detailed account of plant use in the altiplano at this time, H. C. Gibson, "The Percy Sladen Expedition to Lake Titicaca, 1937," *Geographical Journal* 88 (3): 533–42 (1939).

183 **By the early 1960s** John M. Hickman treats this use of totora as an established practice, rather than a new one, in his account of life at this time, "The Aymara of Chinchera, Peru: Persistence and Change in a Bicultural

Context" (Ph.D. dissertation, Department of Anthropology, Cornell University, 1963).

183 **About sixty-five hundred households harvested totora**   The first figure is from Edward M. Dew, *Politics in the Altiplano: The Dynamics of Change in Rural Peru* (Austin: University of Texas Press, 1969), 58; the second is from Dominique Levieil and Gilmar Goyzueta, *Evaluación de la extracción de totora para fines de subsistencia en la Reserva Nacional del Titicaca, sector Puno* (Puno: Ministerio de Agricultura y Alimentación, CENFOR, 1984), 1–24; the third is from Plan Director Global Nacional de Protección, Prevención de Inundanciones y Aprovechamiento de los Recursos del Lago Titicaca, Río Desaguadero, Lago Poopó, y Lago Salar de Coipasa, *Diagnóstico y Estudio de Desarrollo*, sec. 3 (Puno: Proyecto Especial Binacional Lago Titicaca, 1995), 5–8. The net annual contribution of this use of totora as fodder to the regional economy of the altiplano in the 1980s and 1990s was between one million and two million dollars, depending not only on the number of households that harvested totora, but also on the price of meat and the exchange rate between Peruvian and U.S. currency. This is a bit less than the economic value of the annual catch of fish, about three million dollars.

183 **They traveled to cattle fairs**   Details on the new cattle markets can be found in Gordon Appleby, "Exportation and Its Aftermath: The Spatioeconomic Evolution of the Regional Marketing System in Highland Puno, Peru" (Ph.D. dissertation, Department of Anthropology, Stanford University, 1978), 187–211.

184 **Cirilo discussed this problem**   I would like to thank Enrique Mayer for his insights into the use of terms and concepts in this account. I would also like to acknowledge Steve Gudeman's work, which has also strongly influenced this section, and indeed the entire book.

187 **From Rosaspata to Huancané**   The distance from Huancané to the Río Ramis is much shorter than the distance that Cirilo walked with his uncle, cousins, and cattle on other days. On the day they went to Ramis, they had to wait for the ferry—a large totora raft—to carry them across the river.

188 **A report published in 1959**   This report is Ministerio de Agricultura, *Los recursos humanos del departamento de Puno*, vol. 5, sec. B/9 (Lima: Ministerio de Agricultura, Plan Regional para el Desarrollo del Sur del Perú, 1959), 46.

189 **A number of villages decided to add a totora guard**   An account of recent changes in the systems by which villages patrol their territories, set in the northern highlands of Peru, is Orin Starn, *Nightwatch: The Politics of Protest in the Andes* (Durham: Duke University Press, 1999).

190 **And in both cases, the village control over the lake increased**   As I discussed in chapter 4, this case fits in well with Elinor Ostrom's views of the management of common-property resources.

190   **Their tenacity stems as well**   Many factors influence the success of the
       village systems of control over lake resources, particularly the economic
       importance of these resources and the strength of local village institutions
       that set up, enforce, and modify the rules that govern access to them. How-
       ever, since the economic and political aspects of such systems have re-
       ceived a good deal of attention in recent decades, I would like to empha-
       size here the relatively neglected cultural aspects of these systems.

190   **Much as the growth of the Titicaca fisheries**   For a review of the anthro-
       pological literature on protected areas, see Benjamin Orlove and Stephen
       Brush, "Anthropology and the Conservation of Biodiversity," *Annual Re-
       view of Anthropology* 25: 329–52 (1996).

191   **In 1975, the military government**   I would like to thank the CENFOR
       staff, especially Gilmar Goyzueta, for their help in providing me with ac-
       cess to documents and for their generosity with their time in discussing the
       history of the Titicaca National Reserve.

191   **This agency, commonly known by its acronym, CENFOR**   The Ministry
       of Agriculture was called the Ministry of Agriculture and Food between
       1968 and 1980, a change that the military government made to signal its
       concern for addressing the basic needs of the Peruvian people.

192   **Representatives from the league met with the Minister**   The politics in
       the region during this period are described in Lewis Taylor, "Agrarian Un-
       rest and Political Conflict in Puno, 1985–1987," *Bulletin of Latin American
       Research* 6 (2): 135–62 (1987).

193   **The French naturalist Maurice Neveu-Lemaire**   The 1903 map is pub-
       lished in Maurice Neveu-Lemaire, *Les lacs des hauts plateaux de l'Amérique
       du Sud* (Paris: Imprimerie nationale, 1906). The 1927 surveys served as a ba-
       sis for the maps that include the reedbeds, printed on a scale of 1:200,000
       and published in the 1940s: Instituto Geográfico Militar, *Carta Nacional del
       Perú*, hojas 16j, 17i (Lima: Instituto Geográfico Militar). The aerial photo-
       graphs were used in maps of this area printed in the late 1960s on a scale
       of 1:100,000: Instituto Geográfico Militar, *Carta Nacional*, hojas 32-w, 31-x,
       32-x, 33-x, 31-y, 32-y, 33-y, 33-z (Lima: Instituto Geográfico Militar). Aerial
       photographs from the early 1980s appear in Daniel Collot, "Mapa de vege-
       tación de la Bahía de Puno," *Revista del Instituto de Ecología* (La Paz) 2: 49–
       65 (1982); Daniel Collot, Fany Koriyama and Emilia García, "Répartitions,
       biomasses et productions del macrophytes du lac Titicaca," *Revue d'Hydro-
       biologie Tropicale* 16 (3): 241–61 (1983).

194   **Moreover, the density of totora**   The aerial photographs and more recent
       records offer information as well on the density of the totora stands, which
       suggest that the density of the totora is stable. There are some regions
       where totora grows more sparsely, especially where it is crowded by

stoneworts. These plants, a strange kind of giant algae in the genus *Chara,* ordinarily grow in water between five and fifteen meters deep, but are sometimes found in areas that support totora. They concentrate calcium in their stems and can leave a whitish deposit on the lake bottom that suppresses the growth of other plants, including totora. Though they can appear after totora has been harvested, stoneworts do not appear to be a serious threat to the totora beds. Since they cannot survive in shallow water, they die off close to shore in the years when the lake level falls. Wave action can also remove the whitish deposits. The most detailed studies suggest that the distribution of stoneworts is stable, rather than increasing. See Daniel Collot, "Les macrophytes de quelques lacs andins (Lac Titicaca, Lac Poopó, Lacs des vallées d'Hichu Kkota, et d'Ovejhuyo)" (La Paz: ORSTOM, 1980, unpublished report); A. Iltis and P. Mourguiart, "Higher Plants: Distribution and Biomass," in *Lake Titicaca,* ed. Iltis and Dejoux, pp. 241–52.

194   **Of those, twenty-five have distributions**   The CENFOR list was published in CENFOR, *Principales especies de fauna* (Puno: Centro Nacional Forestal, 1978). There are several sources for the ranges of these birds that CENFOR could have drawn on: Maria Koepcke, *Aves del departamento de Lima* (Lima: n.p., 1964), also available in English as *The Birds of the Department of Lima, Peru* (Wynnewood, Penn.: Livingston, 1970; reissued Newton Square, Penn.: Harrowood Books, 1983), and Alfredo William Johnson, *Supplement to the Birds of Chile and Adjacent Regions of Argentina, Bolivia, and Peru* (Buenos Aires: Platt Establecimientos Gráficos, 1972). A more recent source on these birds is Claude Dejoux, "The Avifauna," in *Lake Titicaca,* ed. Iltis and Dejoux, pp. 460–69.

194   **Many other grebe species take flight only a few times a year**   Sources on the short-winged grebe include Jon Fjeldså, "Displays of Two Primitive Grebes, *Rollandia rolland* and *R. microptera,* and the Origin of the Complex Courtship Behaviour of the *Podiceps* Species (Aves: *Podicipedidae*)," *Steenstrupia* (University of Copenhagen Zoological Museum) 11 (5): 133–55 (1985), and Bradley C. Livezey, "Flightlessness in Grebes (Aves: *Podicipedidae*): Its Independent Evolution in Three Genera," *Evolution* 43 (1): 29–54 (1989).

196   **Some of its founding members**   This case shows the importance of links between villagers and national political organizations. In general, the villagers have mobilized themselves to defend their control of the lake without such links; indeed, it is a major theme of this book that such spontaneous political action can be quite effective. However, I would like to underscore the fact that national organizations, a very minor player in this area, have been crucial actors in rural politics elsewhere in Peru. This topic is discussed in Gustavo Gorriti, *Sendero: Historia de la guerra milenaria en el*

Perú (Lima: Editorial Apoyo, 1990), Deborah Poole and Gerardo Rénique, *Peru: Time of Fear* (London: Latin American Bureau, 1992), and Steve Stern, ed. *Shining and Other Paths: War and Society in Peru, 1980–1995* (Durham, N.C.: Duke University Press, 1998).

203 **Like many customary units of measurement** A fundamental source on the topic of measurement is Witold Kula, *Measures and Men* (Princeton, N.J.: Princeton University Press, 1986). I would like to thank my colleague Bill Hagen for suggesting that I read this book.

204 **Dominique and I reviewed a number of these maps** The sketch maps are discussed more thoroughly in Benjamin Orlove, "Mapping Reeds and Reading Maps: The Politics of Representation in Lake Titicaca," *American Ethnologist* 18 (1): 3–38 (1991).

206 **It is striking that the villagers' opposition took such different forms** A useful source on peasant opposition to government programs is James C. Scott, *Weapons of the Weak: Everyday Forms of Peasant Resistance* (New Haven: Yale University Press, 1985).

207 **The lake itself was a powerful reminder** An important source for this notion that landscapes serve as concrete icons as well as abstract symbols is Francis Zimmermann, *The Jungle and the Aroma of Meats: An Ecological Theme in Hindu Medicine* (Berkeley: University of California Press, 1987).

CHAPTER 7. PATHS

210 **The *diarios campesinos* also contain** I spent some time pondering the question of what term to use for these roads and paths. I knew that I wanted a single word in English in order to convey how people in the altiplano use just one word to name them: *ñan* in Quechua, *thaki* in Aymara. The word is readily modified. Villagers speak of the *jatun ñan* (large or principal road) and the *makina ñan* (railroad; literally, "machine road"). The ones who live on the southern shores of the lake speak of the local segment of the vast road network of the Inca empire as the *inka ñan* (or, in the Aymara-speaking areas, the *inka thaki*). This road thus retains its old name as well as its old use, since much of it is in good enough condition for people and pack animals to travel upon. (Details on this road can be found in John Hyslop, *The Inka Road System* [Orlando, Fla.: Academic Press, 1984]. In the time of the Incas, this road was known as the *qhapaq ñan*, the great or chiefly road.) These all contrast with the most common kind, *chaki ñan*, footpath. The Spanish word *camino* names all these *ñan*, but what English word would work best?

I thought for a while about *trail*. It fit the phrase *taruka ñan*, or deer *ñan*, which I had heard in a region a bit up from the lake where these animals are found. It seemed wholly appropriate for some human *ñan* as well. *Trail* was the word that I had used when I wrote letters to my friends to describe the route that Dante, Juan, and I had taken to the summit of Ccapia. It could describe as well the routes that zigzag up the steep rocky ridges behind many lakeshore villages, short cuts that villagers take to some of their fields instead of following the longer, flatter course around the ridges. I thought of one such route I had walked on many times behind Piata. But I rejected the word. Suited to country more wild and unsettled than the altiplano, it did not have the right feel. It also evoked an outdated image of North American Indians—derived half from Boy Scout rituals, half from old western movies—that I wanted to avoid.

A very different alternative popped into my mind: *lane,* a word as linked to peasants and country people as *trail* is to Indians. Its rustic tone appealed to me. The word evoked the narrow *ñan* near the house of the family I stayed with when I visited Amantaní, one of the largest islands in the lake. At the edge of a village, this *ñan* passes between long stone walls that surround fields covered with shrubs that flower during the rainy season, and then continues through a small eucalyptus grove. I thought of the children who drive sheep to pasture along this *ñan;* I recalled the young men who ride bicycles down it, ringing their bells as they pedal in great haste to reach the island's dock before the ferry departs for Puno. This *ñan* was wholly lanelike, but most were not. I realized that the coziness of the word was as exaggerated and inaccurate as the wildness suggested by *trail.*

My choice thus narrowed to two alternatives: *road* and *path.* Always ready for an excuse to use the *Oxford English Dictionary,* I turned to it for definitions of this pair of words. For the former, I found, "an ordinary line of communication used by persons passing between different places, usually one wide enough to admit the passage of vehicles as well as horses or travellers on foot." And for path, "a way beaten or trodden by the feet of men or beasts; a narrow unmade and (usually) unenclosed way across the open country, through woods or fields, over a mountain, etc.; a footway or footpath, as opposed to a road for vehicles." I was already leaning toward *path* as the term I would use, since most *ñan* seemed narrow rather than wide. I made up my mind when I read the last part of the definition. *Footway* brought to mind *chaki ñan,* the most common sort of *ñan.*

I was pleased with the way the contrast between walking and riding played out in these words. The dictionary noted the connections between *road* and *ride,* even though it expressed some caution about etymology, especially for words like *road* and *path,* which are derived from the Germanic branch of the Indo-European language family and hence are less well represented in old documents than Latin words are. This contrast is present, in a far less remote past, in Andean Spanish as well. The word *camino* is connected to *caminar*, to walk, but paths and roads are distinguished by the way that animals, not people, travel on them. A major road would be a *carretera*, a cart road or wagon road, and therefore a road that is wide, smooth, and level enough for a pair of oxen to pull a *carreta*, a cart. A path too narrow or steep for oxen to pull such a vehicle would be a *camino de herradura*, literally a "horseshoe road," along which a horse could walk. Surely *ñan*, on the scale of the *chaki*, the human foot and leg, are paths, not roads.

217   **For the agricultural sector**   These *waru-waru* are discussed in a number of sources: Clark L. Erickson, *Investigación arqueológica del sistema agrícola de los camellones en la Cuenca del Lago Titicaca del Perú* (La Paz: Piwa, 1996), and "The Lake Titicaca Basin: A Precolumbian Built Landscape," in *Imperfect Balance: Landscape Transformations in the Precolumbian Americas*, ed. David Lantz (New York: Columbia University Press, 2000), 311–56; Alan L. Kolata, "Technology and Organization of Agricultural Production in the Tiwanaku State," *Latin American Antiquity* 2 (2): 99–125 (1991); and Joseph Henry Press, *Regenerating Agriculture: Policies and Practice for Sustainability and Self-Reliance* (Washington, D.C.: National Academy Press 1995).

220   **However, the Peruvian government still lists these oil fields**   While this book was being prepared for printing, the issue of petroleum exploration surfaced once again. The October 2001 issue of *Perupetro News*, the official bulletin of the state agency that manages petroleum and natural gas concessions, states, "Perupetro S.A. and the Yukos Oil Co. have reached an agreement on the Technical Evaluation Agreement for Area V in the Lake Titicaca Basin. This agreement is for an area of 1.5 million hectares in the highland region, Department of Puno, where the Pirin field discovered in the last quarter of the nineteenth century is located." Yukos is the second-largest Russian petroleum firm. It was founded in 1993 as part of the transformation of former Soviet state enterprises. Its first years were rocky, but it was able to grow by attracting foreign investment and acquiring other, smaller firms. The future of the global petroleum industry seems particularly uncertain as I write this note in October 2001. The attacks of September 11, 2001, on the World Trade Center and the Pentagon are likely to affect the supply and the demand for this commodity, and may well reduce exploration for some time. Nonetheless, it is once again possible that drilling will begin on the shores of Lake Titicaca.

220   **While in Puno, I heard of a second threat**   PELT has supported the construction of a set of floodgates on the Río Desaguadero. The justification for this project, which cost more than seven million dollars to construct, was that it would moderate the fluctuations of the level of the lake, preventing

flooding at times of high water and reducing the impact of the drop of the lake in dry years. The floodgates were installed in 1999. However, there were several flaws in their design. The engineers did not take into account the fact that water flows from the Río Desaguadero back into Lake Titicaca when the lake level is low and there is a strong flow into the Río Desaguadero from its tributaries downstream of the lake. Such conditions occurred in 1999, and the town of Desaguadero had serious floods as a result. Plans for modifying the floodgates are currently under discussion. In any event, their impact is likely to be more serious in the regions south of Lake Titicaca, rather than on the lake itself.

222 **Some have called it a guerrilla movement** The source for this quotation is Deborah Poole and Gerardo Rénique, *Peru: Time of Fear* (London: Latin American Bureau, 1992), 2.

222 **A brutal civil war ensued** Sources on the Shining Path include Steve Stern, ed., *Shining and Other Paths: War and Society in Peru, 1980–1995* (Durham, N.C.: Duke University Press, 1998); Carlos Iván Degregori, *Qué difícil es ser Dios: Ideología y violencia política en Sendero Luminoso* (Lima: El Zorro de Abajo, 1989), and *Ayacucho 1969–1979: El surgimiento de Sendero Luminoso* (Lima: Instituto de Estudios Peruanos, 1990); Gustavo Gorriti, *Sendero: Historia de la guerra milenaria en el Perú* (Lima: Editorial Apoyo, 1990); and Nelson Manrique, "La caída de la cuarta espada y los senderos que se bifurcan," *Márgenes* 8 (13–14): 11–42 (1995).

224 **As some observers have noted** These observers include Stern, in *Shining and Other Paths,* and Orin Starn, in *Nightwatch: The Politics of Protest in the Andes* (Durham, N.C.: Duke University Press, 1999).

225 **Historians have reexamined large-scale indigenous uprisings** The literature on this topic is extensive and diverse. Two important books that discuss the concept and offer detailed accounts of empirical instances of resistance are James C. Scott, *Weapons of the Weak: Everyday Forms of Peasant Resistance* (New Haven: Yale University Press, 1985), and Aihwa Ong, *Spirits of Resistance and Capitalist Discipline: Factory Women in Malaysia* (Albany: State University of New York Press, 1987). Major reviews of this concept are, for its use within anthropology, Sherry B. Ortner, "Resistance and the Problem of Ethnographic Refusal," *Comparative Studies in Society and History* 37 (1): 173–93 (1995), and, within Latin American studies, Florencia E. Mallon, "The Promise and Dilemma of Subaltern Studies: Perspectives from Latin American History," *American Historical Review* 99 (5): 1491–1516 (1994).

226 **They continue to control much of this world** The phrase "Native Lands in Native Hands" has been used extensively by the Cultural Conservancy, a Native American environmental organization, to convey its core concern of strengthening land stewardship by indigenous peoples.

226   **A recent book bears the provocative title**   This book is Steven C. Topik and Allan Wells, eds., *The Second Conquest of Latin America: Coffee, Henequen, and Oil during the Export Boom, 1850–1930* (Austin: University of Texas Press, 1998).

227   **It rests on the idea**   This phrase is taken from the title of a much reprinted book that first appeared in the 1960s: Albert O. Hirschman, *Journeys toward Progress: Studies of Economic Policy-Making in Latin America* (New York: Twentieth Century Fund, 1963).

228   **As persuasive as it is pervasive**   Anthropological critiques of this notion of development include James Ferguson, *The Anti-Politics Machine: "Development," Depoliticization, and Bureaucratic Power in Lesotho* (Cambridge: Cambridge University Press, 1990); Arturo Escobar, *Encountering Development: The Making and Unmaking of the Third World* (Princeton, N.J.: Princeton University Press, 1995); Akhil Gupta, *Postcolonial Developments: Agriculture in the Making of Modern India* (Durham, N.C.: Duke University Press, 1998); Donald S. Moore, "The Crucible of Cultural Politics: Reworking 'Development' in Zimbabwe's Eastern Highlands," *American Ethnologist* 26 (3): 654–99 (1999); and Marc Edelman, *Peasants against Globalization: Rural Social Movements in Costa Rica* (Stanford: Stanford University Press, 1999).

229   **It is worth pausing a moment**   My sources for this account are Don Kulick, "Language Shift and Language Socialization in Gapun: A Report on Fieldwork in Progress," *Language and Linguistics in Melanesia* 15 (1–2): 125–51 (1987); Don Kulick and Christopher Stroud, "Christianity, Cargo, and Ideas of Self: Patterns of Literacy in a Papua New Guinean Village," *Man* 25 (2): 286–304 (1990); Don Kulick, "'Coming Up' in Gapun: Conceptions of Development and Their Effect on Language in a Papua New Guinea Village," in *Kam-ap or Take-off: Local Notions of Development,* ed. G. Dahl and A. Rabo (Stockholm: Stockholm Studies in Social Anthropology, 1972), 10–34; and Don Kulick and Margaret E. Wilson, "Echoing Images: The Construction of Savagery among Papua New Guinean Villagers," *Visual Anthropology* 5 (2): 143–52 (1992). The quotations are from Kulick, "'Coming Up,'" p. 17.

232   **In Zimbabwe, for example, the Shona word** *budiriro*   The use of this term, and the reshaping of notions of development more broadly, are discussed in Moore, "The Crucible of Cultural Politics." A similar reworking of *development* in Nepal is discussed in Stacy Pigg, "Inventing Social Categories through Place: Social Representations and Development in Nepal," *Comparative Studies in Society and History* 34 (3): 491–513 (1992).

233   **The villagers' notions of time**   Of the extensive literature on notions of time, memory, and history in the Andes, I have been particularly influenced by Olivia Harris, "The Dead and the Devils among the Bolivian Laymi," in *Death and the Regeneration of Life,* ed. Maurice Bloch and

Jonathan Parry (Cambridge: Cambridge University Press, 1982), 45–73; Catherine J. Allen, "Patterned Time: The Mythic History of a Peruvian Community," *Journal of Latin American Lore* 10 (2): 151–73 (1984); Joanne Rappaport, *The Politics of Memory: Native Historical Interpretation in the Colombian Andes* (Cambridge: Cambridge University Press, 1990); Silvia Rivera Cusicanqui, *Pachakuti: Los aymara de Bolivia frente a medio milenio de colonialismo* (La Paz: Taller de Historia Oral Andina, 1991); Peter Gose, *Deathly Waters and Hungry Mountains: Agrarian Ritual and Class Formation in an Andean Town* (Toronto: University of Toronto Press, 1994); Frank Salomon, "Los *quipus* y libros de la Tupicocha de hoy," in *Arqueología, antropología, e historia en los Andes: Homenaje a María Rostworowski*, ed. Rafael Varón Gabai and Javier Flores Espinosa (Lima: Instituto de Estudios Peruanos, 1997), 241–58; and Thomas Abercrombie, *Pathways of Memory and Power: Ethnography and History among an Andean People* (Madison: University of Wisconsin Press, 1998).

234   **Rather than discussing the economic factors alone**   To be sure, there are some broader discourses for change in the altiplano. As shown in Dan C. Hazen, "The Awakening of Puno: Government Policy and the Indian Problem in Southern Peru, 1900–1955" (Ph.D. dissertation, Yale University, 1974), and José Tamayo Herrera, *Historia social e indigenismo en el altiplano* (Lima: Ediciones Trentaitrés, 1982), the 1920s were a period of broad change, with Indian uprisings, the spread of Protestantism, and the opening of schools and marketplaces in the countryside. As Hazen discusses in "Meanings of Literacy in the Third World: The Concepts and Consequences of the *Rijchary* Reform Movement in Highland Peru," *Journal of Library History* 16 (2): 404–15 (1981), there was some use at that time and more recently of the metaphors of *rikchariy*, "awakening," and *jatariy*, "arising." These terms both point ultimately to two paired notions. One is the contrast of night and day, of positive change being like increasing light. The other is the contrast between lying down and standing, of positive change being like getting up. These terms, moreover, may allude to an Andean notion of deep historical time as a succession of epochs. However, the villagers seem to have spoken more simply of ending injustice. They speak of what is just or correct—*chanin*, in Quechua. A key notion in such change has been the idea of the abuse of villagers by state authorities and landlords. The term in Spanish is the cognate *abuso;* Quechua-speakers use a metaphor rooted in humanity.

234   **In the villagers' accounts**   Although this notion of epochs draws on the myths of the Incas, it does not rest exclusively on ideas that were present in pre-Columbian times. Villagers' notions of epochs and transformations draw also on Christian beliefs of creation and of the redemption of human-

ity through the intervention of Jesus. The narratives of national history that are taught in public schools also emphasize the Spanish conquest and the wars of independence as brief periods that separate radically different epochs, and they may have influenced villagers' notions of time as well.

235 **A noted historian has discussed the recurrence of utopian thinking** Alberto Flores Galindo, *Buscando un inca: Identidad y utopia en los Andes* (Lima: Instituto de Apoyo Agrario, 1987).

Acknowledgments

A walk with local villagers on the shores of Lake Titicaca is an exercise in memory, as points in the landscape bring forth stories of the past. A path passes between two low hills and reaches an isolated house with a stone corral where lambs were born, strange ones that all grew up to have two pairs of horns. From a hilltop, a rock can be descried out in the lake where, I learn, a boat crashed one morning years earlier. Crossing a pasture on a ridge, I see the low crumbling walls of an ancient building and hear once again the tales of the Incas who inhabited the region before the arrival of the Europeans.

Writing this book has been a similar exercise in memory. Each section—virtually every paragraph—has touched off recollections of the people who helped me in many ways in the decades since I first visited Lake Titicaca. I would like especially to mention two colleagues, since my years of living and working on the shores of Lake Titicaca began with their assistance. They are Gordon Appleby, whom I have known since our days as graduate students in anthropology in northern California and who was my first host in Puno, and Peter Richerson, a biologist whom I met in our early years as faculty members in environmental studies at the University of California at Davis. Both of them had extensive experience in the Lake Titicaca region and generously shared their knowledge and insight with me at the critical time when I began working there. As I think of them, I would like to acknowledge as well the support of three institutions. The National Science Foundation provided critical financing for the research, and the University of California at Davis gave valuable support in the form of faculty research grants and sabbatical leave. In addition, I spent a sabbatical year at the Lamont-Doherty Earth Observatory of Columbia University; in recognition of this time, during which I wrote drafts of chapters, and of my continued association with that institution, this book has received a Lamont Publication Number, 6152.

There are many other people to whom I also wish to express my deep appreciation. This book would not have been possible without their kind help, and I have not forgotten them. I hope that I have made clear to the readers of these pages that this is a memory-filled book of a memory-filled landscape, and I hope that I have succeeded in showing how crucial it was for me to know Cirilo Cutipa, a man from the lakeshore village of Socca, and other individuals as well. I mention many specific people in the chapters of this book and in the notes to each chapter. I trust that my gratitude to each of them is evident.

Index

Page numbers in italics indicate figures and maps.

Acora district, 24, 191–92, 203, 213
acronyms, 96–97
agriculture, *12, 146, 233;* as assistance, 107; during drought, 132–33; fishing's intersection with, 113–14; and Shining Path, 223; temporal perspective on, 232–33; *waru-waru* fields of, 217; as work, 105, 114–15
Albert, Lake (Africa), 42
Alfaro, Charo, 215–16
Alfaro, René, 21, *86,* 213, 215–16, 219, 223
Allison, Charlene, 246–47*n*
almas perdidas (lost souls): dogs as, 25
altiplano (Andean plateau), *xvii;* archaeological sites of, 42–43; geological history of, 40–42; government maps of, 17–18, *19–20;* indigenous languages of, 52; PELT maps of, 217, 218
Amaquilla village, 160
Amazon River, 118
An American Tragedy (Dreiser), xii–xiv, xxii
Arapa, Lake, 223
archaeological records, 42–43, 120–21

Arequipa, 29, 140, 169, 188
Arguedas, José María, 8–11, 244*n*
arroba (unit of measure), 81, 98, 99
ASARCO, 168
Atacama Desert, 37
Atojja mountain, 23
Atwood, Margaret, xiv
Aymara (native language), xxv, 6; bilingual education in, 199; and collective identity, 65–67; and mapping project, 218; radio broadcasts in, 64, 252*n;* term for *fisherman* in, 52–53; term for *road* in, 269–71*n;* of Urus, 122
ayuda (help), 100–1, 107–8
Azágaro province, 223

Bahía de Puno, 76, 131, 148; CENFOR boundary markers in, 207–8; diversion's threat to, 220–21; floating islands of, *9,* 181–82, 193; sewage in, 219; silverside in, 153; territorial incursions in, 161; totora beds of, 188, 194; totora cutting contracts in, 201–3, 204–5

Baikal, Lake (Siberia), 42

Ballivián, Lake, 42

balsas: construction of, 181, *181;* crews on, 92, 99–101, 108, 255*n;* description of, 122–23, *123;* measurement of, 203; of myth, 80; night fishing in, 129–30; in Palm Sunday festival, 178–79, *179;* poles for pushing, *66,* 200; replacement of, 136, 141; rules for using, 45, 246*n;* statistics on, 136, 168; trawl net fishing from, 124–25, *125,* 259*n;* without registration, 264*n*

Basilichthys bonaerensis. See silverside

basket traps. See *qollanchas*

Battle of Zepita (1823), 26

Billinghurst, Guillermo, 125

bioeconomic models: as development notion, 231; of fishery depletion, 90–91; local application of, 92–94, 253–54*n;* time notion in, 114, 258*n;* use rights factor of, 95–96, 97–98, 254*n;* and work calculations, 98–101, 255*n*

birds, 194–95, 219, 268*n. See also* coots; flamingos; grebes

Blair, Philip, 63

boats. *See* wooden boats

boga *(Orestias pentlandii),* 71, 118, 219, 258–59*n*

Bolivia: author's map of, 18; naval bases of, 158–59; travel between Peru and, 23–35

bolsas (sacks for storing live fish), 170, 171, 230

Brisas del Sur (radio program), 5

Brookner, Anita, xv

brook trout *(Salvelinus fontinalis),* 261*n*

brown trout *(Salmo trutta),* 138, 261*n*

Bustamante, Eufracio, *73, 197;* in confrontation with villagers, 196–98; fishermen census of, 72–73; laboratory budget of, 70–71, 89; retirement of, 216

Bustamante y Rivero (president of Peru), 260*n*

Cachipucara village, 77, 81, 236

canneries, 147–48, 149–51, *152,* 155, 263*n*

Capachica Peninsula, *xiii,* 131, 160; carrying cloth from, *xxvi*

carachi (native fish), 168; in meals, 154; of *Orestias* flock, 119; PELT reports on, 219; trawl net fishing for, 124, 259*n;* types of, 71; vendors selling, 72, *120*

Caretas (newsmagazine), 77

carga (unit of measure), 203

Carino village, 131

carrying cloth, *xxvi*

Castillo, Ignacio, 139

Castillo, Pedro, 78, 139, 143, 149, 216, 231

catch survey: author's plans for, 69–70; economic dimension of, 89–91, 92–94, 98, 253–54*n;* equipment items on, 169–70; FAO guidelines for, 75; fishermen census for, 50–51, 72–74; participants in, 78–80, *79, 85;* pricing factor of, 71–72; training workshops for, 81–83, 99; transfer of data from, 84, 86–88, *86,* 99–100; use rights implication of, 95–96, 254*n;* zones and villages of, 76–77

catfish, 71, 126–27, 219

Catholics, 111

cattle: sale of, 188; totora fodder for, 182, 183, 184–87, 231, 265*n,* 266*n;* urban demand for, 183–84

Ccapia mountain, *30;* ascent to, 29–33; descent from, 38–39; elevation of, 18; grasslands *(puna)* of, 31–32; planning to climb, 21–23; roads to, 24–26, *30;* views from, 33–36; views of, 212

CENFOR (Centro Nacional Forestal): boundary markers of, 207–8; establishment of, 191; measurement concerns of, 203–4; reserve project of, 192–93; totora cutting contracts of, 201–3, 204–5; villagers' opposition to, 191–92, 196, 199–201, 206–7, 227; waterfowl focus of, 194–95

Chandler, Raymond: *The Lady in the Lake,* xiv, xx

Chapman, Don, 75–76

child care, 106–7, 108

Chiripo, Escolástico: drawings by, *123, 179*

Choquehuanca, Dante: background of, 29; climbing Ccapia with, 35–37, 38–40; pond legends of, 32–33

Choquehuanca, Diogenes, 27, 28–29

Choquehuanca, Juan, 29, 31, 32, 35, 36, 39

Christianity, 111, 189, 229, 235; epochal notion of, 274–75*n;* lake imagery in, xxiii–xxiv

Chucuito district, 24; cannery in, 147–48; fish hatchery in, 134, 138, 150, 161, 166; measurement conversion in, 203; structures of, 28

Chucuito Peninsula, 194

Chuquiñapi village (Bolivia), 34, 63

Cirilo. *See* Cutipa, Cirilo

climate: drought conditions of, 131, 132–33, 165; and lake variations, 41–42; temporal perspective on, 232–33; of western vs. eastern cordilleras, 37–38

clinker-building, 262–63*n*

Club Canottieri (sailing club), 70

coca, 31, 77

Coetzee, J. M., 241–42*n*
Cohasía village, 82, 149, 198
Cole, Sally Cooper, 246–47*n*
Colla (Aymara kingdom), 26
Collins, Jane, 244*n*
comités communales (communal committees), 192
Compañía Pesquera Puno, 147, 151
conquest narratives, 224–27
construction: of balsas, 181, *181;* of floating islands, 181–82; in help category, 107; as work, 105–6, 114–15
Contreras, Jesús, 255–56*n*
coots, 195
Copacabana (Bolivia), 24–25, 26, 34, 159, 212
Cordillera de Carabaya, 35, 37
Cordillera Occidental (western cordillera), 28, 37–38, 40–41, 220–21
Cordillera Oriental (eastern cordillera), 35, 37–38, 40–41
Cordillera Real, *12, 23,* 35–36, *36*
Coregonus clupeaformis (whitefish), 133, 138, 261*n*
crafts: in help category, 107; as work, 106
Cutipa, Alejandrina, 214
Cutipa, Cirilo, *xviii, 3,* 22, 143; author's time with, xvi, xviii, 212, 213–15; catch survey role of, 72; on cattle fodder, 184–87; development language of, 231; schoolhouse story of, 214; on sleeping, 253–54*n*
Cutipa, Felix, 213–14
Cutipa, Osvaldo, 213
Cuzco, 140
Cyprinodontidae (pupfish family), 118

Davis, Dona Lee, 246–47*n*
Desaguadero, 24, 26, 36, 271–72*n*
despedidas (farewells). *See* farewells
development (concept): absence of terms for, 231–32; at Lake Titicaca, 230–31; in Papua New Guinea, 229–30; progress notion of, 227–28; tangible paths of, 235–36; temporal perspective on, 232–35, 274*n*
diaries: characteristics of, 102–4, 256*n;* diary-keepers, 102–3, 257*n;* nonwork activities in, 106–8, 256–57*n;* profitability references in, 108–10; road/path references in, 210; source of, 101; time references in, 110–14, 257*n,* 258*n;* work activities in, 104–6
dip nets *(sajjaña),* 125–26, 137, 260*n*
dogs: as lost souls, 25
Dominique. *See* Levieil, Dominique
Dora (Philip Blair's maid), 63–66
double-generations (notion), 234

Dreiser, Theodore: *An American Tragedy,* xii–xiv, xxii
drought, 131, 132–33, 165, 233, 234
drownings, 144

eastern cordillera (Cordillera Oriental), 35, 37–38, 40–41
El Niño events, 165, 233
Escuela de Pescadores Indígenas (School for Indian Fishermen), 51, 148
eucalyptus: groves, 39; poles, 200, 201
Eufracio. *See* Bustamante, Eufracio

FAO (United Nations Food and Agriculture Organization), 50, 74–75, 89
farewells *(despedidas):* to Arguedas's fictional self, 9–11; meals served at, 2, 12–13, 237, 244–45*n;* recollection request at, 3–5
Farfán, Edgar, 70
farming. *See* agriculture
fish: catch estimates of, 149, 150, 151, 163, 169, 218; catch survey of, 69–70, 74–76; fishermen's marketing of, 169–70, 230–31; native species of, 71, 118–19, 258–59*n;* shift in mix of, 168, 219; of Urus, 121; weight measurement of, 71. *See also* carachi; catch survey; catfish; *Orestias;* silverside; trout
Fish Culture Section (United States Bureau of Fisheries), 137
fisheries: bioeconomic model of, 89–90; canneries' impact on, 147–51, 261*n,* 263*nn;* contamination/diversion threats to, 166–68, 219–21, 271*n;* depletion problem of, 90–91; development narrative of, 230–31; fish licensing's impact on, 159–61, 264*n;* floating cage incursions into, 163–66; local vs. outside management of, 45–46, 91–92, 246*n,* 253*n;* military's nationalization of, 155–56; new species' impact on, 133–37; PELT reports on, 218–19; territorial use rights of, 94–96, 231, 254*n. See also* fishermen; fishing
fisherman (term): gender-specific use of, 47–48, 246–47*n;* local equivalents of, 49–50, 52–57; Spanish word for, 50–52
fishermen, *66, 93;* boat crews of, 92, 99–101, 108, 255*nn;* boat names by, 158; cannery's relations with, 147–48, 149–50, 263*n;* as catch survey participants, 78–80, *79,* 81–83, *85,* 99; census survey of, 50–51, 72–74; gendered role of, 48–49, 248*n;* gill net experiments of, 140–41; gill net repairs by, 100, 107; gill net trips of, *xix,* 92–93, 113–14, 253–54*n,* 258*n;* marketing efforts by,

fishermen *(continued)*
169–70, 230–31; migration of, 82, 252–53*n*;
navy's licensing of, 156–57, 159–61, 264*n*;
nonfishing work of, 98, 113, 254–55*n*;
numbers of, 168–69, 218; patience/preci-
sion of, 130; Peruvian vs. Bolivian, 62–63;
prehistory/history of, 119–22; territorial
use rights of, 94–96, 231, 254*n*; village ties
of, 15–16; wooden boats of, *46*, 141–43,
158; work calculations by, 98–101, 253–
54*n*. *See also* villagers
fishing: calculating time spent, 98–101, 112–
14, 253–54*n*; with dip nets, 125–26, 260*n*;
economic returns for, 98, 255*nn*; with fish
harpoons, 126–27; at night, 129–30, 144;
with *qollanchas*, 127–28, *128*, 129; with
scoop nets, 127; technological advances in,
14–15, 136–37; with trawl nets, 123–25,
125, 259*n*. *See also* balsas; wooden boats
flamingos, 37
floating cages, 163–66, *165*
floating islands, *9*, 132, 193, 201, 205; construction of, 181–82
flooding, *23*, 233, *233*
food. *See* meals
*Food, Gender, and Poverty in the Ecuadorian
Andes* (Weismantel), 61–62
Forbes, David, 126
forgetting: as abandonment, 11–13, 244*n*,
244–45*n*; and acronyms, 97; and farewell
request, 3–5; as lover's betrayal, 6–8,
243*nn*; role of paths in, 237; in twentieth
century, 14–15. *See also* memory
Frente de Defensa de la Totora (Totora Defense Front), 196, 268–69*n*
Fulica gigantea (giant coot), 195

Galilee, Sea of, xxiii–xxiv
Gapun (Papua New Guinea), 229–30, 235
gender: complementarity patterns of, 48–49,
247–48*n*, 248*n*; terminology of, 47–48, 246–
47*n*; unmarked in Quechua, 56–57, 249*n*
geological history, 40–42
giant coot *(Fulica gigantea)*, 195
gill nets, *xix*, 168; experiments with, 140–41;
fishermen's trips to, *xix*, 92–93, 113–14,
253–54*n*, 258*n*; time spent repairing, 100,
107
Great Lakes (North America), 137–38
Great Salt Lake (Utah), xxii
grebes, 194–95, 219
Grupo México, 168

haircutting ritual, 214
Hamilton, Burt, 147–48

haqonta (scoop nets), 127, 137
harpoons *(majjaña)*, 126–27, 137
hatcheries, 137, 138, 150, 161, 166
Hilda (author's assistant), 3, *86*, 196–97;
divorce of, 216; fishing data concerns of,
99–100; hiring of, 84–86
Hornberger, Nancy, 248–49*n*
Hotel du Lac (Brookner), xv–xvi, xviii, xx
Housekeeping (Robinson), 241–42*n*
Hoyo, Tomás, 102
Huancané district, 196, 203
Huarisani village, 82
Huatajata village, 141
Huata marketplace, *155*
Huayna Potosí peak (Cordillera Real), 35, 38
Hugo. *See* Treviño, Hugo
Huincalla village, 164
huk'a (unit of measure), 71, 203

ichu (perennial grass), 31–32
identity: cultural vs. economic, 58–59, 249–
51*n*; food's expression of, 61–62; gender,
47–49, 56–57, 246–47*n*, 248*n*, 249*n*; spatial, 59–60, 66–67
Ilave district, 24; Totora Defense League of,
191–92, 196, 206
Illahuamán Chipana, Juan, 244*n*
Illampu peak (Cordillera Real), 35, 38
Illimani peak (Cordillera Real), 35, 38, 145
IMARPE (Instituto del Mar del Perú), *73*;
budget of, 70–71, 89; FAO advisers to, 74–
75, 252*n*; farewell party of, 2–4; fishermen
census of, 50–51, 70, 72–74; focus/respon-
sibilities of, 50; laboratory closing at, 212,
216; *pescador* term of, 51–52; training workshops at, 81–83, 99; villagers' relations
with, 196–98, 227
Inca empire, 25–26, 120–21
Indian (term), 58–59, 60, 249–51*n*
Inland Waters Division (IMARPE), 70
Instituto del Mar del Perú. *See* IMARPE
introduction of species: hatcheries for, 137,
138; to Lake Lanao, 134; to Lake Poopó,
152–53; to Lake Titicaca, 133–34, 137–38,
261*n*; to Lake Victoria, 134
Isbell, Billie Jean, 251*n*
Isla del Sol, 34, 80
Isla Foroba, 117
Isla Soto, 34; in catch survey project, 76–79,
79, 234; description of, 80; intruders on, 82
ispi (native fish), 49, 71, 128, 129, 163–64, 219

James, M. C., 133–34, 137–38, 261*n*
Japanese International Cooperation Agency,
166

jarahui (type of song), 10–11
Jesus Christ: miracles of, xxiii–xxiv; nature and, xxiii–xxiv
Juliaca, 36
Juli district, 24, 32–33
Junsani village, 145

kacharpari (a farewell), 2
K'api villages, 132
Keillor, Garrison: *Lake Wobegon Days,* xii, xxiv
khipu (knotted cords), 256n
Kulick, Don, 229–30

LaBarre, Weston, 265n
The Lady in the Lake (Chandler), xiv, xx
Lago Grande, 18; canneries at, 148; as catch survey zone, 76–77; oil drilling at, 166–67, 219–20; silverside in, 153; view of, 33
Lago Pequeño, 18, 42; cannery at, 148; as catch survey zone, 76; diversion's threat to, 220; incursions into, 160–61; reedbeds of, 194; silverside in, 153, 263n; trawl nets of, 124; view of, 33
Lago Umayo, 194
lakes: as destination, xiv–xvi, 241–42n; geological history of, 41–42; as presence, xxi–xxv, 241–42n; shared experiences of, xxvi–xxvii
lake trout (*Salvelinus namaycush*), 138, 261n
lakeweed, *183,* 184
Lake Wobegon Days (Keillor), xii, xxiv
languages of the altiplano, *52. See also* Aymara; Quechua; Spanish language
La Niña events, 233
La Paz (Bolivia): author's visits to, 62–65, 252n; travel between Puno and, 23–25; trout market in, 140, 147
lata (unit of measure), 81, 98, 99
Levieil, Dominique, 4, 50, *51;* bioeconomic models of, 89–90, 91, 92–94, 253–54n; career of, 211; drawings by, *frontispiece, 125, 142;* fishermen census of, 74; and trout issue, 134; TURF argument of, 95, 97–98, 231, 254n; and wooden boats, 141–43, 262–63n
Ley de Aguas (water use regulations), 191
libros de actas (village record books), 256n
Liga de Defensa de la Totora (Totora Defense League), 191–92, 196, 206
liwi (type of weapon), 178
Lost Lake (Slouka), xxii–xxiii
lovers: as forgetful, 6–8, 243n, 244n; as haughty, 8; as proud, 7–8; as ungrateful, 8

Lupaqa, 24, 26
Luribay, 27

majjaña (fish harpoons), 126–27, 137
Malawi, Lake (Africa), 42
Mamani, Ramón, 102
maps: accuracy of, 19; of altiplano, *xvii,* 17–18; of Ccapia, *30;* dilemmas tied to, 20–21, 26–27; of indigenous languages, *52;* of Lake Titicaca basin, *19;* of PELT project, 217, 218; of totora beds, *185,* 193–94, 267n
Maquera, Julio Constantino, 109, 110, 257n
Maquera, Pedro, 103, 108–9
Marine Institute. *See* IMARPE (Institute del Mar del Perú)
meals: at farewells, 2, 12–13, 80, 237, 244–45n; identity tied to, 61–62; as nonwork activity, 107; from totora reeds, 132, 182–83; types of fish in, 154
measurement. *See* units of measure
Melgar province, 223
memoriales: of Totora Defense Front, 196; of Totora Defense League, 192
memory: floating islands of, 182; of incursions/expropriation, 198–99; of local territorial control, 190, 192, 267n; of readers, 237–39; role of paths in, 236–37; totora story of, 183–87; villagers' ties to, xix–xx, xxv, 3–5, 14–15, 16, 243n. *See also* forgetting
Menchú, Rigoberta, 225
Military Geographical Institute, 20
Ministry of Agriculture, 148, 151, 191, 192, 193, 267n
Ministry of Fisheries, 46, 89; creation of, 156; trout aquaculture projects of, 162–66. *See also* IMARPE (Institute del Mar del Perú)
Misti peak (Cordillera Occidental), 37
Moho district, 60, 158, 169–70
Moquegua, 167, 169
Murra, John V., 254n
myths: of the flood, 34; of the pond, 32–33; of stone balsas, 80

Nadel-Klein, Jane, 246–47n
names. *See* terms
narratives: of conquest, 224–27; of development, 227–32; of lakes as destination, xiv–xvi, 241–42n; of lakes as presence, xxi–xxv, xxvi–xxvii, 241–42n; of night fishing, 144; of Shining Path, 223; of Socca schoolhouse, 214; of telephone's communicative space, 63–67, 252n; of totora as cattle fodder, 184–87; of trout's first appearance, 139–40; of water, xi–xii. *See also* diaries; myths

National Forestry Center (Centro Nacional Forestal). *See* CENFOR
National Science Foundation, 69
navy: boat registration by, 150–51, 156–59, 264*n*; licensing of fishermen by, 159–60, 161, 264*n*
Nazca plate, 40–41
nets: dip, 125–26, 137, 260*n*; scoop, 127, 137; trawl, 123–25, *125*, 137, 259*n*. *See also* gill nets
Neveu-Lemaire, Maurice, 193–94, 267*n*

oil drilling, 166–68, 219–20
Oncorhynchus mykiss (rainbow trout), 134, 138, 261*n*. *See also* trout
Orestias: agassii (*see* carachi); *cuvieri* (umantu), 135; as fish flock, 119; *luteus*, 258–59*n*; PELT reports on, 219; *pentlandii* (boga), 71, 118, 219, 258–59*n*; *puni*, 258–59*n*
"Orgullosa Combapateñita" (song, "Proud Girl from Combapata"), 7–8
Oruno Sport Fishing Club, 152–53
Ostrom, Elinor, 91–92, 95–96

Pacajes (Aymara kingdom), 25–26
Palm Sunday festival, 178–79, *179*
Papua New Guinea, 229–30, 235
Parinacota peak (Cordillera Occidental), 37
Parodi, Tito (author's friend), 22–23
paths: author's choice of term, 269–71*n*; of conquest, 224–27; of development, 227–32; memory's relation to, 236–37; physicality of, 210, 235–36; of Shining Path, 221–24; temporal perspective on, 210–11, 232–35
Paucarcolla cattle fairs, 188
peasant (term), 58–59, 60, 249–51*n*
PELT (Proyecto Especial Lago Titicaca), 217–19, 271–72*n*
Perca village, 202
Peru: during Great Depression, 133; independence of, 122; purchasing maps of, 20–21; resource conservation in, 190–91; Shining Path in, 221–24; travel between Bolivia and, 23–25
Peru: Time of Fear (Poole and Rénique), 222
Perupetro News, 271*n*
Peruvian Cartographic Service, 194
Peruvian Military Geographical Institute, 194
Peruvian Peasant Confederation, 196
pescador (fisherman): use of term, 50–52, 57
petroleum drilling, 166–68, 219–20
Piata village, 139, 149, 174, 231
pichu (unit of measure), 186, 203, 204

Pirín, 166–67
plate tectonics, 40–41
poles (weapons), 200, 201
pollution: from oil drilling, 166–67, 219–20, 271*n*; from Southern Peru Copper Corporation, 221
Pomata district, 24, 25–26, 36, 60, 158
pond legends, 32–33
Poole, Deborah, 222
Poopó, Lake, 118, 152–53, 217
Potosí, 121
Project Underground, 220, 221
"Proud Girl from Combapata" (song, "Orgullosa Combapateñita"), 7–8
Proyecto Especial Lago Titicaca (PELT, Special Lake Titicaca Project), 217–19, 271–72*n*
pueblo olvidado (a forgotten town), 12–13, 244–45*n*
Puma, Dionisio, 129–30
puna (grasslands), 32, 42–43, 246*n*
Puno, 36; apartment living in, 215; author's visit to, 212–13; boat registration in, 150–51, 156–57; CENFOR office in, 191; sewage from, 219; Shining Path movement in, 221–24; travel between La Paz and, 23–25
Puno Sector (Titicaca National Reserve), 193; CENFOR monitoring in, 205–6; totora cutting contracts in, 201–3, 204–5
Pusi district, 196

qatari (sea serpent), 130, 144
qollanchas (basket traps), 127–28, *128*, 129, 137, 211
Quechua (native language), xxv; author's orthography of, 242–43*n*; gender-neutral terms in, 56–57; linguistic structure of, 53–56, 248*n*, 248–49*n*; and mapping project, 218; mix of Spanish and, 6–9, 243*n*, 244*n*; "Shining Path" in, 222; Spanish occupational labels in, 57–58, 249*n*; term for *development* in, 231–32; term for *fisherman* in, 52–53; term for *road* in, 269–71*n*; work-related terms in, 100–1, 255*n*, 255–56*n*
Quispe, Hilaria, 199–201, 226
Quispe, Saturnino, 131–32

racial terms, 7
rainbow trout (*Oncorhynchus mykiss*), 134, 138, 261*n*. *See also* trout
Ramis Sector (Titicaca National Reserve), 193; territorial confrontations in, 196–201, 206
Raynal-Roques, A., 265*n*
reeds. *See* totora (*Scirpus tatora*)
Refuge (Williams), xxii

René. *See* Alfaro, René
Rénique, Gerardo, 222
research projects. *See* catch survey
Richerson, Peter, 70
Río de la Plata, 118
Río Desaguadero, 26, 33, 118, 153, 217, 271–72n
Río Huancané, 33, 82, 167, 220
Río Huenque, 220–21
Río Ilave, 28, 138, 140, 167, 168, 220
Río Ilave delta, 77; Totora Defense League of, 191–92, 196, 206
Río Ramis, 169, 233
Los ríos profundos (Arguedas), 9–11, 244n
roads. *See* paths
Robinson, Marilynne, 241–42n
Rollandia microptera (short-winged grebe), 194–95, 219
rollos (pillories), 28
runa (term for *person*), 56–57, 60
Russian oil consortium, 166–67, 219–20, 271n

Sajjama peak (Cordillera Occidental), 37
sajjaña (dip nets), 125–26, 137, 260n
Salar de Coipasa, 118
Salmo trutta (brown trout), 138, 261n
Salvelinus: fontinalis (brook trout), 261n; *namaycush* (lake trout), 138, 261n
San Juan del Oro, 80
Santa Cruz, General, 26
Santiago de Huata, 12
Sapahaqui, 27
School for Indian Fishermen (Escuela de Pescadores Indígenas), 51, 148
Scirpus tatora. See totora *(Scirpus tatora)*
scoop nets *(haqonta)*, 127, 137
sea serpent *(qatari)*, 130, 144
The Second Conquest of Latin America (Topik and Wells, eds.), 226
Sendero Luminoso (Shining Path), 212, 221–24
Seventh-Day Adventists, 111, 189
Shining and Other Paths (Stern), 222
Shining Path (Sendero Luminoso), 212, 221–24
short-winged grebe *(Rollandia microptera)*, 194–95, 219
silverside *(Basilichthys bonaerensis)*, 45, 168; description of, 71, 151–52, 263n; in Lake Poopó, 152–53; local reaction to, 154–55; PELT reports on, 219; sale of, 71; spawning of, 153–54, 263n
Slouka, Mark, xxii–xxiii
Smyth, A. J., 134, 138

Socca village, 173, 213–14, 231
social categories: of development vs. conquest notions, 228; ethnic vs. class elements of, 58–59, 249–51n; spatial dimension of, 59–60. *See also* villagers
Solomon, Frank, 256n
songs: of farewell, 10–11; of forgetful lovers, 5–8; language switching in, 6–7, 243n
Sopocachi neighborhood (La Paz), 63
South American plate, 40–41
Southern Peru Copper Corporation, 167, 168, 220–21
Spanish language: bilingual education in, 199; electronic media in, 64–65; mix of Quechua and, 6–9, 243n, 244n; term for *fisherman* in, 50–52
Special Lake Titicaca Project (Proyecto Especial Lago Titicaca, PELT), 217–19, 271–72n
Star Wars (film), 55, 65, 248n, 248–49n
Stern, Steve, 222, 223
stoneworts, 267–68n
stories. *See* narratives
Straits of Tiquina, 33, 36, 42, 141, 153
Suárez, Hugo Banzer, 158
Surfacing (Atwood), xiv–xv, xviii, xx

Tanganyika, Lake (Africa), 42
Taquile island, 82
Taraco district, 188, 196
tectonic plates, 40–41
terms: for *accompanying* vs. *helping*, 100–1, 255n; for *development*, 229–30; of ethnicity vs. class, 58–59, 249–51n; gender-specific use of, 47–48, 56–57, 246–47n, 249n; native equivalents of, 49–50, 53–56, 248–49n; for occupations, 57–58, 249n; place-based, 59–60, 251n; racial, 7; of self-labeling, 60–62; Spanish equivalent of, 50–52; for *working* vs. *doing*, 101, 255–56n
territoriality: conquest path of, 224–26; cultural legacy of, 190, 192, 226–27, 267n; fish licensing issue of, 159–61; floating cages issue of, 163–66; and Ramis Sector confrontations, 196–201; slogan for, 226, 272n; spontaneous quality of, 206–7; of totora ownership patterns, 188; use rights principle of, 94–96, 231, 254n
thaya (winds), 35, 144–46
Thoreau, Henry David, xx–xxi, xxii, xxiv
time: activities referenced by, 110; epochal unit of, 234–35, 274–75n; generational unit of, 233–34; for gill net trips, 92–93, 114, 258n; for repairing nets, 100, 107; work's relation to, 98–101, 110–14, 253–54n, 257n, 258n; year as unit of, 232–33

Tiquina, Straits of. *See* Straits of Tiquina

Tiquina naval base (Bolivia), 159, 166

Titicaca, Lake, *19, 23, 185;* biomass of, 218; cannery locations at, 147, 148; catch survey zones of, 76–77; colors of water in, 144–45; conquest narrative of, 226–27; contamination and diversion as threats to, 166–68, 219–21, 271*n;* development narrative of, 230–32; drought at, 131, 132–33, 165, 233, 234; extinction of species in, 134–35; geological history of, 42; memory's centrality to, xix–xx, xxv; native fish species of, 71, 118–19, 258–59*n;* PELT maps of, 217, 218; river system of, 118; size of, xviii, 34; spawning difficulties at, 138–39, 153–54, 263*n;* steamer trip across, 23–24; totora planting in, 176–78; trout cages in, 163–66; trout's introduction to, 133–38, 261*n;* view of, 33–34; villagers' control of, xxv, 45–46, 95–96, 206–7, 254*n*

Titicaca National Reserve, 190; boundary points in, 193, 207–8; establishment of, 193; museum of, 117–18; reserve status of, 192; territorial confrontations in, 196–201, 206–7; totora cutting contracts in, 201–3, 204–5; waterfowl focus of, 194–95

Tok Pisin language (Papua New Guinea), 229–30

Topik, Steven, 226

totora *(Scirpus tatora),* 121, 123, *185;* burning of, 178, 265*n;* as cattle fodder, 182, 183, 184–87, 188, 231, 265*n,* 266*n;* colors of, 176; contracts for cutting, 201–3, 204–5; harvesting of, *175,* 179–80, 189; items made from, 180–82, *181;* meals from, 132, 182–83; measurement of, 203–4; planting of, 176–78; reproduction of, 174, 265*n*

totora beds: CENFOR's patrols of, 199–200; formations/textures of, 174–76; local defense of, 160–61, 191–92, 196, 198; maps of, 193–94, 267*n;* ownership/rental of, 188; Palm Sunday hunt in, 178–79, *179;* stability of, 194, 267–68*n;* threats to, 166–68, 188–89, 219–20

Totora Defense Front (Frente de Defensa de la Totora), 196, 268–69*n*

Totora Defense League (Liga de Defensa de la Totora), 191–92, 196, 206

To Work and to Weep: Women in Fishing Economies (Nadel-Klein and Davis), 246–47*n*

trabajo (work). *See* work

trawl nets *(wayunaqana),* 123–25, *125,* 137, 259*n*

Treviño, Hugo, 21–22, 73, 216; and catch survey, 75–76, 77, 78–79, 79, 84, 88, 89; in con-

frontation with villagers, 196–98; fishermen census of, 73; training workshops of, 81–83, 99

Trichomycterus genus, 118

trout: aquaculture projects for, 162–66; canneries for, 147–48, 149–51, 263*n;* feed for, 163–64; first appearance of, 139–40; hatcheries for, 138, 161; local oversupply of, 146–47; nets for catching, 140–41; night fishing for, 144; silverside's impact on, 153, 154–55; spawning grounds of, 138–39; Titicaca's introduction of, 133–38, 261*n;* weight measurement of, 71

Tupac Amaru (José Gabriel Túpac Amaru), 122

TURF (territorial use rights in fishing), 95–97, 231, 254*n*

Turkana, Lake (Africa), 42

umantu *(Orestias cuvieri),* 135

Umuchi village, 158

United Nations, 228; FAO of, 50, 74–75, 89

United States Bureau of Fisheries, Fish Culture Section, 137

units of measure, 71, 81, 98, 99, 186, 203–4

Urus people, 121–22, 182, 226

Urus settlements. *See* floating islands

Valenzuela, Cristósomo, 217

Victoriano (IMARPE driver), 84, 85, 196–98, 216

vigilante del lago (totora guard), 189

villagers: abandonment concerns of, 3–5, 11–14, 236–37, 244*n,* 244–45*n;* and acronyms, 97; conquest narrative of, 226–27; ethnicity/class labels for, 58–59, 249–51*n;* memory's centrality to, xix–xx, xxv, 14–15, 16, 243*n;* Peruvian vs. Bolivian, 62–63; *pescador* term of, 50–52; place-based labels for, 59–60, 251*n;* self-labeling by, 60–62; in territorial confrontations, 45–46, 190–92, 196–201, 206–7, 267*n;* territorial use rights of, 94–96, 231, 254*n,* 260*n;* time notions of, 232–35, 274–75*n;* totora cutting contracts with, 201–3, 204–5; totora harvesting by, *175,* 179–80; totora planting by, 176–78. *See also* fishermen

villages: in catch survey zones, 76–77; distinctive features of, 173–74; fishermen's ties to, 15–16; fish licensing's impact on, 159–61, 264*n;* floating cages of, *165,* 165–66; number of fishermen in, 73–74; as *pueblo olvidado,* 12–13, 244*n,* 244–45*n;* totora guard of, 189; trout farms in, 162–63; use of term, 60, 251*n*

Vilquechico district, 60, 158
Vilurcuni Peninsula, 160
violence: during cannery operations, 149; of
  civil war, 222–23; against fish licensing
  incursions, 160–61; against floating cage
  project, 164–65; in Ramis Sector, 196–201;
  of Shining Path, 221–22; spontaneous quality of, 206–7; weapons of, 200–1
Viracocha (god), 34, 80
Virgin of Copacabana, 25

Wachtel, Nathan, 121
Waiting for the Barbarians (Coetzee), 241–42*n*
Walden and Civil Disobedience (Thoreau), xx–
  xxi
Walden Pond (Massachusetts), xx–xxi
waru-waru (raised fields), 217
waterfowl, 194–95, 219, 268*n*
wathiya (kind of potato), 213
Waugh, Geoffrey, 90–91
wayunaqana (large trawl nets), 123–25, *125*,
  137, 259*n*
Weismantel, Mary, 61–62, 65
Wells, Allan, 226
western cordillera (Cordillera Occidental),
  28, 37–38, 40–41, 220–21
whitefish *(Coregonus clupeaformis)*, 133, 138,
  261*n*
Williams, Brackette, 244–45*n*

Williams, Terry Tempest, xxii, xxiv
winds *(thaya)*, 35, 144–46
women: as carachi vendors, 72; fishing role
  of, 48–49, *49*, *54*, 125, 248*n*; nonwork activities of, 106–7
*Women of the Praia: Work and Lives in a Por-
  tuguese Coastal Community* (Cole), 246–47*n*
wooden boats, 46; crews on, 92, 99–101, 108,
  255*n*; names of, 157–58; navy's registration
  of, 150–51, 156–59, 264*n*; night fishing in,
  144; poles for pushing, *66*, 200; rules for
  using, 45–46, 65–66; size/design of, 141–
  43, *142*, 262–63*n*; statistics on, 136, 168
work: activities excluded from, 106–8, 256–
  57*n*; diaries' accounting of, 102, 104–6; local conception of, 101, 114–15; profitability
  issue of, 97–98, 108–9, 255*nn*; time's relation to, 98–101, 110–14, 253–54*n*, 257*n*,
  258*n*

Yanaque village, 173–74
Yanarico, Justo, 109–10, 111, 112–13, 258*n*
Yapura village, 202
Yukos Oil Co. (Russia), 271*n*
Yunguyo district, 21–22, 24, 28, 36, 39–40,
  158, 212

Zepita, Battle of (1823), 26
Zepita district, 24, 25, 36, 158

Text: 10/14 Palatino
Display: Snell Roundhand Script and Bauer Bodoni
Compositor: G&S Typesetters, Inc.
Printer and Binder: Sheridan Books, Inc.